Marketing Online For Dummies®

Cheat Sheet

Ways to Use Online Media for Mar...

Internet or Online Service	Use for Marketing
Automated mailing lists	**As a user:** Join mailing lists that contain inf... to your industry.
	As an online publisher: Create an online ma... a relatively simple and inexpensive way to build a strong feeling of community within your customer base.
E-mail	**As a user:** Create a signature file with marketing content for the end of your e-mail messages. Strive to be polite and positive.
	As an online publisher: Standardize key e-mail practices within your company. Use your Web site to offer relevant e-mail addresses for customer use, then carefully manage the (possibly large) number of e-mails you receive.
FTP	**As a user:** Look for programs and files that can be useful for online marketing.
	As an online publisher: Offer interesting programs and formatted reports relevant to your area of business to people who visit you online. Hide the FTP site behind a Web interface to make it easier for visitors to use.
Online services	**As a user:** Join the online service that has the greatest concentration of your customers on it. Join forums and chats relevant to your industry.
	As an online publisher: Consider starting an online service forum on America Online, CompuServe, or both to reach additional customers and potential customers beyond your Web site and Usenet newsgroup efforts.
Push technology	**As a user:** Subscribe to Web sites to get updated when they change, and subscribe to push channels and PointCast to get information about your industry.
	As an online publisher: Use PointCast to create a simple push channel that sends Web pages to users. Include information the user will find valuable, not just your marketing messages.
Usenet newsgroups	**As a user:** Join newsgroups that concern your industry area. Use Deja News (www.dejanews.com) or other search engines to periodically search newsgroups for mentions of your company so that you can respond to any problems before they grow.
	As an online publisher: Standardize key e-mail practices within your company. Use your Web site to offer relevant e-mail addresses for customer use, then carefully manage the (possibly large) number of e-mails you receive.
World Wide Web	**As a user:** Become an expert Web searcher for information on your industry and your competitors; create bookmark files of key sites.
	As an online publisher: Start with a simple Web presence site to allow Websurfers to find basic information about your business online. Then expand with marketing-related content and news.

IDG BOOKS WORLDWIDE

...For Dummies: #1 Computer Book Series for Beginners

Marketing Online For Dummies®

Cheat Sheet

Key Online Marketing Abbreviations

AOL (America Online). The largest online service with over 10 million subscribers. You can use AOL as part of your online marketing efforts, though the highest level of exposure comes from formal marketing partnerships with AOL, which can be very expensive.

BCC (Blind Carbon Copy). A way of selecting recipients for e-mail messages so that recipients don't see every address to which the message was sent.

CIS (CompuServe Information Service). The second largest online service, sometimes referred to as CIS because it's historically been very expensive. CIS is somewhat more business-oriented than AOL, so use a more conservative tone in marketing communications on CIS.

CYA (Cover Your Assets). One of the primary reasons for beginning an online marketing effort today, CYA simply means that you make a move in order to not "miss the party." This is a good reason to start your online marketing effort, as long as you then use what you learn to find better reasons for maintaining and expanding your online presence.

FAQ (Frequently Asked Questions). A document provided by many newsgroups (and sometimes Internet mailing lists) with general information about a newsgroup or mailing list.

GIF (Graphics Interchange Format). A standard for compressed pictures, originally used on CompuServe, and now widely used in online services and the Web. GIF is best used for computer-generated images and other images with few shades of color. GIF images can be embedded seamlessly in Web pages and can also be animated.

HTML (HyperText Markup Language). The code, called *tags* by those in the know, that is added to a text document to make it function as a Web page. Here's a section header in HTML, with one word bold:

```
<H1>Why <B>online</B> marketing is
different</H1>
```

IE4 (Internet Explorer 4.0), NN4 (Netscape Navigator 4.0). Recent versions of the two Web browsers that, together, share about 90 percent of the Web browser market.

IMHO (In My Humble Opinion). One of many Net abbreviations used in e-mail messages, mailing lists, newsgroups, and online service forum postings. Other common ones are BTW (By The Way), FWIW (For What It's Worth), LOL (Laughing Out Loud) and ROTFL (Rolling On The Floor, Laughing). Learn these acronyms, but only use them in instances where you're sure your audience understands them.

ISP (Internet Service Provider). A company that provides dial-up or other kinds of access to the Internet to individuals and businesses. Online services such as AOL and CIS have their own proprietary content, but also serve as ISPs for their users.

JPEG (Joint Photographic Experts Group). A standard for compressed pictures, widely used on the Web. JPEG is best used for photographs and other images with many shades of color and is supported within IE4, NN4, and other browsers.

MSN (Microsoft Network). Microsoft Network is the online service and ISP run by Microsoft. It is less popular than America Online or CompuServe.

ROI (Return On Investment). The percentage of profit or avoided costs generated by an expenditure. ROI is hard to calculate for marketing expenditures because tracing exactly which sales are the result of which marketing expenditures is so difficult. However, you should try to compare ROI for online marketing expenditures versus other marketing expenditures in order to help you allocate resources wisely.

Sig file (signature file). Several lines of text which can be set to appear automatically at the end of your e-mail messages or newsgroup postings. For a marketer, the sig file should contain name, contact info, and the URL of the company Web site.

SIG (Special Interest Group). A term for discussion groups found on commercial online services, also known as *online forums, message boards, roundtables,* or *bulletin boards.* A commercial online service equivalent of Usenet newsgroups.

Spam. Another word for unsolicited commercial e-mail, bulk e-mail, or junk e-mail.

TLD (Top-Level Domain). The three letters at the end of an Internet domain name that denote the type of organization that owns the Web site. For examples, `.com` for a commercial organization or business, `.edu` for educational institutions (four-year colleges and universities only), `.org` for nonprofit organizations.

UCE (Unsolicited Commercial E-mail). Another word for spam.

URL (Uniform Resource Locator). The name for a resource stored on the World Wide Web. A URL such as `ftp://ftp.ourhost.com/users/techdocs/chapter1` designates the Internet service being used, such as `ftp://` for File Transfer Protocol; the Internet domain being access, such as `ftp.ourhost.com`; and, if needed, the pathname and filename of a specific file, such as `/users/techdocs/chapter1`.

WWW (World Wide Web). The number one vehicle for online marketing efforts. (Also, `www.` is commonly found as a prefix to Web site names such as `www.yourcompany.com`.)

®

References for the Rest of Us!®

COMPUTER BOOK SERIES FROM IDG

Are you intimidated and confused by computers? Do you find that traditional manuals are overloaded with technical details you'll never use? Do your friends and family always call you to fix simple problems on their PCs? Then the ...*For Dummies*® computer book series from IDG Books Worldwide is for you.

...*For Dummies* books are written for those frustrated computer users who know they aren't really dumb but find that PC hardware, software, and indeed the unique vocabulary of computing make them feel helpless. ...*For Dummies* books use a lighthearted approach, a down-to-earth style, and even cartoons and humorous icons to diffuse computer novices' fears and build their confidence. Lighthearted but not lightweight, these books are a perfect survival guide for anyone forced to use a computer.

> "I like my copy so much I told friends; now they bought copies."
>
> **Irene C., Orwell, Ohio**

> "Quick, concise, nontechnical, and humorous."
>
> **Jay A., Elburn, Illinois**

> "Thanks, I needed this book. Now I can sleep at night."
>
> **Robin F., British Columbia, Canada**

Already, millions of satisfied readers agree. They have made ...*For Dummies* books the #1 introductory level computer book series and have written asking for more. So, if you're looking for the most fun and easy way to learn about computers, look to ...*For Dummies* books to give you a helping hand.

MARKETING ONLINE FOR DUMMIES®

by Bud Smith and Frank Catalano

IDG
BOOKS
WORLDWIDE

IDG Books Worldwide, Inc.
An International Data Group Company

Foster City, CA ♦ Chicago, IL ♦ Indianapolis, IN ♦ Southlake, TX

Marketing Online For Dummies®

Published by
IDG Books Worldwide, Inc.
An International Data Group Company
919 E. Hillsdale Blvd.
Suite 400
Foster City, CA 94404
www.idgbooks.com (IDG Books Worldwide Web site)
www.dummies.com (Dummies Press Web site)

Library of Congress Catalog Card No.: 98-70125

ISBN: 0-7645-0335-9

Printed in the United States of America

10 9 8 7 6 5 4 3 2 1

1E/SX/QS/ZY/IN

Distributed in the United States by IDG Books Worldwide, Inc.

Distributed by Macmillan Canada for Canada; by Transworld Publishers Limited in the United Kingdom; by IDG Norge Books for Norway; by IDG Sweden Books for Sweden; by Woodslane Pty. Ltd. for Australia; by Woodslane Enterprises Ltd. for New Zealand; by Longman Singapore Publishers Ltd. for Singapore, Malaysia, Thailand, and Indonesia; by Simron Pty. Ltd. for South Africa; by Toppan Company Ltd. for Japan; by Distribuidora Cuspide for Argentina; by Livraria Cultura for Brazil; by Ediciencia S.A. for Ecuador; by Addison-Wesley Publishing Company for Korea; by Ediciones ZETA S.C.R. Ltda. for Peru; by WS Computer Publishing Corporation, Inc., for the Philippines; by Unalis Corporation for Taiwan; by Contemporanea de Ediciones for Venezuela; by Computer Book & Magazine Store for Puerto Rico; by Express Computer Distributors for the Caribbean and West Indies. Authorized Sales Agent: Anthony Rudkin Associates for the Middle East and North Africa.

For general information on IDG Books Worldwide's books in the U.S., please call our Consumer Customer Service department at 800-762-2974. For reseller information, including discounts and premium sales, please call our Reseller Customer Service department at 800-434-3422.

For information on where to purchase IDG Books Worldwide's books outside the U.S., please contact our International Sales department at 650-655-3200 or fax 650-655-3295.

For information on foreign language translations, please contact our Foreign & Subsidiary Rights department at 650-655-3021 or fax 650-655-3281.

For sales inquiries and special prices for bulk quantities, please contact our Sales department at 650-655-3200 or write to the address above.

For information on using IDG Books Worldwide's books in the classroom or for ordering examination copies, please contact our Educational Sales department at 800-434-2086 or fax 817-251-8174.

For press review copies, author interviews, or other publicity information, please contact our Public Relations department at 650-655-3000 or fax 650-655-3299.

For authorization to photocopy items for corporate, personal, or educational use, please contact Copyright Clearance Center, 222 Rosewood Drive, Danvers, MA 01923, or fax 978-750-4470.

 is a trademark under exclusive license to IDG Books Worldwide, Inc., from International Data Group, Inc.

About the Authors

Bud Smith's experience begins on the technical side of the computer industry with recent stints in strategic planning and marketing. Bud was a Jack in the Box fry cook before starting in the computer industry at 21. He was a data entry supervisor, programmer, and technical writer before beginning work as a competitive analyst at Apple Computer. Later Bud was product marketing manager for Apple's QuickTime VR, a product that was both distributed and used mostly on the World Wide Web. Bud is now a full-time author who occasionally joins Frank in a consulting project. A resident of Silicon Valley, Bud never visits the Seattle area, and has no consulting clients there. Bud's writing experience is all in the nonfiction side and includes computer and medical articles as well as a dozen computer books, including *Creating Web Pages For Dummies,* 3rd Edition, with Arthur Bebak, and the recently published *Push Technology For Dummies,* both from IDG Books Worldwide, Inc.

Frank Catalano is a marketing consultant, analyst and business strategist. Frank was a long-time news broadcaster before entering the computer industry. He was a marketing manager for Egghead Software and for the Apple Programmers and Developers Association prior to founding Catalano Consulting in 1992. Frank has worked on projects for a variety of clients including The McGraw-Hill Companies (as an acting VP of marketing), Apple Computer, Corbis, and many others. A resident of the Seattle area, Frank is also a frequent visitor to Silicon Valley, where many of his consulting clients are based. Frank's writing experience includes the Byte Me computer industry column published in Seattle Weekly, science fiction short stories, and contributing a chapter to an earlier marketing book.

ABOUT IDG BOOKS WORLDWIDE

Welcome to the world of IDG Books Worldwide.

IDG Books Worldwide, Inc., is a subsidiary of International Data Group, the world's largest publisher of computer-related information and the leading global provider of information services on information technology. IDG was founded more than 25 years ago and now employs more than 8,500 people worldwide. IDG publishes more than 275 computer publications in over 75 countries (see listing below). More than 60 million people read one or more IDG publications each month.

Launched in 1990, IDG Books Worldwide is today the #1 publisher of best-selling computer books in the United States. We are proud to have received eight awards from the Computer Press Association in recognition of editorial excellence and three from *Computer Currents'* First Annual Readers' Choice Awards. Our best-selling *...For Dummies®* series has more than 30 million copies in print with translations in 30 languages. IDG Books Worldwide, through a joint venture with IDG's Hi-Tech Beijing, became the first U.S. publisher to publish a computer book in the People's Republic of China. In record time, IDG Books Worldwide has become the first choice for millions of readers around the world who want to learn how to better manage their businesses.

Our mission is simple: Every one of our books is designed to bring extra value and skill-building instructions to the reader. Our books are written by experts who understand and care about our readers. The knowledge base of our editorial staff comes from years of experience in publishing, education, and journalism — experience we use to produce books for the '90s. In short, we care about books, so we attract the best people. We devote special attention to details such as audience, interior design, use of icons, and illustrations. And because we use an efficient process of authoring, editing, and desktop publishing our books electronically, we can spend more time ensuring superior content and spend less time on the technicalities of making books.

You can count on our commitment to deliver high-quality books at competitive prices on topics you want to read about. At IDG Books Worldwide, we continue in the IDG tradition of delivering quality for more than 25 years. You'll find no better book on a subject than one from IDG Books Worldwide.

John Kilcullen
John Kilcullen
CEO
IDG Books Worldwide, Inc.

Steven Berkowitz
Steven Berkowitz
President and Publisher
IDG Books Worldwide, Inc.

VIII WINNER
Eighth Annual Computer Press Awards ≥1992

IX WINNER
Ninth Annual Computer Press Awards ≥1993

WINNER
Tenth Annual Computer Press Awards ≥1994

XI WINNER
Eleventh Annual Computer Press Awards ≥1995

IDG Books Worldwide, Inc., is a subsidiary of International Data Group, the world's largest publisher of computer-related information and the leading global provider of information services on information technology. International Data Group publishes over 275 computer publications in over 75 countries. Sixty million people read one or more International Data Group publications each month. International Data Group's publications include: **ARGENTINA:** Buyer's Guide, Computerworld Argentina, PC World Argentina; **AUSTRALIA:** Australian Macworld, Australian PC World, Australian Reseller News, Computerworld, IT Casebook, Network World, Publish, Webmaster; **AUSTRIA:** Computerwelt Österreich, Networks Austria, PC Tip Austria; **BANGLADESH:** PC World Bangladesh; **BELARUS:** PC World Belarus; **BELGIUM:** Data News; **BRAZIL:** Annuário de Informática, Computerworld, Connections, Macworld, PC Player, PC World, Publish, Reseller News, Supergamepower; **BULGARIA:** Computerworld Bulgaria, Network World Bulgaria, PC & MacWorld Bulgaria; **CANADA:** CIO Canada, Client/Server World, ComputerWorld Canada, InfoWorld Canada, NetworkWorld Canada, WebWorld; **CHILE:** Computerworld Chile, PC World Chile; **COLOMBIA:** Computerworld Colombia, PC World Colombia; **COSTA RICA:** PC World Centro America; **THE CZECH AND SLOVAK REPUBLICS:** Computerworld Czechoslovakia, Macworld Czech Republic, PC World Czechoslovakia; **DENMARK:** Communications World Danmark, Computerworld Danmark, Macworld Danmark, PC World Danmark, Techworld Denmark; **DOMINICAN REPUBLIC:** PC World Republica Dominicana; **ECUADOR:** PC World Ecuador; **EGYPT:** Computerworld Middle East, PC World Middle East; **EL SALVADOR:** PC World Centro America; **FINLAND:** MikroPC, Tietoverkko, Tietoviikko; **FRANCE:** Distributique, Hebdo, Info PC, Le Monde Informatique, Macworld, Reseaux & Telecoms, WebMaster France; **GERMANY:** Computer Partner, Computerwoche, Computerwoche Extra, Computerwoche FOCUS, Global Online, Macwelt, PC Welt; **GREECE:** Amiga Computing, GamePro Greece, Multimedia World; **GUATEMALA:** PC World Centro America; **HONDURAS:** PC World Centro America; **HONG KONG:** Computerworld Hong Kong, PC World Hong Kong, Publish in Asia; **HUNGARY:** ABCD CD-ROM, Computerworld Szamitastechnika, Internetto online Magazine, PC World Hungary, PC-X Magazin Hungary; **ICELAND:** Tolvuheimur PC World Island; **INDIA:** Information Communications World, Information Systems Computerworld, PC World India, Publish in Asia; **INDONESIA:** InfoKomputer PC World, Komputek Computerworld, Publish in Asia; **IRELAND:** ComputerScope, PC Live!; **ISRAEL:** Macworld Israel, People & Computers/Computerworld; **ITALY:** Computerworld Italia, Macworld Italia, Networking Italia, PC World Italia; **JAPAN:** DTP World, Macworld Japan, Nikkei Personal Computing, OS/2 World Japan, SunWorld Japan, Windows NT World, Windows World Japan; **KENYA:** PC World East African; **KOREA:** Hi-Tech Information, Macworld Korea, PC World Korea; **MACEDONIA:** PC World Macedonia; **MALAYSIA:** Computerworld Malaysia, PC World Malaysia, Publish in Asia; **MALTA:** PC World Malta; **MEXICO:** Computerworld Mexico, PC World Mexico, PC World Myanmar; **MYANMAR:** PC World Myanmar; **NETHERLANDS:** Computer! Totaal, LAN Internetworking Magazine, LAN World Buyers Guide, Macworld Netherlands, Net, WebWereld; **NEW ZEALAND:** Absolute Beginners Guide and Plain & Simple Series, Computer Buyer, Computer Industry Directory, Computerworld New Zealand, MTB, Network World, PC World New Zealand; **NICARAGUA:** PC World Centro America; **NORWAY:** Computerworld Norge, CW Rapport, Datamagasinet, Financial Rapport, Kursguide Norge, Macworld Norge, Multimediaworld Norge, PC World Ekspress Norge, PC World Nettverk, PC World Norge, PC World ProduktGuide Norge; **PAKISTAN:** Computerworld Pakistan; **PANAMA:** PC World Panama; **PEOPLE'S REPUBLIC OF CHINA:** China Computer Users, China Computerworld, China InfoWorld, China Telecom World Weekly, Computer & Communication, Electronic Design China, Electronics Today, Electronics Weekly, Game Software, PC World China, Popular Computer Week, Software Weekly, Software World, Telecom World; **PERU:** Computerworld Peru, PC World Profesional Peru, PC World SoHo Peru; **PHILIPPINES:** Click!, Computerworld Philippines, PC World Philippines, Publish in Asia; **POLAND:** Computerworld Poland, Computerworld Special Report Poland, Cyber, Macworld Poland, Networld Poland, PC World Komputer; **PORTUGAL:** Cerebro/PC World, Computerworld/Correio Informático, Dealer World Portugal, Mac*In/PC*In Portugal, Multimedia World; **PUERTO RICO:** PC World Puerto Rico; **ROMANIA:** Computerworld Romania, PC World Romania, Telecom Romania; **RUSSIA:** Computerworld Russia, Mir PK, Publish, Seti; **SINGAPORE:** Computerworld Singapore, PC World Singapore, Publish in Asia; **SLOVENIA:** Monitor; **SOUTH AFRICA:** Computing SA, Network World SA, Software World SA; **SPAIN:** Communicaciones World España, Computerworld España, Dealer World España, Macworld España, PC World España; **SRI LANKA:** Infolink PC World; **SWEDEN:** CAP&Design, Computer Sweden, Corporate Computing Sweden, Internetworld Sweden, it.branschen, Macworld Sweden, MaxiData Sweden, MikroDatorn, Nätverk & Kommunikation, PC World Sweden, PCaktiv, Windows World Sweden; **SWITZERLAND:** Computerworld Schweiz, Macworld Schweiz, PCtip; **TAIWAN:** Computerworld Taiwan, Macworld Taiwan, NEW ViSiON/Publish, PC World Taiwan, Windows World Taiwan; **THAILAND:** Publish in Asia, Thai Computerworld; **TURKEY:** Computerworld Turkiye, Macworld Turkiye, Network World Turkiye, PC World Turkiye; **UKRAINE:** Computerworld Kiev, Multimedia World Ukraine, PC World Ukraine; **UNITED KINGDOM:** Acorn User UK, Amiga Action UK, Amiga Computing UK, Apple Talk UK, Computing, Macworld, Parents and Computers UK, PC Advisor, PC Home, PSX Pro, The WEB; **UNITED STATES:** Cable in the Classroom, CIO Magazine, Computerworld, DOS World, Federal Computer Week, GamePro Magazine, InfoWorld, I-Way, Macworld, Network World, PC Games, PC World, Publish, Video Event, THE WEB Magazine, and WebMaster; online webzines: JavaWorld, NetscapeWorld, and SunWorld Online; **URUGUAY:** InfoWorld Uruguay; **VENEZUELA:** Computerworld Venezuela, PC World Venezuela; and **VIETNAM:** PC World Vietnam.

3/24/97

Dedication

This book is dedicated by Frank to his son Michael, who lent his Dad to this book for an unexpectedly large number of long days and nights, with only one break for a visit to Disneyland where they both could be 10 years old. Thanks, Michael.

Author's Acknowledgments

Bud would like to acknowledge Michael Mace, formerly of Apple and now of Silicon Graphics, Inc., for his initial on-the-job tutorial in marketing and strategic planning. He would also like to acknowledge Ken Williams' ongoing efforts to keep him updated on goings-on in the Wintel world during Bud's many years at Apple and since.

Frank would like to acknowledge Ralph Sims of Northwest Nexus, who has been helpful in sorting out the gray areas of newsgroups and other technical stuff.

Both authors would like to acknowledge the Internet community as a whole, which continues to provide answers to questions of all sorts, detailed Frequently Asked Questions documents (FAQs), and much more, even as the Internet changes in ways that aren't always what was intended or even imagined by the people who started it all.

Both authors would also like to thank Viraf Mohta, who created the Directory with our input and many hours of his own research, and the editorial staff at IDG Books Worldwide, Inc., for bringing this project back on track and across the finish line, including Mike Kelly, Acquisitions Editor, Clark Scheffy, Project Editor, and Greg Bulmash, Technical Editor, and many others who shared the work of editing the book when crunch time came.

Publisher's Acknowledgments

We're proud of this book; please register your comments through our IDG Books Worldwide Online Registration Form located at http://my2cents.dummies.com.

Some of the people who helped bring this book to market include the following:

Acquisitions, Development, and Editorial

Project Editor: Clark Scheffy

Acquisitions Editor: Mike Kelly

Media Development Manager: Joyce Pepple

Permissions Editor: Heather H. Dismore

Copy Editor: Kim Darosett

Technical Editor: Greg Bulmash

Editorial Manager: Colleen Rainsberger

Editorial Assistant: Paul Kuzmic

Production

Project Coordinator: E. Shawn Aylsworth

Layout and Graphics: Lou Boudreau, Linda M. Boyer, Angela F. Hunckler, Jane E. Martin, Anna Rohrer, Brent Savage, Deirdre Smith, Kate Snell

Proofreaders: Christine Berman, Kelli Botta, Michelle Croninger, Rachel Garvey, Rebecca Senninger, Ethel Winslow, Janet M. Withers

Indexer: Sharon Hilgenberg

Special Help

William Barton, Copy Editor; Ted Cains, Copy Editor; Constance Carlisle, Copy Editor; Diana Conover, Associate Editor/Online; Mary Corder, Editorial Manager; Kelly Ewing, Senior Project Editor; Wendy Hatch, Copy Editor; Kelly Oliver, Associate Editor/ Quality Control; Diane Smith, Senior Copy Editor

General and Administrative

IDG Books Worldwide, Inc.: John Kilcullen, CEO; Steven Berkowitz, President and Publisher

IDG Books Technology Publishing: Brenda McLaughlin, Senior Vice President and Group Publisher

Dummies Technology Press and Dummies Editorial: Diane Graves Steele, Vice President and Associate Publisher; Mary Bednarek, Director of Acquisitions and Product Development; Kristin A. Cocks, Editorial Director

Dummies Trade Press: Kathleen A. Welton, Vice President and Publisher; Kevin Thornton, Acquisitions Manager

IDG Books Production for Dummies Press: Beth Jenkins Roberts, Production Director; Cindy L. Phipps, Manager of Project Coordination, Production Proofreading, and Indexing; Kathie S. Schutte, Supervisor of Page Layout; Shelley Lea, Supervisor of Graphics and Design; Debbie J. Gates, Production Systems Specialist; Robert Springer, Supervisor of Proofreading; Debbie Stailey, Special Projects Coordinator; Tony Augsburger, Supervisor of Reprints and Bluelines; Leslie Popplewell, Media Archive Coordinator

Dummies Packaging and Book Design: Patti Crane, Packaging Specialist; Kavish + Kavish, Cover Design

◆

The publisher would like to give special thanks to Patrick J. McGovern, without whom this book would not have been possible.

◆

Contents at a Glance

Cartoons at a Glance

By Rich Tennant

"You know, it dawned on me last night why we aren't getting any hits on our Web site."

page 9

"So far our Web presence has been pretty good. We've gotten some orders, a few inquiries, and nine guys who want to date our logo."

page 95

"Yes, I think we should advertise with America Online. Besides, there is no Vladivostok Online."

page 183

"Games are an important part of my Web site. They cause eye strain."

page D-1

"I like getting complaint letters by e-mail. It's easier to delete than to shred."

page 263

"Come on Walt—time to freshen the company Web page."

page 287

Fax: 978-546-7747 • E-mail: the5wave@tiac.net

Table of Contents

Introduction

∙ ∙

*T*he online world is a place of great excitement these days — and the cause of no small amount of anxiety. Businesses have wonderful new opportunities to grow and to extend their relationships with customers — and new types of competitors that may take those customers away. This book will help you make sure that the online world is your friend.

Marketing, as you probably already know, is everything that happens between the manufacturing or creation of a product and its eventual sale to the buyer, including advertising, public relations, product strategy, and more. However, this book is not a marketing primer; for that, and more, see *Marketing For Dummies* by Alexander Hiam (IDG Books Worldwide, Inc.). The job of this book is to tell you and show you how to market your products and services effectively online.

Most people know that the online world includes the World Wide Web, and if you've ever surfed the Web, you've no doubt stumbled across oodles of marketing content, and a large part of this book is accordingly devoted to marketing on the Web. But in this book we also show you that the online world is much more than the Web. Online services, Usenet newsgroups, e-mail, push channels, and more are all part of the online world, and are all potentially useful for your online marketing strategy. We, the authors of this book, have many years of marketing and online experience, and we draw on all of it to tell you how to best use each and every one of these Internet services — and how to prioritize and combine your efforts to create the most effective online presence possible.

Marketing itself can be defined as "the art of the possible." A company has any number of different things it can do to try to improve its products, get more customers, save money, and more; the marketing department's job is to help the company choose what to do and show how to do it most effectively. In the case of marketing online, opportunities for reaching customers are nearly unlimited — but so are opportunities for spending money to build your online presence. What should you do first? In this book we show you how to build your online presence one solid step at a time so that you present an attractive and engaging image of your company and products — without overcommitting at the expense of other necessary marketing efforts.

Who Are You?

One big challenge with many technology-related books is that you need all sorts of qualifications — experience, education, previous reading, and more — to even get started with the book's topic. The *...For Dummies* series excels in providing needed information to the broadest possible range of people, and this book takes that to the limit. You don't have to be a computer programmer, a marketing professional, or anything else special to read and use *Marketing Online For Dummies*.

To get the most out of this book, you should have access to a computer equipped with a modem, and know how to use it. You should either have Internet and World Wide Web access already, or use the MindSpring software on the enclosed CD-ROM to get connected. (Appendix A tells you how to use the software on the CD-ROM.) And you should have in mind some company, product, or cause that you want the world to know more about. That's really about it.

This book does, however, touch on a number of related topics without covering them completely, because they're described in scintillating detail in other *...For Dummies* books. Related topics you may want to read up on include:

- ✔ **General marketing.** If you're interested in learning more about what marketing is and how to get good at it, fast, read *Marketing For Dummies* by Alexander Hiam. Alexander does a good and thorough job of covering marketing topics in a way that lays the groundwork for this book, and for all of your marketing efforts.

- ✔ **Getting online.** *Marketing Online For Dummies* includes tips for marketing on online services, and online services are also a good way to get connected to the Internet. By far the largest online service is America Online. If you want to get online this way, see *America Online For Dummies,* 3rd Edition, by John Kaufeld.

- ✔ **Selling online.** The difference between marketing and selling is sometimes a little blurry, so IDG Books has covered the bases completely by publishing another book along with this one: *Selling Online For Dummies.* When you're ready to help your customers complete the sales process online, Leslie Lundquist, an excellent communicator and expert on secure online transactions, will thoroughly inform you about everything you need to know.

- ✔ **Using and understanding the Internet.** To get the most out of using the Internet and learn some of the details of its history and how it works, see the hit *The Internet For Dummies,* 4th Edition, by John Levine, et al.

To get the most out of the latest Web browsers, which also support other Internet functions like e-mail and newsgroups, see *Internet Explorer 4.0 For Windows For Dummies,* by Doug Lowe, or *Netscape Communicator 4 For Dummies,* by Paul Hoggman.

✔ **Web publishing.** If you want to get off to the easiest possible start in putting up pages on the World Wide Web, see *Creating Web Pages For Dummies,* by Bud Smith and Arthur Bebak.

All of these books are from IDG Books Worldwide, Inc. You can find out more about any of these books from the *...For Dummies* Web site at www.dummies.com.

As for computer platforms, we're very much aware that the computing world is not entirely made up of PCs running Windows 95; both of us have used other platforms extensively and have done work for Apple and for Unix-based companies as well. The vast majority of the information in this book applies equally well no matter what kind of a computer you're using; if your computer can connect to the Internet and run a World Wide Web browser such as Microsoft Internet Explorer 4.0 or Netscape Navigator 4.0, you're in.

However, most people out there using the Internet are running Windows, and most of the software programs available for using the Internet and creating content for the Internet come out on Windows first, and other platforms later or not at all. (As we point out in the book, some professional-level software is available first and foremost for Unix, and if you ever become a full-time Webmaster, you may find yourself using Unix extensively. But that's a different topic than what we cover in this book.) So the software on the CD-ROM that accompanies this book is mostly for Windows 95, with a good set of Macintosh programs provided as well. Screen shots of software and Web pages in this book are created mostly on a PC running Windows 95, with some from a Macintosh. Variety is, after all, the spice of life.

The few sections of the book that have specific steps that you need to follow on your computer are specifically written and tested on Windows 95, though they are nearly identical in most cases for the Macintosh and Unix versions of the same programs where such versions exist.

It's Not a Seedy ROM

The CD-ROM that comes with this book is packed with software that will help you get online and establish a strong online marketing presence. The majority of the software is for Windows, but the CD-ROM includes a nice set of Macintosh programs, too. The programs on the CD-ROM were used in creating the examples and screen shots in this book. For details of what's on the CD-ROM and how to install the software, see Appendix A.

Well-Attended Conventions

In this book, a *convention* is not necessarily something you have to book a hotel room for. Our conventions are standard ways of structuring specific types of information that you find in this book, such as steps and instructions. (One example of the use of a convention is the use of italics for the word "convention" the first time it appeared at the start of this paragraph; when you see a term in italics, a definition of it soon follows.) Here are the conventions for this book:

- Things that you, the reader, are asked to type, as well as specific instructions that you need to follow in a set of numbered steps, are shown in **bold.**

- New terms are printed in *italics*.

- Information used in specific ways is formatted in a specific typeface. This book uses a special typeface for *URLs* (Uniform Resource Locators), which are the addresses used to specify the location of Web pages and other Internet resources. For example, the URL for the *...For Dummies* series is as follows:

  `http://www.dummies.com`

  In most of this book, we omit the `http://` from Web addresses, because you don't actually have to type it into your Web browser.

- Related, brief pieces of information are displayed in bulleted lists, such as the bulleted list that you're reading right now.

- *Right-clicking* means clicking on something onscreen while using the right mouse button. If you are left-handed or for some other reason have changed your mouse settings in Windows, you may need to use a different mouse button to achieve the effect of right-clicking on something. Also, right-clicking doesn't have a direct equivalent on the Macintosh, which only uses a single button on the mouse. For the Macintosh, the commands you choose by right-clicking in Windows are usually available via program menus.

- Numbered steps are used for instructions that must be followed in a particular sequence. This book has several sets of sequential steps that tell you just how to perform the different tasks that, when taken together, can make you a successful online marketer.

To make the steps brief and easy to follow, we use a specific way of telling you what to do. Here's an example of a set of steps:

1. **Start your Web browser.**

2. **Go to the Web site** `www.swsoft.com`

   The Southwest Software home page appears.

   Note: This is a real site, check it out!

3. **Click on a link in any of your areas of interest: Links, Products, or Tech Briefs.**

The Party of the First (and Second) Part

To make finding things in this book easier for you, we divide it into parts, which separate chapters into nice, easily located, related groups. Here's a quick guide to the parts in this book; use it to navigate your way through as you read.

Part I: Getting Started with Online Marketing

You need to know a few basics to use the online world effectively for marketing. For example, you need to know what Internet services are available for you to deliver your marketing messages; just as important is knowing who's out there in the online world for you to reach with your marketing effort. And the online world is not only a place for you to do marketing; it's also a great place to find information for all your marketing planning, both online and *offline*. (We use the term *offline* to mean everything that isn't online, such as all your traditional marketing efforts.) As soon as you know who's there and how to reach them, you're ready to plan out your online marketing effort, and this Part concludes with a step-by-step description of how to create just such a plan.

Part II: Marketing on the World Wide Web

Part II is your tour — we think it's a tour de force — of how to establish an effective presence on the most popular Internet service of all, the one that's captured imaginations around the world, the World Wide Web. Ever wonder why some companies have a great Web *URL* (Web address) that's easy to remember, and others don't? We tell you how to get the right Web URL for your online marketing work. Then, in three easy-to-follow chapters, we tell you how to build your own Web presence, either as a *DIY* — that's British for a "Do It Yourself" project — or working with other professionals, whether employees of your company or hired consultants. After reading this Part, you'll know just how to get what you want from your Web marketing effort.

Part III: Marketing with Other Internet Services

Other online technologies, such as newsgroups, e-mail, Internet mailing lists and more, tend to get ignored in the understandable rush to do marketing on the World Wide Web. However, these technologies can be less expensive to use, yet just as effective in creating and maintaining an online marketing presence — and when used in combination with a Web site, they can make the difference in effectively reaching your customers and potential customers. In Part III we give you the scoop on how to use each of these additional online technologies effectively and also give you our take on what the next few years will bring for online marketing opportunities.

Part IV: The Marketing Online For Dummies Internet Directory

The funky yellow pages used for this part tells you that something different is going on here. This part is where you can find a directory of Internet resources — including Web sites, newsgroups, and mailing lists — to help you in your online marketing effort. Each entry in the directory gives you an address and a quick description of a site or service that offers valuable information for the online marketer.

Part V: The Part of Tens

The Parts of Ten are fun, but have serious information about things to do in online marketing, things not to do, and pointers to some of the best *offline* resources to use in creating your online marketing presence.

Part VI: Appendix

This book's Appendix is not something you'd want removed — it's a guide to how to install and use the software on this book's CD-ROM.

Icons Used in This Book

To help you make your way through this book, we've added five icons that help you find specific kinds of material:

Warning icons alert you to online marketing challenges and traps you may easily fall into if you're not careful. Even though online marketing is new, we've been around the block a few times already and can warn you about enough of the potholes to help keep you from having to call a tow truck.

This icon points out references to software that's on the _Marketing Online For Dummies_ CD-ROM.

This icon lets you know when we cover some information that is good to keep in mind and commit to memory. The information may be a point that we make, usually at greater length, elsewhere in the book, or it may be something new that you want to pay particularly close attention to.

Points to things that go into some technical detail — things you may want to know, but don't necessarily need to know. You can skip these and read the text, skip the text and read these, or both.

The Tip icon flags specific information that may not fit in a step or description, but that will help you create better Web pages.

Part I
Getting Started with Online Marketing

The 5th Wave   By Rich Tennant

"You know, it dawned on me last night why we aren't getting any hits on our Web site."

In this part . . .

The online world is a whole new arena for marketing, one with many opportunities — but also its own history and rules. Use this part to become familiar with using online resources effectively, learn more about who's online, and find out how to start extending your marketing efforts to reach this new audience.

Chapter 1

The Online World

· ·

In This Chapter

▶ Introducing the Internet

▶ Using the Web

▶ Who's using the Internet

▶ How the Internet is used

▶ Working in the online world

· ·

*I*n order to market effectively, you need to know the territory in which you're operating. As with most new territories, what most people know about the Internet is a mix of fact and folklore. The Internet is so new, and still changing so fast, that just keeping up with it can seem like a full-time job.

Never fear; in this chapter we introduce you to the various actors that make up the Internet, starring, of course, the World Wide Web, but with many supporting players such as e-mail and push technology. Then we describe who's on the Internet — something you need to know *before* you decide how much or how little to invest in your online marketing effort. We finish up by describing some of what people do with their online time; the habits (both good *and* bad) of the people that you're trying to reach can either help or hurt your online marketing efforts, so you need to know as much as you can about them.

Do You Need to Market on the Internet?

Because the Internet in general, and the Web in particular, have received so much hype, many companies have been swept up by a "gold rush" mentality, spurring them to get on the Internet and the Web quickly with the threat of otherwise missing out on the next big thing. If you're wary of technological flashes in the pan (given the demise of the 8-track tape, CB radios, and CP/M computers, maybe you should be), you're excused for wondering if you really need to market on the Internet.

The Internet versus the Web

In many cases, people use terms such as *online world, Internet,* and *World Wide Web* more or less interchangeably. That's okay, and it reflects some interesting realities about the online world. (Okay, you got me already: When we say "the online world," we mean the whole thing — the Web, e-mail, traditional online services such as America Online, and all else that depends on being wired. Basically the online world is anything that you can connect to with your computer and a modem.)

At present, the World Wide Web is the most exciting place in the online world, and your company or product Web site should be both the starting point and the linchpin of your online marketing effort. However, you need to use other Internet services, plus traditional online services, to complement and support your Web presence. Some of the other Internet services may someday even rival the Web in the number of crazed computer users that they attract. So don't be confused when you see terms such as *Internet, Web,* and *online services* all used more or less interchangeably; they're just different parts of the online elephant that everyone is trying to put to work for themselves.

In this book we give you a lot of cautionary notes about how to avoid overinvesting or foolishly investing in an online presence, and a heavy investment in online marketing is not for everyone. However, we think that nearly all businesses need to have a clearly defined online strategy, including goals, methods to use in meeting those goals, and ways to measure success.

Though businesses vary tremendously in how many online customers they have — for example, a large percentage of computer buyers are online, but only a small percentage of car buyers — the people who *are* online include most of the opinion-makers and trendsetters. Someone buying a can of soup made by your company may never see your Web site; but someone writing an article about trends in soup marketing is almost sure to try to look you up. (You do want your company to get mentioned in the press, right?) And increasingly, grocery-store buyers making decisions about what to stock are going to start their work by looking online, too. (And, of course, you want your company to be considered early in major buying decisions.)

So you need to market online. But just what is *marketing?* Basically, it's communications between a company and a customer that influence the customer to buy a product or service from the company. Those include not only outbound communications like advertising and public relations, but things like surveys, customer focus groups, demographic research, and so on. This book shows you how to market your company, your products, and your services effectively online.

Marketing divides people up into groups called, strangely enough, *markets*. A market is a group of people who are conscious of themselves as a group and who communicate with one another on topics of shared interest that relate to your product. People who share a profession, gender and age groups, people who share a nationality, or people who have a specific role in a family — child, parent, grandparent — are all markets. An important part of marketing online is knowing which markets you're trying to reach and where to find them online — this book helps you do just that.

Being online — especially having a decent-looking company Web site — is becoming as important as being in the phone book. If you want people to contact you at all, you'd better be listed. Elsewhere in this book, we explain the basics of creating a competent online presence cheaply, and we go into detail for people who want to go beyond simple *online presence* into proactive online marketing. But start by making sure that each product, service, or company that you're involved with has at least a basic, effective online marketing effort. The next section introduces the different pieces that make up the online world.

Introducing the Internet as a Marketing Tool

What is the Internet? It's a big mess — a mix of good and bad ideas, shaken, stirred, half-heated, and served buffet-style. More seriously, the Internet means many things to many people, but luckily we can give you a simple answer as to what it really is.

The Internet is simply an *inter-network:* that is, a way to connect many smaller computer networks and computers with one another. The reason folks call it *the* Internet, and not just *an* internet, is that the Internet is the one network that connects most of the computers on Earth, so it deserves to be recognized as one specific thing. What makes all this connecting possible is that the Internet has a set of unifying standards. Though doing so is simplistic, you can think of the Internet as just a whole bunch of wires that carry messages compatible with each other.

Each different kind of content that goes over the Internet is called an Internet *service;* e-mail is one Internet service, and the Web is another. An Internet service meets agreed-on, public standards so that any computer on the Internet can access the particular service, using any of a variety of available software packages. These standards are based on *protocols,* each of which is like a language that the computers on the Internet speak when they want to transfer a particular kind of data. When people talk about the Internet today, they're not just talking about the underlying wiring; they're talking about the various Internet services and protocols that they use or have heard about.

An Internet service is different from an online service like America Online, which has its own proprietary standards controlled by a single company, not open standards agreed on by all players like the Internet.

One such Internet service is used to transfer any kind of file between computers. This service is known commonly as *FTP,* which stands for File Transfer Protocol. The kinds of files that you can send with FTP include text documents, computer programs, graphics, sound files — just about anything. E-mail and newsgroups, each using their own specific protocols, emerged as early, text-only Internet services. The Web, another service with, again, its own protocol, became wildly popular by adding graphics to the mix. And push technology, a new kind of Internet service closely tied to the Web, turns the Internet inside out by periodically delivering information on a sort of subscription schedule determined by the user, not just at the moment that the person is actively seeking information. Expect to see more new Internet services, and lots of growth and change in existing ones, over the next few years.

Introducing the Web

The World Wide Web (or just *Web* for short) is the most talked-about online invention ever. Hyped beyond belief in the world press and the force behind rags-to-riches stories like that of Netscape Communications, Inc., the World Wide Web is one of the great business stories of all time.

Luckily, the sizzle does come with some real steak. As we explain in detail later in this chapter, the Web has tens of millions of real users who collectively spend millions of hours a day *surfing the Web.*

Using the Web is made possible by software programs called *Web browsers,* the runaway leaders being Netscape Navigator and Microsoft Internet Explorer. In this book we show Internet Explorer in our screen shots, because it's available on the CD-ROM at the back of this book and because in our opinion, it's a somewhat better browser than Netscape Navigator. The things that we like best about it all relate to the fact that it integrates different functions together very well; for instance, searching, using push technology, and making your browser work well with Windows are all easier from within Internet Explorer. But Netscape Navigator is also an excellent tool, and hopefully the two will continue to compete aggressively for years to come.

From a marketer's point of view, the Web is best understood as a collection of glossy company reports that can be accessed only by a still small but growing group of unusually influential people. But side by side with the company and product information is college course material; personal home pages that describe hobbies, children, and pets; online pornography; political advertising; and anything else that you care to name. A glossy corporate home page is shown in Figure 1-1, and a personal home page is shown in Figure 1-2. The Web is a wild world.

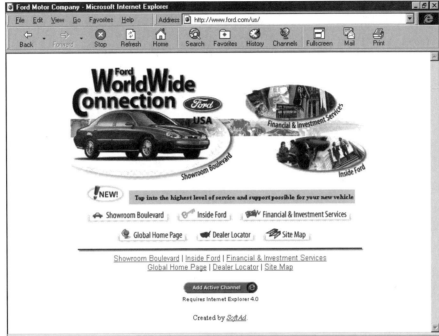

Figure 1-1:
The
corporate
look of
the Web.

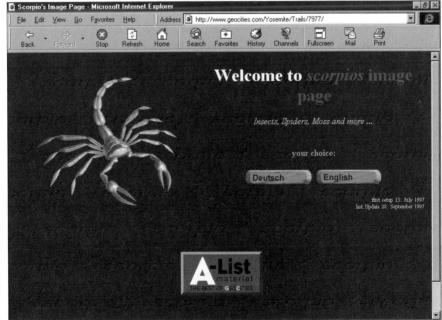

Figure 1-2:
The
personal
look of
the Web.

The Web is one of the best tools ever invented for marketing. Unlike television commercials, which force themselves on the viewer, Web sites are accessed only by users who *want* to see them — our message is reaching people who want it. But to get people to stay with you, you need to use an enticing style.

Shouting above the noise on the Web is impossible. You can't get in people's faces on the Web like you can with a television or radio commercial or even a print ad; people can click the Back buttons on their browsers to leave a site even faster than they can turn the page of a magazine or find the TV remote hidden in the crevices of their couch. The trick is to put up a competent, easy-to-use Web site, and then help the people who want to find you do so. (Speaking of making sure your Web site is found, in Chapter 7 we show you how to get your site registered with the various *search engines.* Chapter 2 covers using search engines in order to find marketing-related information on the Web.)

Belying the hype about its importance, and despite the efforts of some people to spice it up with audio and video, the Web is for the most part a *cool* medium: quiet, informative, and useful. To use it effectively, lead with information mixed with just enough graphical eye candy to attract a reader. An effective Web site works much like the *advertorial* inserts that you see in magazines like *Time* or *Newsweek,* mixing *advert*ising and edi*torial* content. Count on the Web being an increasingly important part of your marketing efforts in the years to come. Chapters 4–7 cover the ins and outs of building and publicizing your marketing Web site.

E-mail and mail lists: Unsung online heroes

E-mail is probably the biggest single reason the Internet has become the success that it is today. For a long time, the online world was a hodgepodge of incompatible online services such as *BIX, Delphi,* and *MCI Mail,* each with its own proprietary network and separate protocols. The Internet at this point was used almost entirely by the U.S. government and colleges. But people on each online service wanted to be able to send e-mail to friends and colleagues who used other services. To allow this interaction, the proprietary online services had to add *Internet gateways* (connections to the Internet) for e-mail to flow through from one person on one network to another person on another network. Businesses followed suit with their in-house e-mail systems, and the Internet grew rapidly, setting the stage for the Web and other online resources.

Even in this age of the multimedia Web, e-mail is still mostly text-only, with no formatting (such as **bold**, <u>underline</u>, or *italics*) and no graphics; it even retains quaint and annoying problems such as a tendency to break a message up into many shorter lines. However, e-mail is an increasingly important communications medium and a key part of online marketing.

Like real mail (or *snail mail* — the kind delivered by the U.S. Postal Service), e-mail is a tempting channel for marketing. People have become used to getting advertising offers in their regular mail, though *junk mail* is the disparaging term for this kind of mailing, showing what many people think of it. But e-mail, unlike much regular mail, feels very special to people; they seem to take their e-mail in-boxes more personally than they do their postal mailboxes. So when you're using e-mail for marketing, proceed with caution, as we explain in detail in Chapter 8.

The most important things to remember when using e-mail for online marketing are two do's and a don't:

- ✔ **Do make sure that you respond to e-mail sent to people within your company.** If you put an e-mail address on a popular Web site, you can easily get flooded with e-mail. Make sure that you don't ignore any prospective customers you bring in and that they receive quick and appropriate responses.

- ✔ **Do try to ensure that e-mail sent to people outside of your company is positive and informative.** Every one of those e-mails is, at least in part, a marketing message.

- ✔ **Don't send unwanted e-mail, such as the mass e-mail *spam* that some companies send to prospective (that is, soon to be *ex*-prospective) customers.** Most recipients ignore spam e-mail; others respond aggressively, with angry notes or even *mail bombs,* automated mass mailings back to the sender that can choke the sender's mail system.

Listservs, or *mail lists,* are one of the most useful forms of e-mail, especially from a marketing point of view. A mail list is simply a list of people who ask to be informed about a given topic. A short exchange of messages from a mail list is shown in Figure 1-3.

Both e-mail messages and mail lists are marketing tools that are best used with a light touch, not explicitly as marketing vehicles but as technical and information pieces that also support your marketing messages. We describe the effective use of e-mail and creating, maintaining, and influencing a mail list in Chapter 8.

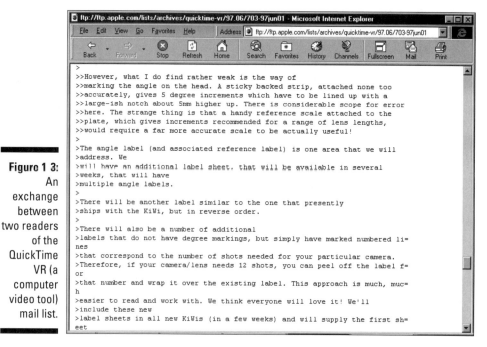

Figure 1-3:
An exchange between two readers of the QuickTime VR (a computer video tool) mail list.

Newsgroups: The threat and the promise

Remember the Pentium scare from winter 1994? A university-based PC user tested the math functions on his new Pentium computer and found that the Intel chip produced a series of errors in certain unusual but not-unheard-of circumstances. Some of the people he corresponded with used *Usenet newsgroups* — online discussion areas for messages on specific topics — to post his findings and ask others to repeat his tests. They did. They confirmed the problems and then asked Intel what it was going to do.

The folks at Intel ignored the postings at first. Then they responded, clumsily. Then they tried to belittle the problem. Then they tried a software fix. Then an exchange plan. Finally, Intel had to offer to recall and replace all the Pentiums sold up to that point, a huge expense both in dollars and in damage to the positive public image Intel had enjoyed.

Such is the exciting world of Usenet newsgroups. (Although similar forums exist on online services and on Web sites, Usenet is the biggest with tens of thousands of newsgroups and millions of messages posted.) Employees of different companies, acting with little or no supervision, slander one another and each others' products with abandon. Crazy conspiracy theories circulate, companies overreact, underreact, lie, and threaten users.

Of course, a lot of good things go on in newsgroups as well. Problems get solved, customers get reassured, people have a good time, and no one gets (physically) hurt. Figure 1-4 shows a newsgroup posting. But the potential problems are what first compel the attention of online marketers.

To effectively use newsgroups to respond to customer concerns and get your marketing information out to the world, you have to ask people in your company to see themselves as representatives of your company to the outside world, to avoid being negative, to be attentive, to be positive and helpful, and to let others inside the company know of any problems they hear about. You can help yourself by making sure that your marketing messages are at least as well understood by people in your company as they are by the press and customers for whom you create them. We describe in detail how to find and use newsgroups in Chapter 10.

America Online and online services

Online services are the reason that so many computer users first got modems. Early modems were poky things that ran at 300, 1200, or 2400 bits per second (bps), less than one-tenth the speed of the mighty 28.8, 33.6, or

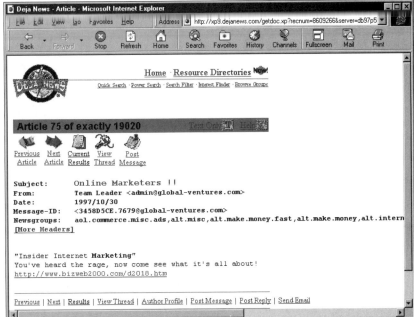

Figure 1-4: Newsgroups can be Dr. Jekylls or Mr. Hydes.

56 kilobits per second (a thousand bits per second, or Kbps) modems of today. A wondrous profusion of online services sprang up, each one meeting slightly different needs.

Now the world of online services has narrowed to a single behemoth, America Online — which recently purchased its chief rival, CompuServe — and several much smaller services. Recently topping 10 million users, America Online has three times as many users as its closest rival, the Microsoft Network, and more users than all other online services combined. AOL is also the largest single gateway to e-mail, Usenet newsgroups, and the Web.

America Online and its remaining rivals are like a microcosm of the open Internet, with graphical presentations somewhat like Web pages, proprietary e-mail interfaces that can exchange text messages and files with almost anyone, and newsgroup-type areas for messages. Figure 1-5 shows the interface for America Online. Online services can be wonderful resources for people new to the Internet, with services such as free Web page hosting — that is, they'll let you put your Web page on their Web server for others to view — and technical support from groups of fellow users who are often very expert on a variety of topics, including using computers and the online world.

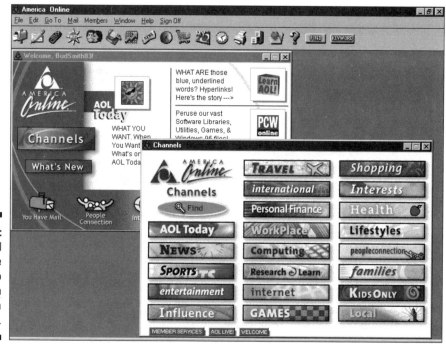

Figure 1-5:
People all over the world go online with America Online.

What about using online services for online marketing? Well, the Web is a popular destination for online service users and others, so you should focus your initial efforts on the Web — you reach the most people that way. Then research the major online services to see if any of them have the kind of mix of people that you're looking for as customers. For example, CompuServe has a strong presence of business-oriented users; with America Online, you reach more consumers at home and more Macintosh users. Barnes and Noble, for example, has an exclusive, multimillion dollar arrangement with America Online to market and sell its books on that service. For more details on how to use online services for online marketing, see Chapter 10.

Online services also do a great job of getting new people online so they can bask in the glow of your online presence. If the success of your online marketing effort requires getting more of your existing customers online, so you can build a stronger, ongoing relationship with them, encouraging them to sign up for an online service is a great way to do it. Getting people online and other ways to use the power of America Online and other online services are described in Chapter 10. You can also use an Internet Service Provider (ISP) to get people connected; Mindspring is one such ISP, and you can get online with Mindspring using the CD-ROM in the back of the book.

Push technology

Push technology is the latest way to get your message out across all that wiring to all those connected people. In its current, infant state, push technology takes on two main forms. The first and best-known incarnation of push technology is the PointCast Network, a nicely designed interface to news and information services, as shown in Figure 1-6. The Web address (or more technically, the *URL,* or Uniform Resource Locator) for PointCast, Inc., is www.pointcast.com; you can download the software for free.

The newer form of push technology, *Web channels,* is built up from pushed Web site information, accessed through the PointCast Connections service, through the Internet Explorer browser, or through the Netscape Netcaster push tool. The Netcaster approach is based on a technology called Castanet from Marimba, Inc., an innovative company that uses the popular Java programming language to support highly functional push channels. The PointCast and Internet Explorer approaches are incompatible with the Netscape approach.

Push technology works very much like the Web. Instead of surfing to Web sites, push users subscribe to *channels.* The channels automatically deliver new information to the user at regular intervals, anywhere from once an hour to once a week or more. Users can also choose to get information on demand. Instead of viewing content through a Web browser, push users use

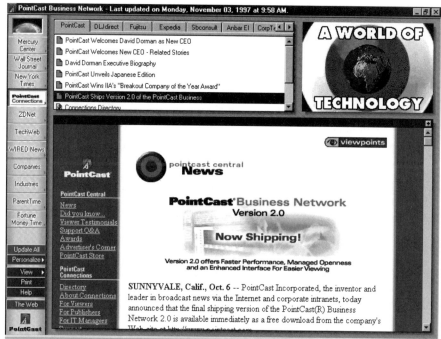

Figure 1-6:
PointCast is
the leader
in push
technology.

software called a *push client*. The Internet Explorer 4.0 browser has the push client built into the browser, which may be more the trend of the future. In the Netscape Communicator package, the push client is a separate application.

For online marketing purposes, push technology has both good and bad points. The good news is that people who subscribe to your push channel can get updated information from you on a regular basis. The bad news is that they won't subscribe just to get marketing material or ads. To attract and hold users, you need to create an information-rich channel in which marketing messages are present, but in an understated way.

Compared to other things that we describe in this book, push technology is really on the cutting edge technologically, with Microsoft and Netscape waging a fierce standards battle and users having to deal with the incompatibilities that result. Push technology is really good, though, for making sure that the people who *want* to see your messages can and for creating a feeling of community among users. We explain in Chapter 2 how you can use push technology to stay well informed. For even more information, check out *Push Technology For Dummies* by Bud Smith (IDG Books Worldwide, Inc.).

Finding Your Online Market

The population of the online world is different than the population of the U.S. or of the world as a whole. In deciding how much time, energy, and money to spend on your online marketing efforts, you really need to take some time to find out who's online and compare that to who you are trying to reach in your marketing efforts. Then you can size your online efforts to match your expected rewards.

To find out more about who's a member of the online world, you can refer to a survey from the Graphics, Visualization, and Usability (GVU) Center at the Georgia Institute of Technology. GVU's WWW User Survey, as it's called, uses a survey form on its Web site to collect data about the Websurfing public, as shown in Figure 1-7. You can also refer to other surveys that we mention in this chapter and that are available online; however, those other sources tend to be either less complete than GVU's WWW User Survey, or charge money for the results.

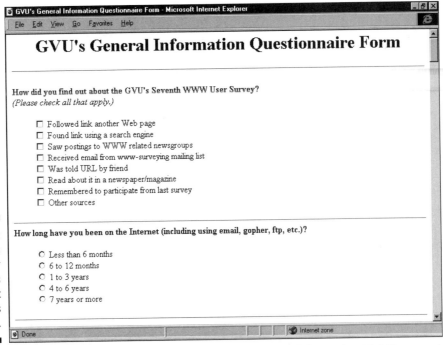

Figure 1-7:
GVU's
WWW User
Survey tells
you a lot
about who's
on the Web.

Statistics are an attempt to capture a snapshot of current realities, and can be accurate to within a few percentage points — or can be thoroughly biased, misrepresented, and misused. The statistics quoted here are the best freely available ones we could find. Projections are an attempt to *guesstimate* the future, and so are inherently unreliable unless you have Nostradamus on your payroll, or read tea leaves. We suggest that in your marketing planning for the online world, and indeed for all your marketing planning, you rely heavily on statistics and very lightly on projections. For a very entertaining look at the problems with projections, see the Robert X. Cringely column on the subject at `www.pbs.org/cringely/archive/dec397_main.html`.

The results from GVU's WWW User Survey are fascinating when you look at them from a marketer's point of view. You can find the survey's results at `www.gvu.gatech.edu/user_surveys`. (That's an underscore character near the end of the URL, not a space.) In the next few sections we describe some of the survey's findings, which are consistent with other surveys and with our own experiences, as well as their implications for online marketing.

People like to talk about how fast the online world is changing, but the results from GVU's WWW Survey are actually becoming increasingly consistent from one survey period to the next. Though the number of Internet users is growing rapidly, close to doubling in less than a year, the characteristics of the user population — for example, the percentage of males versus females, types of professions represented, and so on — now change little in

How GVU's WWW User Survey works

GVU's WWW User Survey is managed and licensed by Georgia Tech Research Corporation. It's available on the Web at `www.gvu.gatech.edu/user_surveys`. (This Web link and other Web links in this chapter are on the CD-ROM at the back of this book if you want to get to them quickly without doing the keyboard calisthenics.) The GVU survey has run for four years and may be the single best freely available source of information about Web users.

The GVU survey works in the following way: Twice a year, the survey's directors solicit Web users to fill out a survey form. They use press releases, links, online ads, and other forms of publicity, plus a chance at a small cash prize, to induce people to fill out the survey. About 20,000 people take the survey in a one-month period. The GVU Center then analyzes the results and posts them on the Web.

The GVU survey does have a few flaws. Because users take it voluntarily, instead of being picked randomly, it's skewed toward more frequent Internet users (who are more likely to see the ads and links) and toward those who are willing to take the time to fill out the survey. However, the data from the GVU survey corresponds very closely to other surveys, such as the Find/SVP random telephone survey of American Internet users. Overall, the GVU survey is an excellent starting point for finding out who's on the Web and starting the process of finding out how many of your potential customers are online.

the six months between surveys. You can make decisions about your
Internet presence today with relatively good confidence that the Internet
population, though larger, will still look much the same by the time you
implement your decisions.

Online user profile

Who's online? First off, almost everyone who's online uses the Web. According to the Find/SVP 1997 American Internet User Survey, the home page of
which is shown in Figure 1-8, about 90 percent of all people who are online
use the Web. (The other 10 percent use e-mail or a commercial online
service, such as America Online or the Microsoft Network, but not the Web.)
A summary of the Find/SVP survey results is available at `etrg.findsvp.com/`
`internet/overview.html`. Following are the implications of the prevalence
of Web use and other conclusions that can be drawn from the GVU survey,
the Find/SVP survey, and other surveys of the online and offline worlds.

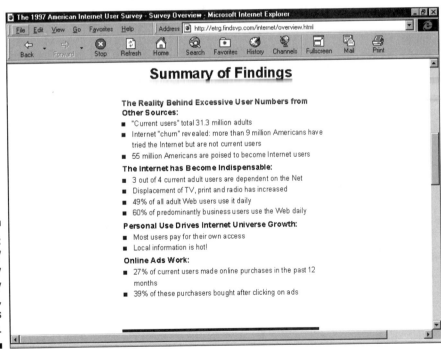

Figure 1-8:
The Find/
SVP survey
is very
thorough,
but details
cost money.

✔ **Over 30 million people are online.** About 30 million people — less than 1 percent of the world's adult population — are online. Of the 120 million or so computers in active use, only one-fourth are connected to the online world. **Implication: The Internet is not the best way to reach a mass worldwide audience.**

✔ **The online world is very American.** According to GVU's WWW User Survey, 80 percent of respondents are American, with 7 percent in Canada or Mexico, 7 percent in Europe, and the rest scattered elsewhere. America Online, the leading non-Web online service with over 10 million users, is also very American, as its name implies. Find/SVP expects the number of American households online to double by 2001, some details of the Find/SVP survey are shown in Figure 1-9. **Implication: Online efforts that are focused first on the American market are more likely to get results.**

✔ **Within America, the Internet is bicoastal.** In the U.S., only California and New York have more than 1 million Internet users, according to Find/SVP. Also high in Internet usage are the rest of the Northeast, the rest of the West Coast, and the Southwest (excluding Texas). **Implication: For regional services, target Californians and New Yorkers first.**

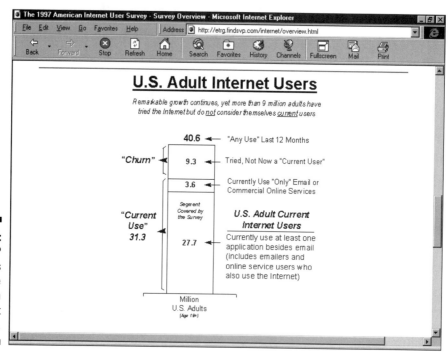

Figure 1-9:
Find/SVP
site shows
where
American
Internet
users are.

✔ **The online world speaks English.** Almost all American online users speak English first; as do many online Europeans. Among Europeans, only about half think that having online information in their native language is important. (European and Asian computer users are commonly multilingual and are accustomed to using software in English or in a mix of English and local languages.) Among other languages, online users speak German, French, and Japanese (in order of popularity). **Implication: You can reach most of the online world with an English-only online presence.**

✔ **The online world is mostly male.** As a consumer population grows, it tends toward mirroring the overall population, so the fact that the Web is maintaining about a two-thirds male to female ratio as it grows is surprising. **Implications: Your online marketing effort reaches mostly men.**

✔ **Online users are well-off.** The mean household income of Web users is about $58,000 a year, according to the GVU Survey. The U.S. Census bureau says that the mean U.S. household income, by contrast, is about $41,000 a year, according to information posted at www.census.gov. **Implication: Use the Web to reach people who are upper-middle-class (or even *rich*).**

✔ **Most users are ages 25–50.** About a fifth of Web users are 19–25, much higher than their percentage in the population, and about one in eight are over 50, less than their percentage in the population. Two-thirds of Web users are 25–50. **Implication: Use the Web first to reach younger people.**

✔ **Half of all online users work in the field of computers or education.** About 30 percent of Web users do computer-related work; 14 percent are students, and other educational occupations make up about 10 percent more, according to GVU's WWW User Survey. Because computer and educational occupations and, to a lesser extent, other professionals make up so much of the online population, most other occupations are not found in the online world as frequently as in the offline world. **Implication: Companies with computer-related and education-related products and services should invest heavily online; others should be more cautious.**

Some facts and implications are obvious, and their effects on your marketing strategies are easy to utilize. However, others may take longer to grasp. For example, in the offline world, older people tend to be richer; the fact that the Web has both a younger-than-average population and a richer-than-average population means that it must have a very high percentage of people who are both young *and* rich. (Maybe that means you can think about marketing gold-plated skateboards on the Net? We doubt it.)

Also interesting is that so far only a few groups are truly flocking to the online world. Nearly every American who works in a computer-related profession is online. Knowledge workers — such as journalists, analysts,

The "online market"

The online market can also be viewed as a collection of pieces of different markets — 20 percent of American men, 10 percent of American women, most computer professionals, and so on. This view of the online market is what maps best to your existing marketing efforts. Use the information in this book and elsewhere — especially the detailed employment information in GVU's WWW User Survey and the American geographical usage breakdown in the Find/SVP Survey — to calculate what percentage of each of your existing target markets is online. Use this information to help figure out how much of your marketing budget to spend online versus elsewhere.

and others — are also heavily online. Of all adult American males, about 20 percent are online. In contrast, older people, women, non-professionals, and non-Americans just don't make up much of the online population. If you have products or services aimed at these smaller online markets, spend slowly and carefully on your online marketing efforts.

For companies who have — or are willing to create — products and services that fit the characteristics of the demographics that we outline in this chapter, the online world can be a *very* rewarding place. Young, rich, professional, male Americans are one of the more free-spending groups on the planet. And Internet users include a disproportionate number of those who influence opinion in America and elsewhere, so your online efforts to reach them have impact far beyond the online world itself.

Online users and occupations

One of the best-understood ways to describe the target market for your products and services is by your target customer's occupation. You probably have at least an intuitive understanding of what lines of work your current and desired customers are in — and also an understanding of what lines of work your customers are *not* in. A good way to get a handle on how ambitious your online effort should be is to find out how many people in the occupations that you're trying to reach are online.

For a quick look at major occupational groups and their presence online, with details for male versus female, USA versus Europe, and age group, you can go to some cool pages at GVU's WWW User Survey:

1. **Connect to the Internet and start your Web browser.**

2. **Go to GVU's WWW User Survey Web site home page at** www.gvu.gatech.edu/user_surveys.

    The GVU Survey home page appears.

3. **Click on the link for the most recent survey. (Higher-numbered surveys are the most recent; the 7th Survey is the most current at the time of this writing.)**

The page for the survey that you chose appears.

4. **Scroll down and click on the Graphic Presentation of Tables and Graphs link.**

The Graphs and Tables of the Results Web page for the survey that you chose appears.

5. **Click on the General Demographics link.**

The Web page scrolls down to links for general demographic questions.

6. **Click on the Major Occupation link.**

The Web page with links to the Major Occupation graphs and tables appears.

7. **Examine the table and graphs for the areas that interest you.**

One of the available graphs, graph of major occupations split by location (All versus U.S.A. versus Europe) is shown in Figure 1-10.

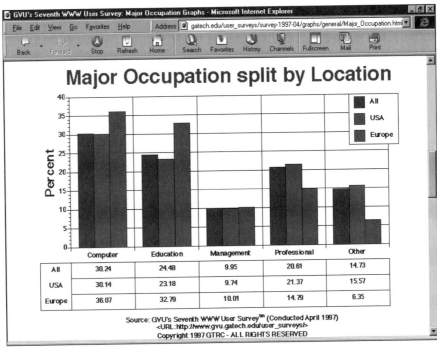

Figure 1-10:
The GVU
Survey tells
you who
does what,
in general.

Like other demographic data, the GVU Survey employment information data does have limitations. The GVU tables don't compare employment of online users to overall employment, nor do they tell you what percentage of people in a given occupational field are online. The information in the GVU tables isn't totally helpful for every marketing effort, because what you probably want to know is what percentage of people in a given occupational field are online so that you know how many of them you can reasonably hope to reach via your online marketing efforts.

A good place to look for broad-brush occupational data is the U.S. Department of Labor Bureau of Labor Statistics Web page. One table that we find helpful is called Employment by Major Occupational Group, available at stats.bls.gov/emptab6.htm. It splits the 130 million or so people in the U.S. workforce into nine major occupational groupings. Some selected data from this table is shown in Table 1-1. Note that professional specialty occupations, a key marketing target online, is projected to be the third-largest and the fastest-growing group. Also note that, unlike the GVU data, the table doesn't include students.

Table 1-1	The U.S. Bureau of Labor Statistics Projected Employment for 2005	
Occupation	*2005 projected employment (in millions)*	*Projected growth 1994–2005 (percent)*
Total	144,708	13.9
Executives, administrative, and managerial	15,071	16.8
Professional specialty occupations	22,387	29.3
Technicians and related support occupations	5,316	19.7
Marketing and sales occupations	16,502	18.0
Administrative support, including clerical	24,172	4.3
Service occupations	24,832	22.7
Agricultural, forestry, fishing, and related occupations	3,650	−3.0
Precision production, craft, and repair occupations	14,880	5.9
Operations, fabricators, and laborers	17,898	4.4

Here is one way to get a finer focus on who's online by occupation:

1. **Repeat Steps 1 through 4 in the previous steps to reach the tables and graphs for GVU's most recent WWW User Survey.**

2. **Click on the General Demographics link.**

   The Web page scrolls down to links for general demographic questions.

3. **Click on the Occupation – Actual Positions link.**

   The Web page for the Actual Job graphs and tables appears, as shown in Figure 1-11.

4. **Examine the table for the jobs that interest you and note the results.**

   The top job areas represented in the GVU's WWW User Survey, rounded to the nearest full percentage point, are Student (K–12 and College), 17 percent; Programmer, 9 percent; Educator (K–12 and College), 6 percent; Manager, 4 percent; Engineer, 3 percent; Microcomputer, 3 percent; and Retired, 3 percent. Other is 27 percent. Marketing professionals and writers are a mere 1 percent each.

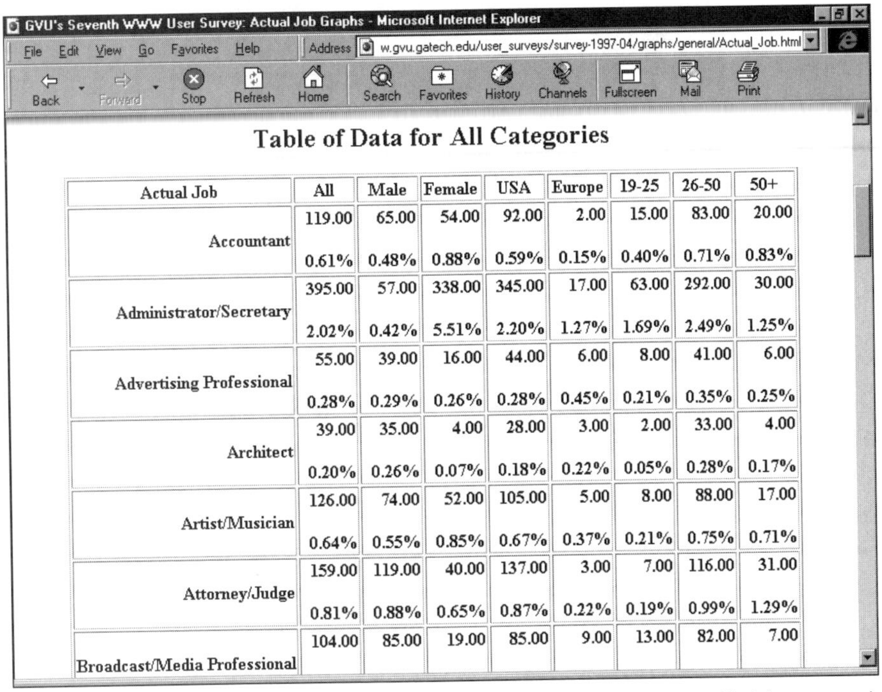

Figure 1-11:
The GVU's
WWW User
Survey also
tells you
who does
what,
specifically.

GVU's Seventh WWW User Survey: Actual Job Graphs - Microsoft Internet Explorer

File　Edit　View　Go　Favorites　Help　　Address w.gvu.gatech.edu/user_surveys/survey-1997-04/graphs/general/Actual_Job.html

Back　Forward　Stop　Refresh　Home　Search　Favorites　History　Channels　Fullscreen　Mail　Print

Table of Data for All Categories

Actual Job	All	Male	Female	USA	Europe	19-25	26-50	50+
Accountant	119.00	65.00	54.00	92.00	2.00	15.00	83.00	20.00
	0.61%	0.48%	0.88%	0.59%	0.15%	0.40%	0.71%	0.83%
Administrator/Secretary	395.00	57.00	338.00	345.00	17.00	63.00	292.00	30.00
	2.02%	0.42%	5.51%	2.20%	1.27%	1.69%	2.49%	1.25%
Advertising Professional	55.00	39.00	16.00	44.00	6.00	8.00	41.00	6.00
	0.28%	0.29%	0.26%	0.28%	0.45%	0.21%	0.35%	0.25%
Architect	39.00	35.00	4.00	28.00	3.00	2.00	33.00	4.00
	0.20%	0.26%	0.07%	0.18%	0.22%	0.05%	0.28%	0.17%
Artist/Musician	126.00	74.00	52.00	105.00	5.00	8.00	88.00	17.00
	0.64%	0.55%	0.85%	0.67%	0.37%	0.21%	0.75%	0.71%
Attorney/Judge	159.00	119.00	40.00	137.00	3.00	7.00	116.00	31.00
	0.81%	0.88%	0.65%	0.87%	0.22%	0.19%	0.99%	1.29%
Broadcast/Media Professional	104.00	85.00	19.00	85.00	9.00	13.00	82.00	7.00

Source: GVU's WWW User Survey, www.gvu.gatech.edu/user_surveys.

This data gives you a pretty good idea as to who's online by occupation. To find *penetration* information — for example, what percentage of all managers are online — you need to compare the percentage of online users in that profession to the total number of people in that profession. Though surveys vary in how they define each profession, you may already have a pretty good idea what percentage of workers fall into the employment categories that interest you. Otherwise, use other resources, including the many online resources that we identify in the Directory, to help you in your search.

One good source for very detailed occupational data for the U.S. workforce is the U.S. Department of Labor's ALMIS, or America's Labor Market Information System, Web page. You can search for specific occupations by state or for the entire country. Figure 1-12 shows the search form that you fill out to generate results. Go to `ecuvax.cis.ecu.edu/~lmi/lmi.html` to start looking.

You certainly can get more detailed data about who's online — by profession or by any other attribute — from a research company working in the online world, but you probably have to pay for the data. If the information hasn't already been developed, you may have to commission a custom report — a very time-consuming and expensive prospect. The steps described in this section give you a way to get a quick, free rough cut on the data that you need. (So even if you pay for more detailed information, you have a way of reality-checking the results that are given to you!)

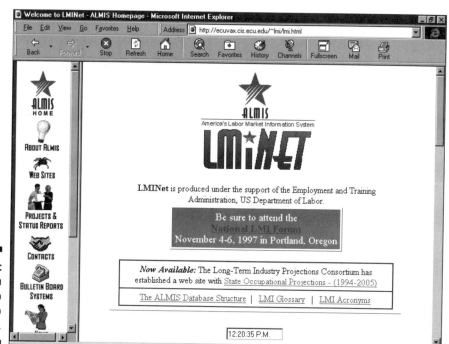

Figure 1-12:
Search
ALMIS to
see who
does what.

Ask your customers

You may eventually need to know just how many of your actual and prospective customers really are online. The best way to find out is to ask them! You can get a rough estimate just by talking to a few dozen of your customers. For somewhat more detail, use a phone survey or a mailed survey form. Check trade associations and other sources for free research relevant to your business. To get detailed quantitative data specific to *your* customers, consider hiring a market research firm. (Of course, that's expensive, which is why in this chapter we point you to as much free data as possible!)

Computer characteristics of online users

When you're designing and testing your Web site or deciding what messages to send to the online world, knowing about the computing environment of the people out there is often valuable. Knowing what kind of computer setups people are using can help you design your Web site and other aspects of your online presence in a way that lets you reach more people, more effectively. Here are a few details about online computing:

- ✔ **Macintosh users are online en masse.** Although only about 4 percent of personal computers sold this year will be Macintoshes, about 26 percent of all GVU Survey respondents use Macs. Other surveys show less Mac access —10 percent or so — but still more than the Macintosh market share would indicate. **Implication: Macintosh users are a big online market.**

- ✔ **Unix users are influential.** Although only about 5 percent of respondents to the GVU survey use Unix, don't forget that the Internet started on Unix and many influential *Webmasters* (people who create and maintain Web sites) and others still use Unix. **Implication: Don't insult Unix users.**

- ✔ **Sixty percent of all Internet access is from the home.** Frequent Internet users, such as those who tend to take the GVU Survey, spend most of their online time at home — though they may be working or seeking work-related information. **Implication: Don't assume users are in the workplace when they log on.**

- ✔ **Two-thirds of users have slow modems.** Although many Web sites work well only when accessed with a fast, network-based Internet connection, two-thirds of all Web use is done at modem speeds of 33.6 Kbps (kilobits per second) or less. **Implication: Design your online presence for users with slow modem; that is, keep huge graphics and other fat files to a reasonable level.**

✔ **Half of users have small screens.** About half of all users have monitors 15" or less in size, and more than half run at 800 x 600 resolution or less. Figure 1-13 shows different screen sizes running a typical Web site. (To show differences in what users experience, this figure shows a Macintosh running Netscape Navigator 4.0 in contrast to most other screen shots in this book that are taken from a PC running Internet Explorer 4.0.) **Implication: Design your online presence for small screens.**

You can't stereotype online denizens as Windows 95 users sitting in offices with fast Internet connections and big screens. A student with a Macintosh in his dorm room, or a computer programmer sitting at home with her PC, a dial-up modem, and a medium-sized screen, are just as common in the online world. Don't swing for the fences in your online presence; create a look that's easy on the user's eye, that comes onscreen quickly, and that fits well on a small screen. (For even more info on screen size, see Chapter 6.)

How Is the Internet Used?

Elsewhere in this chapter we show you the major tools of the online world and tell you quite a bit about who's online — both vital concerns for any online marketing effort. Now we peel back the covers on what people actually *do* online. Some of the facts may surprise you!

How people use online resources

Knowing who's online, as we describe in the previous section, is very helpful in deciding how strong of a marketing effort to make in the online world. Knowing how people use online resources helps you target your marketing effort where it does the most good. Here are some facts about how people use online resources and the relevant implications for your marketing efforts:

✔ **The Web is the online heavyweight.** As we mention earlier in this chapter, 90 percent of all online users — about 28 million people in America alone — use the Web. The Web is also the most flexible and best-known online medium. **Implication: Concentrate your online marketing efforts on the Web.**

✔ **Nearly everyone online uses e-mail.** E-mail is the killer application of the online world; however, using it for mass mailings (*spamming*) is *very* unpopular, as we describe in Chapter 8. **Implication: Use e-mail in online marketing, but proceed *carefully and courteously*.**

✔ **Only half of online users use newsgroups.** This information is courtesy, once again, of GVU's WWW User Survey. As we describe in Chapter 10, newsgroups are not good marketing vehicles for everyone — but you can't ignore them either. **Implication: Use newsgroups sparingly.**

Figure 1-13:
Typical
Web screen
shots at
640 x 480
pixels,
800 x 600,
and
1024 x 768.

✔ **Users are online frequently.** According to the GVU Survey, 85 percent of users log on daily; half of them are online for a total of more than 10 hours a week. (Many users report giving up time watching TV for the Web or other online activities; others even do both at once.) Although this high usage rate may somewhat reflect the fact that the GVU Survey attracts more frequent users, the result is generally supported by other surveys as well. **Implication: The online world gets a lot of its users' attention.**

✔ **Reference is the greatest use of the Web.** The GVU Survey lists the most frequent uses of the Web as reference, news, and product information. Figure 1-14 shows the ZDNet site, which combines all three. **Implications: Put product info online; add reference material to your site to get more users.**

✔ **People are working on the Web.** Two-thirds of users pay for their own online access. Online users spend the largest amount of their time gathering information, followed by searching, browsing, working, and educating themselves, all of which are done by more than half of users. Entertainment, communicating, and especially shopping don't get the same investment of time. **Implication: Take your site seriously — your users do.**

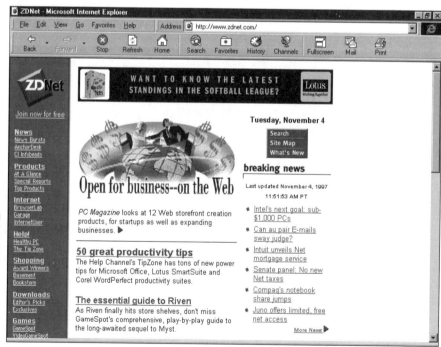

Figure 1-14:
ZDNet
combines
reference,
news, and
product
information.

You can see that people take their online time seriously; people who surf the Net do so often, they find the Net valuable, and they work hard to track down the information that they want. What all this information means is that despite the efforts of many sites to provide eye candy with animation, video, and so on, you can achieve many of your online marketing goals simply by putting up information that you want people to see and by making it as easy to find as you can.

If you do want to put in extra work to attract people, again, going high-tech may not pay. Valuable reference information, such as some tables of data about the industry that you're in, may attract more users — and more of the type of users that you want — than whizzy multimedia features. Take your users seriously, and they'll return the favor.

How people surf

If you're trying to attract people to your Web site, knowing how they use the Internet and what they don't like are two very valuable pieces of information. Here are some tips:

- ✔ **People find sites with search engines.** To find specific sites, more than 80 percent of people use search engines and links. (We show you how to earn a black belt in online searching — or at least defend yourself until help can arrive — in Chapter 2. In Chapter 7, we cover the process you need to follow to make sure that your site appears on the various search engines so that your future online customers can find your site.) Other sources are printed media, friends, and Usenet. **Implication: Make sure that search engines and other sites point to your site.**

- ✔ **People use bookmarks for browsing.** The most popular techniques that people use when casually browsing the Web are bookmarks, search engines, and typing in known URLs. **Implication: Encourage users to bookmark your site.**

- ✔ **The biggest problems are speed, broken links, and finding sites.** Two-thirds of users cite Internet speed as a major problem; half mention broken links; and a third mention finding sites. **Implications: Keep your Web page(s) small and well maintained.**

- ✔ **Users are concerned about censorship, privacy, and navigation.** Censorship is the leading concern of Internet users, with about one-third of users naming it as their primary concern, according to GVU's WWW User Survey. One-quarter of users name privacy concerns, and the GVU Survey includes a lot of information about what users think should be done to protect their privacy. Navigation concerns are next, with about one in eight users worried about getting around the Web and the Internet as a whole. **Implication: Protect user information and make your Web site easy to use.**

> ✔ **People won't pay to surf.** About two-thirds of all users say they would not pay to surf a site, and they back this up with their behavior; very few sites that started out charging money have survived. The only large-scale exception is adult-oriented material, which is the biggest moneymaker online. **Implication: Don't plan to charge for access to your site.**

The facts listed here reinforce some good advice that you'll hear over and over again, in this book and elsewhere: Publicize your URL, make your Web site easy to find with a search engine, and keep it up-to-date by adding new information and eliminating broken links.

Working in the Online World

You picked up this book to help yourself do effective marketing work online. In this chapter we give you a lot of information to help you get a handle on the online world, what the pieces are that make it up, who's in it, and how to start matching your marketing goals to it. Here are some lessons you can carry forward as you use the rest of this book:

> ✔ **You have to be online.** No, not everyone is online, but the people who are online are young, well-off, and influential; if you're not reaching them, you can be sure that your competitors are. You don't have to wrench your business up by the roots and replant it on the Internet; but if you ignore the online world, you do so only at your peril.

> ✔ **Start with the Web.** The Web is the big banana of the online world. Start your online efforts by planning now to create a Web site if you don't have one or regularly update your site if you do.

> ✔ **Use other Internet services.** You have to be aware of Internet newsgroups to protect yourself from flames, rumors, and worse; on the plus side, Internet newsgroups are a popular way for people to get URLs. E-mail is an important part of your Web and overall online strategies. Use the detailed information in this book to consider each Internet service separately and decide how best to use it.

> ✔ **Take a moderate approach. Shakespeare's line from *Macbeth* applies to too many Web sites: "a tale told by an idiot, full of sound and fury, signifying nothing."** Online users want easy-to-navigate, fast-loading, up-to-date Web sites that look good on a medium-sized screen. They want product and reference information and don't want to work hard to get it. You don't have to bet your company on a big, fancy online presence, just be competent, accurate, informative, and up-to-date.

The rest of this book shows you how to create an effective online marketing presence as quickly, easily, and cheaply as possible.

Chapter 2

Finding Marketing Information Online

. . . .

. . . .

*O*ne of the biggest challenges that you face in your marketing effort is time. Because the responsibilities of marketing are so broad, from corporate strategy to pricing decisions to packaging design, finding the time to do everything can be difficult. Sometimes it seems that you don't even have enough time to do *anything*.

One of the many things that you may not have had time to do, in between tending to your other responsibilities, is to become an expert user of the Internet and the Web. You may find yourself too busy in meetings, on the phone, writing that strategic plan, and so on, to spend much time surfing the Web, let alone finding the gems of marketing information and interaction that are out there.

Yet being *wired* — that is, plugged into appropriate online mailing lists, Web sites, chats, and other sources — is nearly a prerequisite for success in marketing these days. If you want to create a robust online presence, you need to know what's going on in the online world.

This chapter shows you how to become a savvy searcher for online marketing resources. As you find the resources that you need, you get a firsthand look at what is — and isn't — out there. You can see what kinds of marketing sites are already available, how various companies and individuals have crafted their online presence, and get an idea of what your current and potential customers may expect of you in the online world.

Using Online Marketing Resources

You can use online resources to meet some of the following key marketing information needs:

- ✔ **Market definition and *segmentation*.** If you're involved in creating a new product, ask yourself: For what market is your product or service intended? For an existing product that has a market, ask yourself: Do other related markets that may be more profitable exist? Online resources can help you with the key marketing activities of defining and *segmenting* your market — that is, identifying groups of customers who may be interested in your product.

- ✔ **Market trends and demographics.** Is your target market growing? Shrinking? Do demographic trends support your marketing plans? Or do demographic trends undermine what you thought was a great idea?

- ✔ **Assessment of the competition.** What's the competition up to — both online and in the offline world? You can find out about both of these areas of activity online. For instance, competitors often let valuable information, such as features of upcoming products, leak in online newsgroups.

- ✔ **Opportunities and *buzz*.** What new opportunities are coming up? Who's hot — or not? Figure 2-1 shows the news page for CNET's NEWS.COM, a leading resource for online news, at www.news.com. The online world, being the cutting edge place that it is, is full of information about what's on the horizon.

After you know where to look, you can fill much of your need for marketing information in all these areas online.

Use the Directory in this book and on the CD-ROM as a starting point for creating your own list of top marketing resources.

Though you may need only a modest online presence to match your offline competition, watch out for online-based competitors — either an established, well-known company who starts selling online or a new online-only organization. If you start hearing back from your customers about new online-only competitors and you start losing sales to this new competition, your need to go online increases in a big way. To meet this kind of challenge, do everything in this book to bolster your online marketing presence and then take a look at *Selling Online For Dummies* by Leslie Lundquist (IDG Books Worldwide, Inc.) to move into online sales as well.

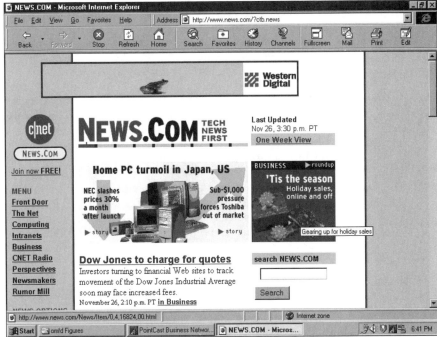

Figure 2-1:
CNET's
NEWS.COM
has the
latest online
news.

Hi-tech is tops online

While Internet users vary, they do have a few things in common: They're all computer users, and they're all on the Internet. Though this information may sound obvious, figuring out the implications of commonly understood facts is the source of many marketing insights. The implication here is that on the Internet, you can expect to find an awful lot of information about things like computers, the Internet, and high technology in general. You can also expect to find a reasonable amount of information about things that techies are interested in — investment information, certain obscure TV shows, movies (such as anything with "Star Trek" in its title), and some of the more esoteric intellectual pursuits. However,

the Internet has a dearth of information about most other things, such as farming or sculpture.

How useful online marketing resources are to you is likely to depend on how your interests compare to the interests of North American computer-using techies. If you're in the computer field or a related area, you can probably find a great deal of online information that's of interest to you. If not, finding what you need is tougher. Rest assured, though, that as the Internet continues to grow, the marketing resources available in nontechnical areas of interest will improve.

Goals and costs of online searches

After you get the hang of online searching, it's a lot of fun, and it turns up a seemingly never-ending stream of results. You may never find exactly the key fact that you wanted to know when you started, but you're bound to find out several other worthwhile things along the way. However, this apparent serendipity actually underscores a problem common to many types of online efforts: The Web can be fun, interesting, and seemingly valuable, but at the end of the day, it doesn't always do enough to help pay the bills. And how are you going to justify that faster Internet connection you need if you can't show the value of what you do online?

The main cost of most online searches is your time. Though you can spend a lot of money with online resources like Lexis-Nexis and Dialog (a couple of searchable online resources that cost money to use), your time is still likely to be more valuable than the bills you run up. And as we note at the beginning of this chapter, time is the one thing that people doing marketing work never have enough of.

So have a clear goal in mind at the beginning of an online search and keep your eyes on the prize. Figure out what you want to know and how long you plan to spend trying to find out. Then when that amount of time expires, stop, and go to Plan B — which may be calling someone, sending e-mail to a knowledgeable source, or even hiring someone to investigate for you. Just don't allow yourself to spend hours searching for information, get distracted by the CoffeeCam Web site (`www.menet.umn.edu/coffeecam/`) that shows whether anyone has made coffee yet, and find yourself wondering two hours later why you went online in the first place.

Strengths of online resources

The advantages of using online marketing resources are that they tend to be cheap, timely, and fast. Online, you can find some free information on almost any topic, even if that information is simply a phone number to call or some suggested book titles on the particular topic. With a little experience, you can do an effective initial search yourself. Often, especially in the fast-paced world of marketing, all you need is a quick rough answer or even just some clue as to what that answer may be. Online resources are great for that.

The Web, newsgroups, mailing lists, *pushed* information, and online services all have their share of the latest and greatest information. Where these online resources tend to be lacking is in depth, completeness, and perspective. Given that almost all online information is free, the providers rightly feel that they've done you a favor by telling you anything at all. They don't feel obligated to provide comparative information or context. In addition, partly because the Web in particular is so new and partly because online resources tend to delete old information to make room for newer stuff, reliable historical information is lacking.

However, this quick turnover of information, though it may seem like a drawback, can be used to your advantage: Look for breaking news, recent press releases, customer questions, and general *buzz*. Then use traditional printed resources and ask knowledgeable people for depth and perspective.

Many books like this one provide long lists of online marketing resources. This book includes a Directory section with lots of links to good marketing resources, but we also believe in the old saying: "Give a person a fish, and you feed them for that day; teach that person how to fish, and you feed them for a lifetime." No one can provide you with all the specific online resources that you need for your job. However, we can provide you with techniques that will continue to serve you well as your needs and the Internet's resources change. So study the techniques on Internet searching in the next section and push technology later in this chapter, and use them to build your own connections into the online world.

Following the experts

As you search for information online, think about the process in relation to planning your own online presence. People with a strong online presence are, to a certain extent, experts. However, because the online world is still new, even the experts make lots of mistakes! Here are some of the potential pitfalls to online marketing and how they relate to your own planning:

- ✔ **Hard-to-find Web sites.** The Internet has no secret search engines or places to go where all the cool people find sites easily — if you have trouble finding company or product information on the Web, lots of other people are having the same problem. Think about how you can make your own company and product information easy to find. Chapter 7 covers the details.

- ✔ **Slow-loading Web pages.** If you get frustrated waiting for someone's graphics-rich Web page to load, keep that in mind when you design your own Web site. If your site is too slow to load, people won't stick around to see it.

- ✔ **Missing information.** Often people quickly find a site and then waste many minutes trying to find information that should be front and center. For instance, many companies don't give their real-world address or a main switchboard phone number for people who want more information. D'oh! Organize your site in such a way that it answers common informational needs, and at the very least provide numbers and addresses for more conventional methods of communication.

- ✔ **Unanswered criticism in newsgroups and mailing lists.** You can find some of the most amazingly harsh criticism of companies in their own company-sponsored mailing lists and in newsgroups online — but what's even more amazing is that it often goes unanswered. Think about how to respond effectively and constructively to online criticism of your company or product. Chapter 10 discusses this issue in more depth.

- ✔ **Flame mail.** Many times companies respond to criticism, whether harsh or gentle, with flame mail of their own. Think about how to get everyone who speaks for your company online to do so in a positive way. The old adage "fight fire with fire" definitely does *not* work online.

- ✔ **Unanswered registrations and e-mail.** Do you like it when you register at a Web site or send e-mail, and never hear anything back? Visitors to your Web site won't like it if you do the same thing to them. Think about how to interact effectively with people who send you information and e-mail, and make sure that you respond to all e-mail messages and site registrations. Chapters 8 and 9 go into more detail on e-mail.

- ✔ **Privacy concerns.** Ever wonder what happens to that registration information you give online? So will people who register at your Web site. In fact, according to the GVU's WWW User Survey discussed in Chapter 1, people place a value on their personal information and want to trust you before giving it. If they don't have a feeling of trust, they often enter false information. Think about how much information you ask people to give you online and how to tell them what you plan to do with it.

Searching Out Marketing Opportunities on the Internet

Most people who use the Internet know how to search it; as we mention in Chapter 1, more than 80 percent of Internet users use search engines. However, few people know even the rudiments of truly effective searching.

Building up your bookmarks

In marketing, you can't afford to be the last one on your block to hear something — and being first gives you a big advantage over your competitors! As you search the Internet, build up a robust list of *bookmarks* (or *favorites,* as they're called in Internet Explorer) so that you can easily revisit valuable sites for new information. We suggest spending some time making your bookmarks list a valuable resource — here are some tips:

- ✔ **Create subject folders.** Don't make your bookmarks list an unorganized catchpot for all your personal and business interests. Create subject folders for areas of interest — partners, the competition, demographics, marketing offline, marketing online, and more. Subject folders can make your future online searches much faster and more productive.

- ✔ **Create *frequency* folders.** Create folders for sites that you want to visit daily, weekly, monthly, and just occasionally. (Don't be afraid to put the same link in a subject folder and a frequency folder.) With frequency folders, you can put your all-too-brief Websurfing time to the best use.

- ✔ **Prune early and often.** About a century ago, a candidate in a U.S. election used the irreverent catchphrase, "Vote often and early, for James Michael Curley." Although you're not really allowed to vote more than once per election, you *can* trim your bookmarks list frequently. Get rid of any links that you haven't used lately and are unlikely to need again in the near future. (If you need a link in the *far* future, you can find it by searching again.) The less deadwood in your bookmarks, the more you use them.

- ✔ **Share your bookmarks.** One way to elevate the level of discussion among your colleagues is to give them the opportunity to be as well informed as you are. Send your bookmarks to them as an e-mail attachment and then show them how to bring your bookmarks into their own bookmarks list. If you have people working for you or with you on a project team, sharing bookmarks is a great way to get everyone on the same (Web) page.

- ✔ **Know how to use your browser well.** Netscape Navigator 4.0 and Internet Explorer 4.0 each have their own tricks for searching, managing bookmarks, retrieving previously visited links, and more. (Because searching is so important when using the Web for online marketing, we give you some general information about searching using both browsers, later in this chapter.) Pick the browser you like and use it.

You can find Internet Explorer 4.0 on the *Marketing Online For Dummies* CD-ROM or download the latest version of either browser from the Web: www.microsoft.com for Internet Explorer 4.0 and www.netscape.com for Netscape Navigator.

Which browser is better?

Internet Explorer and Netscape Navigator are both excellent browsers, each with their own advantages. Having used both over the years, we think that in the latest versions, both numbered 4.0, Internet Explorer is a step ahead of Netscape Navigator, mainly because its push technology, searching, history, and other capabilities are better integrated. However, if you're already used to Netscape Navigator, stick with it and upgrade to Netscape Navigator 4.0 if you haven't already.

Using Internet Explorer 4.0 for searching

One of the most important tools for using the Internet effectively is a good set of bookmarks of top Web sites relating to online marketing and your industry. The way that you find cool Web sites to bookmark is by searching. And Internet Explorer 4.0, with its high degree of integration, makes searching easy.

Internet Explorer 4.0 is a key search tool because it has a new feature for searching that puts the search hits down the left edge of the browser window and the searched-for Web page to the right of the search area, as shown in Figure 2-2. To switch search providers, just choose a different one from the pull-down list. Having the search hits listed on the left allows you to very quickly and easily scan through them to see which one you want to investigate further. After you find something that's worth looking at full screen, just click the Search button again to hide the search area and use the full browser window for viewing the site.

We usually don't like *frames,* a technique that Web authors use to display the Web page as two or more separate frames, also known as panes. But Internet Explorer uses frames well, so in this case, pane is a good thing.

Pull-down list of search providers

Search window   Search button

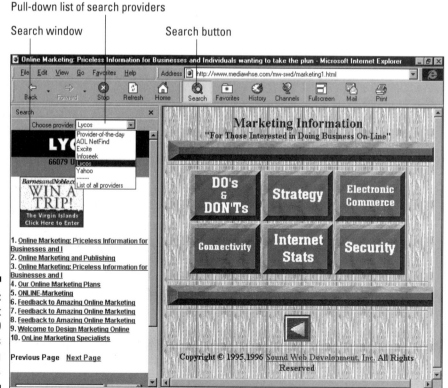

Figure 2-2:
Internet
Explorer 4.0
makes
searching
easy.

For the section on Yahoo!, later in this chapter, we show you how to access the Yahoo! Web page directly, because you get more complete information that way. But for quick searches, the Internet Explorer 4.0 Search button is the way to go.

Follow these steps to do a quick search in Internet Explorer 4.0:

1. **Start Internet Explorer 4.0.**

2. **Click the Search button or choose Go⇨Search the Web.**

   The Search pane appears, as shown in Figure 2-2.

3. **Choose a search engine from the pull-down menu of search providers.**

   We like Excite as a search engine — its search display includes many useful options for fast searches. These options are especially beneficial for the fuzzy kinds of searches online marketers sometimes have to do, such as searching for everything about corn oil — a product whose name includes common words that have many meanings.

   You can choose the last option, List of all providers, to see a Web page that lists over a dozen search engines, including specialty engines for searching Usenet newsgroups, chat sites, and more. The Web page for the list of all providers is shown in Figure 2-3.

Figure 2-3: The List of all providers option shows many more search choices.

4. **Enter the term(s) that you want to search for and then click the Search button.**

   Your top ten search results appear in the Search pane, as shown in Figure 2-4 with a search for information on "online marketing." Here are some things to notice about the results that appear in the Excite Search pane:

   - **Title.** The actual words that appear in the search pane are the Web page titles. Web page titles are hidden HTML entries that do not appear in the Web pages themselves. See Chapter 5 for details on how this works.

   - **URL.** Rest the cursor over a title to see the URL (Uniform Resource Locator — the address) of the Web page. The URL can sometimes give you a clue as to whether you want to visit the Web page. (For instance, you may recognize a company name, or a college or personal site may be more or less likely to have the kind of content you want.)

   - **Summary.** Click the Excite icon next to any site to display the *site summary*. The site summary is the first words that appear in the body of the site's HTML code, including comments. (See Chapter 5 for more details on HTML.) Click the Excite icon again to hide the site summary.

   - **More Like This.** Within the summary, click the `More Like This` link to update the search and find more sites like the one summarized.

   - **Confidence level.** Excite gives a rating to how strongly the site matches with your search terms. As you look at matches, keep an eye on the confidence level; where it drops sharply, your odds of finding what you're looking for drop as well.

5. **Click a search link to view the Web page in the Web page pane.**

   Viewing the Web page while keeping the search results visible in the Search pane is a fast and easy way to preview search links to see if they're what you want, or to continue the search if you need to keep looking.

6. **Click the View Full Screen option at the bottom of the Search pane to view your search results full-screen, as shown in Figure 2-5.**

   Use the options in the View Full Screen Web page to refine your search. These options are especially useful when your search words have multiple meanings, like *graphic* (graphic equalizer? computer graphics?) or *Apple* (Apple computer? Apple records? Golden delicious apple?).

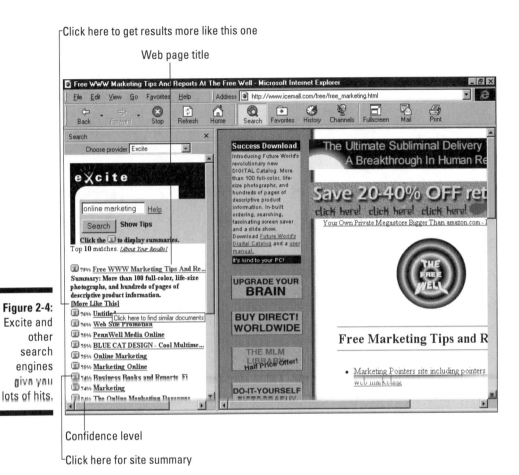

Figure 2-4:
Excite and
other
search
engines
give you
lots of hits.

Click here to get results more like this one

Web page title

Confidence level

Click here for site summary

7. **Click the Previous and Next buttons to move through your search hits. Continue viewing summaries and Web pages until you find a site that you want to explore more.**

Using Netscape Navigator 4.0 for searching

Netscape Navigator has long been the best browser; but in its 4.0 version, it's now roughly equivalent in capabilities to Internet Explorer 4.0. It's still the best choice for organizations that need a single browser that works on many platforms, and Netscape is working on future capabilities — most notable, a unified, cross-platform desktop — that may allow it to move back ahead. So if you're accustomed to Navigator, sticking with it is worthwhile.

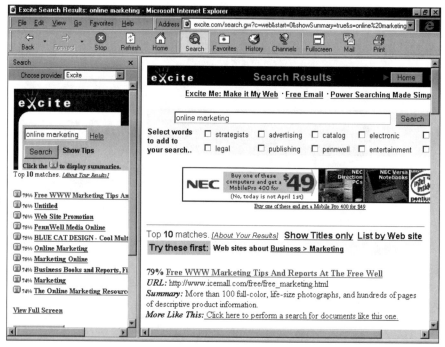

Netscape has a powerful search capability that includes all the features of Internet Explorer searches except for the ability to drive the search from a pane of hits down the left-hand side, as shown back in Figure 2-2. Instead, in Netscape, you go directly to the full-screen display, which is a time-saver if you frequently end up going to the full-screen display anyway. Follow these steps to do a search in Netscape Navigator 4.0:

1. **Start Netscape Navigator 4.0.**

2. **Click the Search button or choose Edit➪Search Internet.**

    The Search page appears. Navigator automatically chooses a search provider for you.

3. **If the search engine you want is not already chosen, choose it from the buttons that list search providers.**

    The Search page appears with a window where you enter your search term(s), as shown in Figure 2-6. The search display for Excite includes options that are particularly useful for online marketers, such as site summaries.

    Unlike Internet Explorer 4.0, you don't have to make an extra menu choice to see additional search options; all the choices are available by simply scrolling down the search page.

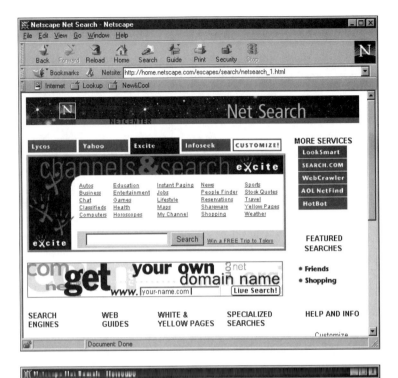

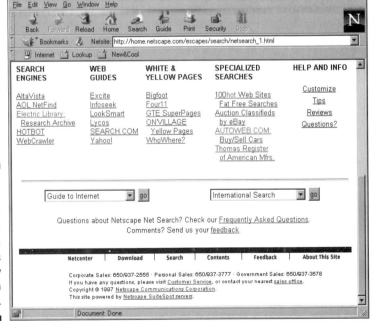

Figure 2-6:
The
Netscape
search
page
includes
many
search
options.

4. **Enter the term(s) that you want to search for and then click the Search button. In Figure 2-7 we searched for the term "marketing online."**

   Your top ten search results appear in the Search window, as shown in Figure 2-7 with a search for information on online marketing. Here are some things to notice about the results that appear in the Excite Search window:

   - **Title.** The actual words that appear in the search pane are the Web page titles. These hidden HTML entries do not appear in the Web pages themselves. See Chapter 5 for details on how titles work.

   - **URL.** In Netscape Navigator searches, unlike Internet Explorer searches, you immediately see the URL (Uniform Resource Locator — the Internet address) of the Web page, which can give you a clue as to whether you want to visit this site.

   - **Summary.** The site summary is the first words that appear in the body of the site's HTML code, including comments. In Navigator, unlike Explorer, you don't have to do anything extra to see the summary.

   - **More Like This.** Within the summary, click the More Like This link to update the search and find more sites like the one summarized.

   - **Confidence level.** This option gives you Excite's rating of how strongly the site matches with your search terms.

5. **Use the options at the top of the hits list to find out more about your results.**

   Excite finds any predefined categories that match your search words and gives you the chance to go straight to the category. We find a lot of good marketing links this way. You can also click the appropriate link to view only the titles of the search hits or list the search hits in order by Web site.

6. **Use the options at the bottom of the hits list to find out more or to fine-tune your search.**

   At the bottom of the hits list you see the same options that we describe in Step 5, plus additional terms that you can click to check them, which includes them in your search. For instance, you may choose to add the term *advertising* to a search for online marketing information.

7. **Click the Previous and Next buttons to move through your search hits. Continue viewing summaries and Web pages until you find a site that you want to explore more.**

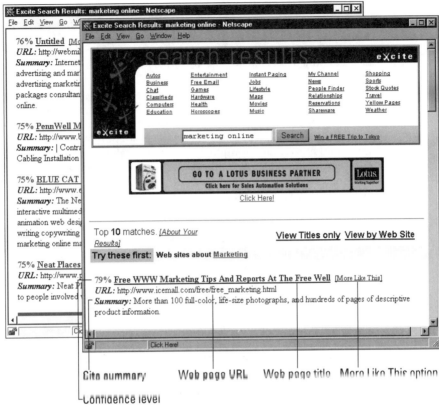

Cito summary   Wob pago URL   Wob pago title   Moro Liko This option

Confidence level

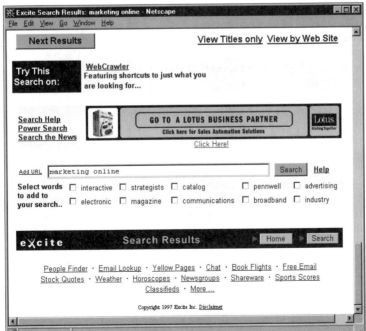

Figure 2-7:
Netscape
Navigator
gives you
the details
up front.

Using Yahoo! for category searches

One valuable tool that works well with any browser — including older versions of Internet Explorer, Netscape Navigator, and other browsers — is Yahoo! Certain online tools and resources continue to amaze us, and Yahoo! is one of those winners. Yahoo! was a Web pioneer, started by three now-famous Stanford graduate students who created a directory of Web resources for fun. The Yahoo! service became more and more popular, and more and more demanding of their time, so they quit school to create a company. Yahoo! is now a Silicon Valley stalwart and a company that looks like one of the long-term winners on the Web. (Yahoo! is just the kind of success story that you may be looking to duplicate in your own online marketing efforts!)

Cool, you say, but what's so great about the Yahoo! search engine? From the beginning, Yahoo! has used a staff of literate — not necessarily technically adept, but literate in the English department sense of the word — to categorize Web sites for easier searching. Yahoo! organizes the Web in much the same way that the Dewey decimal system organizes a library.

The strengths of Yahoo! are a good match for online marketing because the categories match the way that regular people think. For instance, if you want to look at all the companies in a given field, you can use Yahoo! to go down five or six levels deep into a very narrow category of companies and then search within that narrow category. And Yahoo! frequently shows you related resources — such as industry directories and online mailing lists — as you do your search.

When you want to find all the good resources in a given field, Yahoo! is your best starting point. And when you want to search within a narrow area — do a search that gets you marketing winners, but not stock market winners — Yahoo! is the way to go.

You should always set aside a chunk of time for a thorough Web search, but have at least a half hour free before starting a search in Yahoo! You're likely to find so much interesting stuff that you may miss lunch while you're searching the Web and bookmarking useful sites.

In our screen shots we use the Internet Explorer 4.0 browser, but Yahoo! works just as well in other browsers. Because Yahoo! works poorly in the Internet Explorer 4.0 Search pane, and takes real advantage of the extra space if you give it a full browser window, you may want to do a full-screen Yahoo! search. Here's how:

1. Start your Web browser.

2. Go to the Yahoo! Web site at `www.yahoo.com`, as shown in Figure 2-8.

Consider bookmarking the Yahoo! Web site or even making it the default home page that appears after you start your Web browser. (Yahoo! isn't the most popular site on the Web for nothing.) The My Yahoo! feature lets you set up your own news feed so you can get specific news for marketing or your industry; you can also look for people online (always valuable for keeping in touch with your marketing contacts), get free e-mail (get your kids on e-mail!), and more. (We were so enthralled that we even stopped to look at the Yahoo! in-house job listings, but nothing was a good fit.)

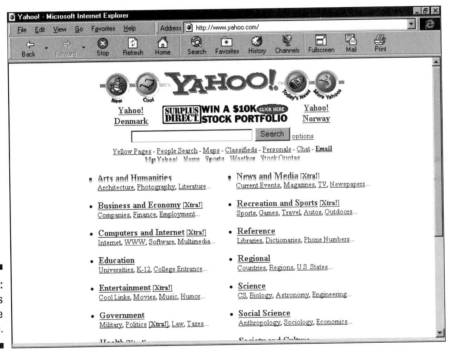

Figure 2-8:
Yahoo! is effective and fun.

3. Click on a category that interests you.

The Yahoo! page for the category that you chose appears; an example is shown in Figure 2-9. Note these major features:

- **Restricted search.** You can search for certain keywords within a certain category. This capability alone can save you a lot of search time. For instance, to find out about marketing resources in your industry, click your way down into the category that describes your industry. Then enter the word "marketing," click on the second radio button to narrow the search to the current category, and then click on the Search button.

- **Highlights.** Just below the search entry text box are some options that change depending on the category you're in. Look here for news, chats, and other kinds of specialized information.

- **Subcategories.** The subcategories are carefully chosen and sensible, even as you drill down into obscure areas. (Just remember that Yahoo! started at Stanford and that a lot of bright undergrads worked on the Yahoo! database.)

- **Featured links.** Yahoo! lists certain links that fit the category, such as key resources and newsgroups, in alphabetical order beneath the subcategories. This listing is great for finding resources to use in online marketing. You can find some gems here, but also some dogs; don't stop your search with the featured links list.

4. Continue moving among categories and doing searches within categories until you find the area that you need.

5. Enter search terms to find the specific information that you need.

The search results appear, as shown in Figure 2-10. Notice that search terms are highlighted within both the category and specific site information listed.

If you already have an online presence (or after you do), make sure you show up in Yahoo! in the categories that fit your business; if you don't, contact the folks at Yahoo! to make sure they classify you correctly. Because Yahoo! is so widely used, it constitutes free advertising that you can't ignore. See Chapter 7 for details on how to make sure you show up in Yahoo!

As you search in Yahoo! and other search engines, be sure to keep an eye out for mailing lists, online chats, newsgroups, and other non-Web resources that you can use to stay informed.

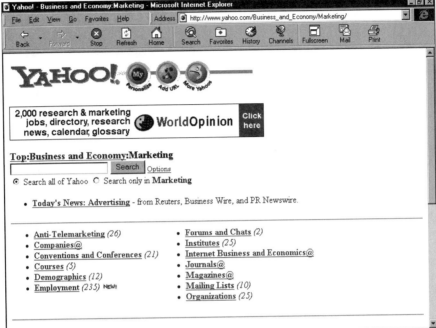

Figure 2-9:
Yahoo!
categories
are deep
and wide.

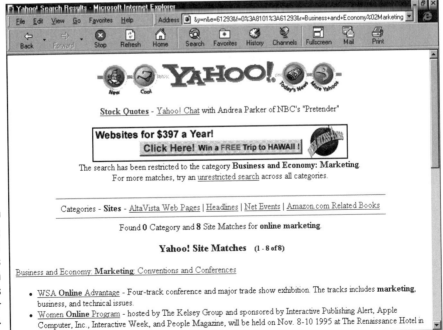

Figure 2-10:
Do Yahoo!
searches
within
categories
for better
results.

After you type in a URL in Internet Explorer 4.0, it attempts to complete the URL for you based on the first letters that you type in and the letters in URLs that you've typed in the past. Because few URLs start with a *y,* you can usually get to Yahoo! by choosing File⇨Open and then typing **www.y.** Internet Explorer completes the URL for you and brings up Yahoo! In Netscape Navigator you can reach a Web site simply by entering the middle part of any URL that starts with `www.` and ends with `.com`. For example, to reach Yahoo, choose File⇨Open Page, then type **yahoo**. Netscape Navigator completes the URL for you and brings up Yahoo!

Using other search engines

Though Excite and Yahoo! should get you most of what you need, other search engines have strengths as well. You can access a variety of search engines from Microsoft's Search page, shown back in Figure 2-3 (`home.microsoft.com/access/allinone.asp`), or the Netscape Navigator search page, shown in Figure 2-6 (`home.netscape.com/escapes/search/netsearch_1.html`). However, when you use these search pages, you're cut off from some advanced options that are available only if you go to a particular search engine's Web site. To get more options, go straight to the search engine's home page. Here are the home pages for some of the search engines highlighted on the Microsoft and Netscape search pages and elsewhere:

- ✔ **AltaVista.** A fast search engine is especially valuable for an online marketing search, which often requires many tries to narrow down a topic. The AltaVista search engine is fast and complete in its features. You find it at `www.altavista.digital.com/`.

- ✔ **HotBot.** *Wired Magazine's* HotBot may be the fastest search engine of all. Go to `www.hotbot.com`.

- ✔ **Newsgroups.** Deja News is a specialized search engine for newsgroup postings. These postings can serve as a giant database of user comments on your products and your competitors' products. Deja News can also help you find newsgroups related to your industry area that you may want to join, as we describe in Chapter 10. Look for it at `www.dejanews.com`.

- ✔ **Chat.** For a guide to chat activity, check out Yack at `www.yack.com`. For online marketing, participate in chats about your industry and about online marketing topics.

✔ **Four11.** Recently acquired by Yahoo!, Four11 is the leading provider of white-pages-type directory services to help you find e-mail and real addresses of people — information you often need for online marketing efforts. ("I wonder where old Bud went, I'd like to hire him for a consulting job.") You can access Four11 through Yahoo! or directly through its Web site at `www.four11.com`, shown in Figure 2-11.

✔ **MetaCrawler.** *Meta* means all-encompassing, and *crawler* refers to Web crawlers, programs that automatically search the Web and index the results. As its name implies, MetaCrawler queries several leading search tools simultaneously to get very complete results, with duplicates removed. Using a search engine like this may cut your search time a bit. Check out MetaCrawler at `www.metacrawler.com`.

✔ **SEARCH.COM.** The CNET Web site has spun off a monster site for all kinds of online searches at `www.search.com`.

If you want to get really good at online searching, check out *World Wide Web Searching For Dummies,* 2nd Edition, by Brad Hill (IDG Books Worldwide, Inc.).

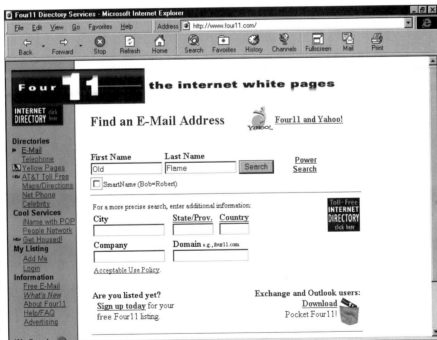

Figure 2-11:
Four11 helps you find people.

Searching specialized databases

Although the Web is a rich and wonderful resource and more and more high-quality information is moving to the Web, it still can't match the resources of paid databases like Lexis-Nexis or Dialog, which are among the best-known resources for specialized business and legal information. The trouble with these services is that they not only cost more money than Web sources (most of which are free), but require more time and knowledge of the specialized search languages that they employ. (True, these databases offer some free services via the Web, but you're likely to get sucked into using the paid ones to get the best information; and though they *do* offer easy interfaces, you're likely to need to use the difficult ones to get the most detailed information in a reasonable amount of time.)

Although figuring out how to use the paid databases can be worth the time and money, discussing the tradeoffs and how to use their information is really beyond the scope of this book. If you need a search done thoroughly and quickly, find a professional researcher with Lexis-Nexis or Dialog expertise. If you want to try it yourself, go to the Yahoo! category for this kind of service, www.yahoo.com/Business_and_Economy/Companies/Information or start your search from within America Online or CompuServe, each of which offer a selection of paid databases, low pricing for occasional searches, and support for using the paid databases effectively.

Getting Information Pushed to You

Something that's helpful to most online users and nearly perfect for marketing is *push technology,* a relatively new kind of Internet service that delivers information directly to you. Push technology has been much-hyped but has now achieved broad acceptance; it's integrated into the new versions of the leading Web browser suites — as part of Internet Explorer 4.0 and in the separate Netscape Netcaster 4.0 push client — and the leading push program, PointCast 2.0, has over a million active users. Marimba's Castanet technology continues to rack up design wins as well.

If you want the complete story on push, read Bud's book *Push Technology For Dummies* (IDG Books Worldwide, Inc.).

Push programs send you up-to-date news and information on any topic that you choose; the best programs also provide many links to the Web. This way push doesn't replace your Websurfing time; instead it just makes your Web time more efficient. The programs push to you the information that you know you need; then you can find important related information by following links from pushed stories back to the Web and by Websurfing on your own.

The three major push platforms are PointCast 2.0, the updated push client program from the company that's the leader in push technology; Internet Explorer 4.0, with push features integrated into the Web browser; and Netscape Communicator, the suite of online tools for Netscape that includes not only Netscape Navigator 4.0 — the latest version of the industry-leading Web browser — but also Netscape Netcaster, a powerful push client. You can use any of these platforms or all three to get information pushed to you.

For the online marketer who wants to create a push channel, push technology presents both a problem and an opportunity. The opportunity is that users who subscribe to your push channel are giving you the ability to automatically send them marketing messages as often as they choose to update the channel. The problem is that users typically won't subscribe to an all-advertising push channel; you have to include enough useful information to make it worth their while.

Following are some tips and tricks for using PointCast 2.0, the leading push-only product available. Not only is PointCast a pioneer in push technology, and a great way to keep up-to-date, it's also an effective carrier of advertising. As you use PointCast, consider the best way to publicize your own online marketing efforts.

Staying up-to-date with PointCast

PointCast is the original push application; its most frequently used option is the PointCast Screen Saver, shown in Figure 2-12, which displays current stock quotes and headlines when you're not using your computer. (This feature was amazing to people when PointCast was first introduced in early 1996; now it's commonplace.)

PointCast needs to connect to the Internet to receive information updates. It works with either a dial-up modem connection or a direct connection via a network. See the Help files within PointCast for more information.

How does the push part of PointCast work? Well, your computer regularly requests updates from PointCast servers on the Internet. After you set up PointCast, you don't have to go Websurfing to get updated information; it's sent to you automatically on a schedule that you set. And then PointCast takes over your screen when it's idle — kind of a pushy thing to do! — and puts the info right in your face. (You can turn off the PointCast Screen Saver component if you want to.)

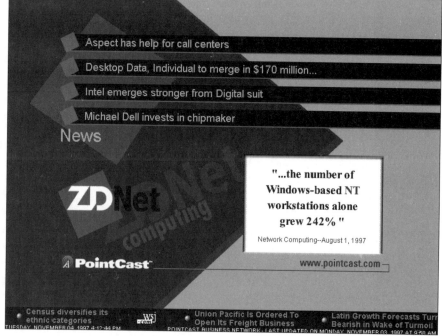

Aspect has help for call centers

Desktop Data, Individual to merge in $170 million...

Intel emerges stronger from Digital suit

Michael Dell invests in chipmaker

News

ZDNet computing

"...the number of
Windows-based NT
workstations alone
grew 242% "

Network Computing--August 1, 1997

PointCast

www.pointcast.com

Census diversifies its ethnic categories
WSj.com
Union Pacific Is Ordered To Open Its Freight Business
Latin Growth Forecasts Turn Bearish in Wake of Turmoil

TUESDAY, NOVEMBER 04, 1997 4:12:44 PM   POINTCAST BUSINESS NETWORK, LAST UPDATED ON MONDAY, NOVEMBER 03, 1997 AT 9:58 AM

Figure 2-12:
The PointCast Screen Saver takes over your screen when you're not using your computer.

Although it's been a big success by almost any measure, PointCast has also gotten a lot of criticism. For instance, the PointCast Screen Saver, neat as it is, can also be a distraction. And when many PointCast users on the same corporate network get updated at once, the network can get bogged down. Finally, you can accomplish similar results — that is, push information to people — with e-mail; you just can't include the pretty pictures.

On the up side, most marketing types need lots of information, and PointCast is an especially good tool for people in marketing, as we describe in the next section. In addition, PointCast has introduced several free tools to make its use on corporate networks easier on network administrators; see the PointCast Web site at www.pointcast.com for the latest information on these tools.

Eight excellent PointCast channels for online marketing

As a PointCast user you're allowed to have up to 11 PointCast channels, 9 channels that you choose plus the Connections superchannel — you can have as many individual PointCast Connections as you want — and the nearest regional newspaper to you. Here are eight of my favorites:

✓ **The Connections superchannel:** This channel is an easy pick, because it has so many specialized channels contained within it. Finding just a couple of Connections that meet your needs can be a big help in staying up-to-date. (Personal highlights: the Mining Company's Internet Industry, Marketing, and Usnenet sites; the Internet Advertising discussion list; and David Strom's Web Informant newsletter.)

✓ **The Industries and Companies channels:** The Industries channel allows you to track up to ten industries from among almost 50 choices. With Companies you can track any 25 companies that have a stock ticker symbol. Together they're a great way to keep up with your industry and the competition.

✓ *The Wall Street Journal:* Now you can get a steady dose of *The Wall Street Journal* — considered by many to be a business necessity — without getting ink on your fingers or paying for the interactive version subscription.

✓ **ZDNet and CMPnet:** Two excellent sources for computer industry and online news, ZDNet focuses more on products, including downloadable shareware, and CMPnet covers industry news.

✓ **The Weather channel:** You can get weather reports for your own area by picking up the paper or turning on the radio, but with the Weather channel, you can get weather reports for places you're traveling to or where your friends and colleagues live and work. The weather is one of the few sure and safe conversation-starters, and being plugged in to the weather as it's happening to the person on the other end of the phone or e-mail exchange can be fun.

✓ **Wired News:** Overhyped, annoying in its graphical design, and rude in its tone and approach, *Wired* magazine is still one of the most powerful voices for the online world, both reflecting and influencing online culture. Wired News is a good vehicle for keeping up and a good source for ideas as you plan and implement your own online marketing efforts. The Wired PointCast channel is shown in Figure 2-13.

The Connections superchannel and the Companies and Industries channels deliver a lot of company press releases along with regular, independently written news. This is not a bad thing — getting the company's viewpoint can be valuable. Just remember, *caveat lector* (let the reader beware) — do be aware of the source of any news you read.

Keep track of what you like and dislike about the PointCast Connections channels that you subscribe to. Think about how a PointCast Connections channel can help your company stay close to users.

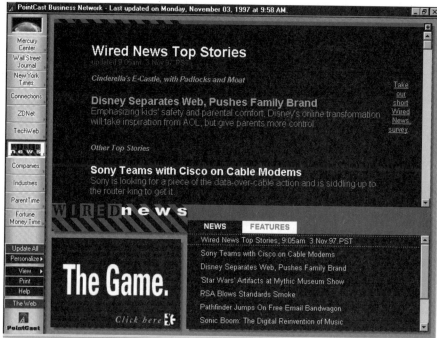

Chapter 3

Effective Online Marketing

- -

- -

*W*e're reminded of an old saying from the days when computers were first being used to automate business processes (no, not "If it ain't broke, don't fix it."). The saying is: "Taking a bad process and putting it on the computer doesn't make it a good process." The upshot of this cliché was that you often had to fix your business processes before computerizing them, or you would just end up with an expensive mess.

The same holds true of your online marketing efforts. If you have a poor or incomplete marketing effort offline, you end up with a poor or incomplete marketing effort online.

Does this mean you can't do anything online until you fix every conceivable problem in your existing marketing effort? Not at all. But it does mean that you should keep your online marketing effort modest until you have your overall marketing effort operating effectively. Remember, unless you're starting an Internet-based business, most of your customers are not online. For most businesses, online marketing is the tail; the rest of your marketing effort is the dog. The dog should wag the tail, not the tail wag the dog.

So to mount an effective online marketing effort, you start with modest goals; meet those; add more ambitious goals; meet those; and so on. At each step in your online marketing effort you think of marketing resources you wish you had in the offline world, such as white papers, data sheets, press releases, Q & A (Question and Answer) documents, and others. By building your online presence gradually, you give yourself the opportunity to budget for and develop traditional and online deliverables together and reinforce one with the other.

This chapter tells you how to plan your overall online marketing effort so that it succeeds the first time out. However, while planning is vital for the longer term, the "just do it" philosophy (also known as "ready, fire, aim") has a long and honored role in the online world as well. If you're really in a hurry to get something up online, use Chapter 4 to start researching and securing your domain name, and Chapter 5 to create an initial Web site. This covers your, uh, *derrière* until you can complete and implement the more thorough planning process described in this chapter.

Assessing Your Overall Marketing Effort

The first step in creating an effective online marketing presence is to quickly assess your overall marketing effort. Nearly every traditional marketing resource you have can be used to help make people aware of your online marketing effort, and almost every marketing document, ad, white paper or other resource you have or create can be *repurposed* — modified and reformatted, but with the content left basically intact — for use online. So knowing where you stand in the offline world is vital to going online effectively.

You need to look at your current marketing effort for your company and for each part of what you sell — the products and services that are the reason for your company's existence. Then you can best decide how you want to represent yourself online.

What's your role?

If you're part of a small company or organization, you may be responsible for the whole enchilada: the company's strategy, products, services, public relations, and online presence. But for medium-size and larger companies, you may be responsible for part of the picture: a division of the company, or a specific product or service.

Unless you have all the levers in your own hands, you need to work with others to create an effective online presence, and mesh it smoothly into the traditional and online marketing efforts of the rest of the company. And even if you only own part of the picture, and even if some of the decisions we discuss here are likely to be made by others, go through all the steps in this chapter. They help you understand the roles and perspectives of, as well as communicate effectively with, the other participants in your marketing effort as you make all the pieces of the puzzle work together.

Assessing your current company-level marketing efforts

To effectively market your company you need to understand its strengths, so you can use them in marketing, and its weaknesses, so you can help alleviate them through new product development, partnerships, and other efforts. Start the process of better understanding your company by asking yourself some questions.

- **What does your company sell?** List all the products and services that your company sells. (If you work for a really big company, and you're only taking a small part of it online, restrict your answers to your division or product group.) Then come up with one short phrase that describes the majority of your product and service sales. Typical answers may be auto tires, computer software, or forestry services. That phrase tells you where to best direct your initial online marketing effort.

- **Who are your customers?** List the major groups of customers that you have. Your customers may include home-based professionals, home-makers, middle managers, or golfers. If you know your customers well, you already have a mental image of each type of customer, or even know one or more representatives of each type. Match up your major customer groups with the information about the demographics of the online world in Chapter 1 to identify those among your customers who are most likely to be online.

- **What differentiates your company from other companies?** For instance, don't say you're "fast" unless your company is the fastest in some measurable way, or at least close and working on getting to Number 1. And don't say you're "customer-oriented" unless you have the customer feedback or customer service awards to prove that you are among the most customer-oriented companies in your area of business. "Largest" is good — but largest in what market? Use the information in Chapter 2 to help you do a search of your competition online to identify your own advantages. Hopefully you end up with one or two differentiators for which you have good, solid backing.

Don't be surprised if you can't come up with much that makes your company stand out from the crowd; many companies, at certain points in their existence, don't really have strong qualities that differentiate them from the competition. But if you don't have any at this point, it's a warning signal that you're vulnerable to competitors who do differentiate — and when they do, it will be at your expense. If your company is FredCo, they'll tell customers they're "faster than FredCo," "more customer-oriented than FredCo" and, eventually, "larger than FredCo." Start thinking now about what differentiating qualities you want to develop.

A good example of the importance of differentiation is a company both of us have done work for (one as a consultant, the other as a seven-year employee): Apple Computer. Shortly after it was founded, Apple had the *best-selling* personal computer, the Apple II. When it lost that distinction to the IBM PC, Apple moved on to selling the *easiest-to-use* personal computer, the Macintosh. But when Microsoft Windows helped the PC close the ease-of-use gap, Macintosh differentiation eroded. Lately the company has taken to selling the *fastest* personal computers with its G3 series. This new differentiation seems to be attracting some big-spending, high-end customers and helping the company return to profitability — though the jury is still out on the ultimate fate of the company.

Also assess your existing company marketing efforts. Gather together your logo, some stationery, any company-level press kits you have, catalogs, press releases, print ads, TV and radio commercials, annual reports, speeches by company officials, any Web pages you already have, and so on. Think of some familiar company logos — your local bank, the nearest fast food restaurant, computer companies, car manufacturers (many of them have changed their logos in recent years to update their market presence), your competitors, and so on. What kinds of impressions do these various logos give you? Most likely, a bank is fairly formal and simple, giving a feeling of reliability, security, and straightforward business. A car manufacturer wants to display something about the type of car it produces — Cadillac uses a coat of arms to suggest royalty and luxury, while Ferrari uses a rearing horse to show off its muscle and race-proven speed. Now look at your own company logo and see if it supports your company's marketing well. If it does, use it online; if not, consider replacing it and rolling out the new logo as part of your online marketing effort. Figure 3-1 shows the home page of a company that creates logos; if you need help with a new logo, you can find many such companies on the Web.

Don't try to completely remake your company's image online. Because the online world is new as a major force in society, and because only certain groups of people are online in any numbers, your online marketing effort directly affect the degree to which your company is seen as technologically savvy — a strong online presence can reset the bar on how "with it" your company seems technically. Use the online demographics information and resources in Chapter 1 to help tailor the image you project online to the people within your targeted customer groups who are most likely to be online. But otherwise, don't overreach. For instance, your online marketing effort can't make a conservative company image into a wild and crazy one overnight. Understanding your company's traditional marketing presence makes you much more effective in your marketing efforts online.

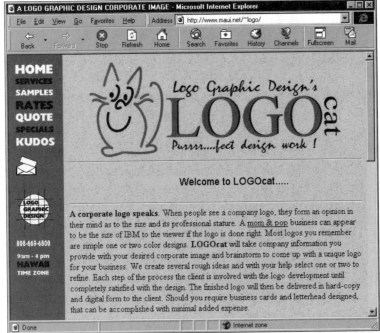

Figure 3-1:
The home
page of a
company
that does
company
logos.

If your company's image really does need a makeover, your online efforts can be a key part of that change. Consider hiring an experienced consultant to help make a concerted push in this direction. Just don't try to make over your company's image only in the online world; until that overall company image makeover gathers steam, your online presence should reflect the image your company has today.

Marketing at the company-level online

Many people who end up finding you online are primarily interested in finding out where you're located, what business your company is in, how many employees you have, how much money you make (revenues), and how much you keep (profits). Having a competent, basic online presence at this company level is very important.

Company marketing, whether online or offline, is somewhat vague and amorphous. Think of those "image" advertising campaigns that you often see on TV for large companies in areas like financial services or computing services. They don't sell you anything, and you may not even ever buy anything directly from the company. They just lay the groundwork for the company's more targeted marketing efforts.

Making it so

One common mistake at this point in the marketing process is to come up with differentiators for your company and products that you'd *like* to be true instead of that *are* true. So if you come up with an adjective that describes how you'd *like* to be able to present your company or products, think about how you can "make it so." Identify training programs and practices that you can put in place to make your company the best at customer service; for instance, auto repair companies and others talk about the checklists their personnel use to make sure that they do a complete job. Investigate ways to improve your product to make it the fastest or easiest to use; look at the practices of competitors who claim these differentiators now, and figure out how to meet, then beat them.

Changing what your company is doing to make its products more marketable is where marketing becomes part of a company's overall business strategy, and is part of why marketing is so important to companies (and why so many company CEOs tend to come from the marketing side of the company). In taking the time to think through these issues, and make needed changes in products and services, you're making it possible to better market those same products and services in the offline world and online as well.

The job of company-level marketing is to communicate the key attributes of your company and create a base of recognition with the customer for your more targeted, product-based marketing efforts. Such efforts also help market your company to potential investors. Figure 3-2 shows the home page of Superscape, a medium-sized company with a good understanding of how to market their company and products online.

Assessing current product marketing efforts

Your products can be physical things people buy, services, or some mix of the two. You may have packaged one or more services in a very product-like way by standardizing what gets done, rates, duration, and so on. If you haven't already done this, consider doing so. By packaging services in a product-like way, you make it easier for people who visit you online to compare your offerings to those of other companies.

In this book we generally use the word "products" to refer to products, services, and mixed product/service packages. If there's a concern or an idea that's specific to services, we point that out. In general, just think of your products as whatever the specific things are that people buy from you.

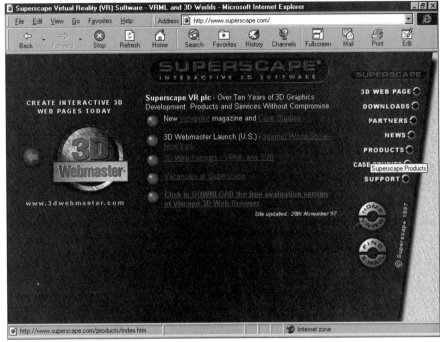

Figure 3-2:
Superscape's
strong
presence
online, with
pointers to
products.

Now think about what differentiates each of your products, or each service that you market as a product. If you think your product is the best for its purpose, decide what "best" means for your kind of product. List ways to back up your claim to be the best if it's challenged. For instance, your product may be made of higher-quality materials, created by more experienced people, or used by customers who themselves have a reputation for doing good work. If your product is the cheapest, define the term more exactly as lowest purchase price, lowest cost of ownership, or some other aspect of low cost.

To gather evidence for your claims, use the Web and other online resources described in this book. Chapter 2 tells you how to efficiently search online. The Directory section not only includes Web sites but also newsgroups and other online resources that have valuable marketing and product information.

Wrack your brain for product differentiators and work to back them up; undifferentiated products are not only vulnerable to competition, they're hard to make much profit from. Figure 3-3 shows a Web page for a product that doesn't mention competitors directly, but instead shows off its differentiation.

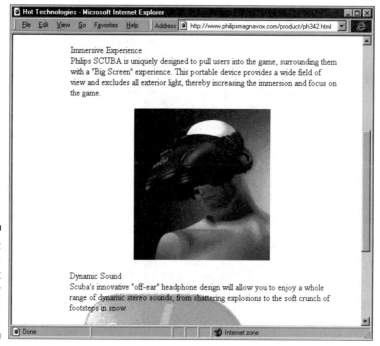

Figure 3-3:
Here's a
product that
knows why
you need
to buy it.

Start your online product marketing effort by assessing the existing marketing materials you have for the product, but don't feel too limited by them: You're more likely to have success in remaking the image of a product online than in remaking the image of a company. A company's image usually reflects some realities about the company's history, current practices, and executive staff that are hard to change. Product images are more susceptible to "spin," as long as they're based on identifiable product realities.

Consider how to change your product's current image online. For example, you may be able to better emphasize the technical advantages of your product to the online audience than you've been able to manage offline. In marketing a lawnmower, you can include detailed photographs and explanations of what "makes" your lawnmower so special more easily online than in a typical print advertisement. If your online effort works, you can then consider how to reflect the change in your offline marketing efforts.

Marketing your product online

You can do a tremendous amount with product marketing online — everything from putting up a single, simple Web page to an entire Web site with accompanying efforts on e-mail, in newsgroups, on online services, and more. You can also decide whether to sell all, or just a selection of your company's products online — see *Selling Online For Dummies* by Leslie Lundquist (IDG Books Worldwide, Inc.) for details.

You can also address the fuzzy line between products and services online as we discuss in the "Assessing current product marketing efforts" section. Figure 3-4 shows an example of a Web site hosting service marketed as a product online — all in a single Web banner ad.

A concise example of marketing a service like a product

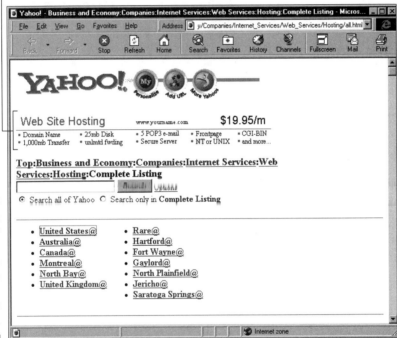

Figure 3-4: Tie up your service in a nice package and voilá! It's a product.

Marketing online for the sole proprietorship

What if you're pretty much a one-person band — an independent consultant, author, freelancer, or other lone wolf? Do you need an online presence? If you size the effort carefully, the answer may well be *yes.*

Is your traditional marketing sufficient?

As you look at your company and product marketing materials, you may notice that some marketing pieces you'd like to have are missing. This is normal; just about everyone can use a brand new or updated data sheet, marketing plan, Q & A, white paper, or what have you.

If you find that your overall marketing effort is lacking; if you can't identify strong company and product differentiators and see those reflected in a reasonable number of marketing materials for each of the audiences you need to reach, then you have a bigger problem than an online marketing effort alone can solve. The best way to jump-start online marketing is by borrowing logos, layouts, ad copy, and other resources from your existing marketing materials — if those are missing, the online marketing effort becomes much more expensive and difficult.

If this case sounds familiar, you need to create an overall marketing plan now. *Marketing For Dummies* by Alexander Hiam (IDG Books Worldwide, Inc.) can be a real help. Then decide on either a reality-first or an online-first plan. If few of your customers are online, create a limited online presence to cover yourself while you build up your traditional marketing portfolio. But if many of your actual or prospective customers are online, consider developing a reasonably strong online marketing presence first, then extending it to print, broadcast and so on. In either case, working on your online marketing can be a catalyst for creating a strong overall marketing effort.

If you're like most people working independently today, you're probably already using online resources for communications, to develop a feeling of community with others doing similar work, and for research. If not, your first order of business is to get online. The easiest way to do this is by getting an account with America Online or with MindSpring, the Internet Service Provider (ISP) whose Internet access software is on the *Marketing Online For Dummies* CD-ROM. See Appendix A for information on how to use the software on the CD-ROM.

Unlike most larger businesses, an online-first marketing effort may make sense for you. As an independent, most of your marketing efforts so far have probably been informal, person-to-person efforts. You probably have at least some of the basics like business cards, stationery, and a fax number; but mass mailings, Yellow Pages advertising, and other small-business marketing tools are probably more than you need, considering their cost.

If this is your situation, a modest online presence makes perfect sense. A small Web site describing you and listing some of your accomplishments serves as a seemingly external validator of your success and technical savvy. Unless an unusually small number of your current and potential customers or clients are online, consider creating a simplified and scaled-down but professional-looking version of the business Web presence site described in detail in Chapter 5 and use other low-key online marketing efforts described in this book.

Matching Your Customer Base to the Online Community

You've looked at your existing marketing effort, probably finding a few holes in the process, and hopefully getting some new ideas about what your company's image is, how each of its products and services should be marketed, and what traditional marketing resources you need to develop. You're also probably pretty excited about creating or improving your online presence. Good, because now it's time for your first reality check.

The reality check is simply this: How many of your current and potential customers are online? Use Chapter 1 to get a good idea about the big picture of who's online and discover how to research how many of your customers are online already. In Chapter 2 we show you how to search online resources to investigate who else is already online trying to reach your customers. Unless your customer base includes groups that are online in high numbers, consider creating a modest initial online presence and then improving your traditional and online marketing efforts in tandem.

You need to carefully research your customer base — which can mean anything from simply asking all your own contacts to commissioning a formal study — to find out how many of them are online. Ask your customers what they expect from you online, and whether they are frustrated or disappointed with your lack of an online presence. Ask them what Web and other online resources they find useful, and how they use them. (Don't be surprised if what they want isn't "gee-whiz" multimedia stuff but solid information about your company and industry that they can use in their work.)

You can get a general idea of your customer base's online profile by matching up your current and potential customers to groups that are or aren't online, as we describe in some depth in Chapter 1.

Here are some of the products and services that strongly need to be online:

✔ **Computer products.** Absolutely anything having to do with computers should be online. Not only are computer users and computer professionals very heavily represented online, as you may expect, but people are also very much aware of their computer use while online. They want and expect to find computer-related products and services online.

✔ **Educational products.** Almost anything having to do with education is a good subject for an online effort. Not only are a large proportion of students online, but so are many of their parents. Students and parents both are receptive to college, university, and private school recruitment, educational CD-ROMs, books, tapes, you name it. Even if it's just an eraser or a box of chalk, your educational product needs to be online. Figure 3-5 shows an online site for education products.

✔ **Products marketed strongly to professionals.** Computer and educational professionals are most strongly online, but are followed closely by other kinds of professionals. And while people often surf the Web aimlessly at work, they feel good about surfing sites that contain information or products helpful to them in their work.

✔ **Any product with a high-tech edge to it.** Having the latest high technology in your products is an important way to create highly differentiated (read: highly profitable) products, and many people strongly associate high technology with the Internet. You need a strong online presence to support your claim to be on the technical cutting edge, and to reach customers who are receptive to these kinds of claims.

Match up your customer profile against who's online not only for your company as a whole, but for individual products and services as well. You may find that some are better candidates for early development of your online presence.

You may have less need to be online if your customers are lower-income, aren't American, work outdoors, are craftspeople, or are unlikely to own or use computers. If you ask around, whether formally or informally, about which of your customers are on the Internet, and get little response, you can probably build your online presence more slowly.

What if my customer base is typically not online?

Maybe comparing your customer base to the online community described in Chapter 1 shows that not many of your customers are online, leading you to think you don't need to do anything online at all. However, three strong arguments against doing nothing exist.

Well, first

First, remember that almost any business has some potential and current customers who are online, and that press, analysts, investors, and other influencers are online heavily. This argues for at least some online presence.

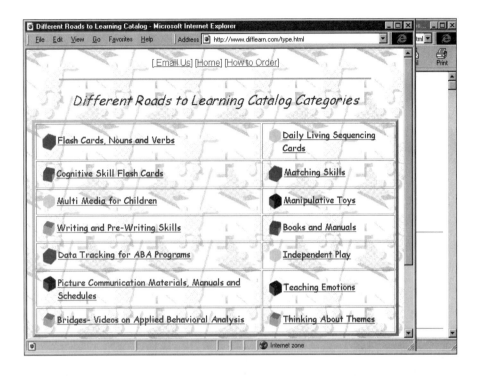

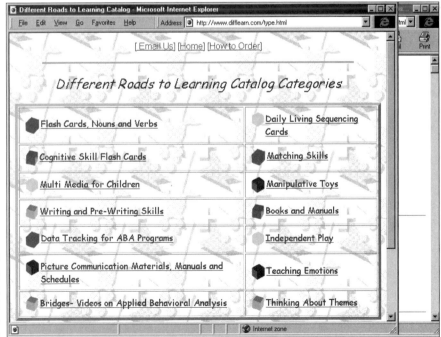

Figure 3-5:
Time to get educated online.

The tricky point here, though, is that you aren't likely to impress these people with a disproportionately large online presence. What they do need to see is an up-to-date, simple, up-to-date, competent, up-to-date, complete, online presence. Did we mention that these people will think poorly of you if you don't keep your online presence up-to-date?

If your site is outdated, you may become the beneficiary of unwanted attention like the Cob-Web award, which noted sites that hadn't received needed updating. (Ironically, the Cob-Web award's Web site went several months without updating, then was taken down.)

And second

The second reason you need at least a basic online presence, almost no matter what business you're in, is that the current limitations on who's heavily online are unlikely to last. According to the GVU's WWW User Survey (covered in Chapter 1) and other resources, the types of people who spend much time online haven't been changing very fast, even as the number of Internet users quickly grows. However, there aren't many youngish, well-off, male American computer professionals left who aren't already on the Internet, and someone's adding to the number of users. Also, lower-cost computers and systems like WebTV are bringing new people onto the Internet. If it continues to grow anything like it has in the past, the Internet will have to attract people who are currently underrepresented online. As your customers and potential customers get wired, you don't want their first cyberspace experience to be getting a bad impression of you from your hard-to-find, out-of-date, or even completely missing Web site. Get your feet wet online today so you can be ready to dive in fully tomorrow.

And finally, third

The third reason you need some online presence is the unpredictability of marketing in general, and Internet marketing in particular. Many companies have failed in their Internet objectives, while others have succeeded beyond their wildest dreams, and there's quite a bit of unpredictability as to who will and who won't do well. Keeping your initial effort modest reduces the risk of failure; but getting some presence online quickly improves the odds that you can build it into a big success.

What if my business is local?

How much should you invest in your online presence if you operate only in a limited geographic area? For most online users, using online resources to find, for example, the nearest copy center or café, is next to impossible. And for local businesses it can be difficult to decide how much effort to put into a new, globe-circling medium that can reach tens of millions of people, 99.99 percent of whom are guaranteed not to be within driving distance of your store.

If your local area is relatively low-tech in terms of its Internet use, then consider going slow. (The Find/SVP study described in Chapter 1 includes a map of the U.S. that shows which states have high and low percentages of online use; for marketing in non-U.S. countries, consult local resources.) But if you're in an area with high Internet usage, consider charging ahead. Size your effort to match a realistic estimate of the number of visits you're going to get from people who are locals and therefore potential customers. And take extra steps to publicize your online presence in local media, and in Web sites, newsgroups, and so on that have a strong local flavor. Figure 3-6 shows a Web page from Sidewalk, Microsoft's Web service for local information. Services like this are increasing quickly in number and impact.

Figure 3-6: Microsoft's Sidewalk is a leading localized online resource.

Use the information on searching in Chapter 2 to find other local resources that are already online, and make the effort to trade pointers with them — include a link on your Web site to theirs, and ask for a link from their Web site back to yours. To find an initial list of local resources, go to www.yahoo.com and click on the Regional link to find resources in U.S. states and cities and foreign countries.

Assessing What Your Competitors Are Doing Online

A key step in deciding on how big an online marketing effort you want to mount is to assess the online presence of your competitors. You have no doubt already encountered your competitors' online presence in several ways: visiting their Web site or otherwise seeing them in the online world, seeing their press releases, business cards, and other traditional marketing materials with pointers to their online presence, and hearing from your customers and colleagues what they've seen your competitors doing online. (If none of your direct competitors has an online presence, look at similar businesses that operate in a slightly different geographic area or business area.) Also take a look at the online presence of suppliers and customers, any industry or trade groups that your company is part of, and others who you work with. Use the categories in Yahoo! (www.yahoo.com) to find larger and more established industry segments; for newer and smaller industry areas, use a fast, wide-ranging search engine like HotWired's HotBot (www.hotbot.com).

Creating a comparison chart

Looking around and gathering impressions is very valuable, but the thing that's really going to help you is to compare and contrast the online presence of your most direct competitors with your own. Doing so is not as hard as it sounds; all you need to do is make a simple chart briefly describing key aspects of your competitors' online presence.

The best way to create such a chart is to restrict it to quantitative aspects: questions that can be answered by a yes or no, a number, or a short, factual phrase. Stay away from qualitative judgments, such as "lousy" or "slow" or "beautiful," for now. Making objective decisions is most easily done when they are based on objective facts, and working through your findings with others is much easier if you initially stay away from value judgments and stick to "just the facts, ma'am," as Jack Webb used to say on *Dragnet*. An example of this kind of chart is shown in Figure 3-7.

Here's one way to create such a chart. Take a large piece of paper and create four columns — one narrower one for features of the online presence, and three wide ones for your top three competitors. (You may want to add more later, but start with three to help you focus.) Then create rows for key aspects of their online presence. The first few rows should be simple ones that you can fill out with check marks for yes, *X*'s for no, or a number or short phrase. Examples include Web site (yes/no), active in newsgroups (yes/no), has customer mailing list for customers to subscribe to (yes/no), online service area (yes/no).

FEATURES	MAP CENTRAL	MAPS BY THE BEACH	OUTDOOR CLUB'S MAP NOOK
Web site	No	Yes	Yes- page on Outdoor Club's site
Active in newsgroups?	No	No	Yes (Outdoor Club, occasionally Map Nook)
Online mail list	No	Yes	Yes- for Outdoor Club, not Map Nook
Online service forums	CompuServe forum	No	AOL area for Outdoor Club
Web URL	x	www.beachmaps.com	www.outdoorclub.com/ mapnook
Number of Web pages	x	12	Dozens for Outdoor Club, one for Map Nook

Figure 3-7: Size up the competition on paper.

The most important part of your online presence, and the most expensive part to develop, will almost certainly be your Web site. So go into some detail on your competitors' Web sites. Create rows for different aspects of the Web sites: Web URL, number of pages (estimate if there are many), e-mail address for feedback, sales locations listed, online selling, uses graphics, uses multimedia, uses push technology.

Don't get caught up in an online arms race to have the biggest, most expensive online presence. Adding advanced technologies like push and animation to a simple, one-product site can be overkill and cause more problems than they solve. Chapters 5–7 discuss creating an appropriate Web presence for your company and its products and services.

Now create a new row and, for each competitor, list the major areas of that competitors' Web site. Areas might include About the Company, Products, News, Technical Support, and Feedback. If you're feeling energetic, put the number of Web pages in each area in parentheses after the area name.

Finally, create one box for what you've been itching to write down this whole time: your opinions, or more formally, your *qualitative observations*. Note one or two plusses and one or two minuses that stick out for each competitor — things like whether the site has complete descriptions of products, fast- or slow-loading pages, well-written text, and most vital of all, whether the site is up-to-date. Note if a site has major categories missing or present compared to the others. You can also note whether the site is ugly or attractive — but don't be surprised if others disagree with this or any other qualitative assessment that you make. Don't feel you have to write a lot about every competing Web site; if a site is competent, but not spectacular, you may not have anything to say here.

If you are really only concerned about a specific product, you may still find performing the company-by-company comparison described in the previous few paragraphs very valuable; the company online presence often forms the base for the product online presence. You can easily use the same exercise we describe in the previous few paragraphs for any products you want to market. Create categories that reflect the features and appropriate marketing resources for the kind of product you're interested in, then assess each competitor in those categories.

After you're done, step back and take a look at the overall chart. Think about changing the comparative points for clarity or adding one or two competitors for completeness. Consider recopying your chart on a clean sheet of paper or recreating it in a word processor or spreadsheet program for neatness. Show it to a few colleagues and see if they understand it.

Using your completed chart

At the end of this exercise, you probably have some bad news and some good news. The most likely bad news is that at least one of your competitors is doing much more online than you are. If you're anything like us, seeing just how much your competitors are doing online can make you feel very nervous. As you consider the cost and effort to match or exceed your competitors' efforts in the online realm, you may find yourself in need of a stiff drink, a walk in the park, or the rest of the day off.

The likely good news is that the analysis you just did to create your chart gives you a tremendous amount of information and many good ideas for your own online presence. The areas (newsgroups, e-mail, and so on) of the online world that your competitors do (or don't) use, the size of their Web site, the areas they cover, and the overall impression their online presence gives are invaluable touchstones for you to use in planning your own effort. This chart is also a great motivator for getting your colleagues to understand the importance of getting online and getting management to approve the money and personnel you need to make it happen.

Sizing up your online-only competition

Take time to search the Web for online-based competitors — competitors that complete most or all of the sales cycle online. If you're a local plumbing company, this is not such a big concern; no one can fix a leaky sink over the Web. But if you're a retailer, wholesaler, or consultant, you need to know just how much your current customers can accomplish without ever leaving their keyboard. Figure 3-8 shows the Web site of Amazon.com, a Web-based bookstore that has posed a significant challenge to retail bookstores everywhere without ever opening a storefront of its own.

One way to find online sales sites is to search for keywords associated with online sales. One good keyword is the word *order*. If you use the Boolean operator + to combine the category you're interested in with the word *order* you're likely to find Web pages for online sales. For instance, if you use the search engines described in Chapter 2 to search for "books + order" then you're likely to get a link to the order page of Amazon.com.

Figure 3-8:
Anyone
anywhere
can buy
books
online from
Amazon.com.

If you have significant online-based competition then people can browse, buy, and specify delivery options online, all without actually going anywhere, and all without giving you a second thought, or any chance for the business. Though most such competition is relatively small in volume now, it will only grow in the years to come. Consider separately investigating and evaluating online-based competitors. You may decide to launch an online sales effort yourself.

Sizing Your Online Marketing Effort

If you've worked your way from the start of the chapter to this point, you've assessed your overall marketing effort; matched your customer base against who's online; and analyzed what your competitors are doing online. This work, combined with the ongoing Internet hype we're all subjected to, may induce a certain degree of panic on your part.

Take a deep breath and relax. It's still early in the Internet game, and only a tiny portion of American commerce — let alone commerce in other countries — actually occurs on the Internet.

What if they're not online?

Throughout this book we advise a conservative approach to building your online presence, mostly because we've seen so many overdone Web sites that went up with incredible speed, enthusiasm, and expense, and then quickly turned into liabilities because of poor initial design and infrequently updated content.

Another reason for a conservative approach is that getting going from a standing start takes time. If one or more of your competitors already have a complete, competent online presence — or, worse (for you), an exciting, innovative, technically excellent Web site and solid use of other online services — and you have little or no presence online, you need all the time and money you can muster just to catch up.

On the other hand, if your investigation of the competition reveals that your competitors are not online, or that they have limited or poorly executed online presences, you may want to roll the dice and make a stronger initial effort — one that *beats,* not just meets, the competition. Though the biggest bubble of Internet hype occurred a few years ago, people continue to be fascinated by the ever burgeoning online world. If you can make a concerted effort that results in online leadership, you benefit twice: once by the positive impression you make online, and again by the positive impression you make when you trumpet your leadership in the offline world.

Don't bet the farm (or the company) on this kind of effort; your competitors can always surprise you with a sudden online makeover while you're working on your own, and the positive marketing impact you make with your online effort still takes time and work to translate into sales. But business is often about taking some chances, and the online opportunity might be one worth taking.

While it's too late to get in on the first round of Internet mania that has gripped the world's media over the last couple of years, you can have the advantage of being able to benefit from the lessons learned as fortunes were made and, just as often, lost in the initial bubble of online enthusiasm. You may well be better off launching a sustainable and steadily growing Internet presence now than if you had gone through the booms and busts that have occurred to date. (One estimate we saw quoted in *PC Magazine* is that 20 percent of all business Web sites will be closed down over the next couple of years as many companies walk away from unprofitable investments. You don't want to be among the manic, but neither do you want to be among the depressed.)

Choosing an online marketing position

So now it's time to size the initial online presence you want to achieve — the base from which you build in the years to come. Grab the comparison chart you made in the previous section — if it's a bit out of date, you may want to visit those sites again, or perhaps do another search for any other competitors. Remember that your competitors are the benchmark against which your customers, the trade press, and your management and share-holders or other investors measure you. Then make an initial decision as to where you want to be on the continuum of online innovation:

✔ **Innovator.** Maybe you want to be an innovator online. This means that, compared to your competitors, your online presence is larger, more expensive, and has more gee-whiz features. As an innovator, some of your online efforts are expensive failures; others succeed so well as to get you noticed outside your industry and your traditional markets. You're the first to introduce online selling, and you work to increase your online sales even if they aren't initially very profitable. You spend significant amounts of money in the offline world to advertise your online presence, and try to partner with other leaders.

✔ **Fast follower.** One smart way to play the innovation game is to be a *fast follower*. This means that you watch your competitors' efforts and others online for good ideas and adopt them, while avoiding expensive mistakes by letting others make them instead of you. If you do this right, you spend less online than your most aggressive competitors and, unlike them, every dollar you spend counts. You keep a healthy balance between your online and traditional marketing efforts.

✔ **Competitor.** Another reasonable approach is to create an online presence that is in the middle of the pack. You may occasionally do something innovative, but in most areas you wait for solid evidence of success or failure before adding new directions to your online effort. Your expenditures are low; their impact high. Your traditional marketing efforts take priority over your online ones.

✔ **Conservative.** You may well decide that your business needs are best met by having a minimal online presence for now, letting competitors take the lead and instead spending your marketing money in other areas. As an example, Figure 3-9 shows the single Web page that Cosmo Software, a division of Silicon Graphics Inc., initially put up for Cosmo Worlds, a 3-D authoring package. It simply announced the product's presence. (They've since expanded the site greatly.) Or you may not spend much on marketing at all, preferring to put your efforts into other areas of your business. In this scenario, you spend very little online.

Your position on this continuum of online innovation may or may not be tied to how innovative you are in other areas of your business. You don't necessarily need to be a top-flight technical innovator with your products to take a leadership position in your online presence. Do avoid causing confusion among your online visitors, though. If your overall company culture and marketing efforts typically take a conservative approach, don't suddenly go wild in your online marketing approach. If you do decide to be innovative, do it in a lower-key way, with a classy overall design and without getting in customers' face too much in the look or content of your site. Lead in the useful content and features of your site, rather than in the use of advanced Internet technologies or whizzy design features.

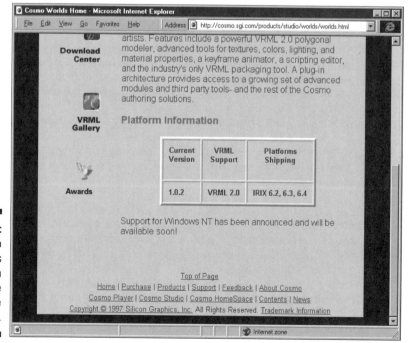

Figure 3-9:
Cosmo
Worlds
started with
a single
Web page
online.

Dividing your effort among the various online areas

Your initial online marketing effort will consist of specific efforts in one area, some areas, or all of the areas of the online world; compare what your competitors are doing and your own company's needs and decide what to do in each area:

✔ **Web site.** This is the crux of your online effort, and we cover building a marketing Web site in Chapters 4–7. If you are currently lacking much of an online presence or don't have one at all, put your efforts here first. Looking at your competitors' Web sites gives you a pretty good idea of what you need to attain at least an acceptable Web presence in the eyes of your customers. If you're behind, consider catching up to the extent possible with a reasonable initial effort. If you're already doing pretty well online, set your goals using a combination of competitive concerns and customer needs.

✔ **E-mail and listservs.** A minimal online effort should include employee guidelines for using e-mail in a way that supports your company's marketing effort, as described in Chapter 8, or creating a *listserv* mailing list for online customer support (so-called because one popular program for creating them is called LISTSERV), as described in Chapter 9.

✔ **Newsgroups.** Even a minimal online effort includes monitoring relevant newsgroups, even if that just means doing a Web search using Deja News (as we describe in Chapter 2) to see if your company is being mentioned in the newsgroups. A moderate online effort is likely to include having someone in your company actively participate in newsgroups. See Chapter 10 for details.

✔ **Online services.** Consider monitoring relevant forums, including competitors' forums, in online services. (Don't even try to keep up on all the chat rooms! But do consider having an account on each major online service and checking in occasionally.) A robust online effort may include starting a forum of your own for customer support on one of the online services. See Chapter 10 for more information.

✔ **Push technology.** After you have a competent Web presence, push technology is a good way to make a version of your Web content either very available, or even downright inescapable, to your customers who are online. Chapter 2 has details. However, if you're not where you want to be on the Web yet, don't push your luck (forgive the pun) by overcommitting to push technology.

Budgeting and resourcing your online effort

Your position on the online innovation continuum for each Internet service also depends on the resources available to you. You need people in your organization who have time to help and sufficient knowledge of HTML development tools for your Web site, as well as knowledge of the other online services. On the other hand, you can go with outside help, but that may require a larger budget. Writing skills are critically important for a strong online presence. If you have strong writing skills in your company now, great; otherwise you may have to look for an outside source at greater expense.

If you want to see more information about the importance of good writing on the Web, see an interesting article — with examples — on this topic in Web Week at www.webweek.com/97/May5/undercon/graphics.html.

If you don't have the resources available to get out of the gate fast, start slowly, and build steadily to a stronger online presence. First aim for the position of "Competitor" in your online presence (as we describe in the "Choosing a online marketing position" section), and then show others in your company how that benefits you. Gather positive comments about your Web site from visitors, including business partners, customers, and others. Keep copies of e-mail messages that come in through your Web site and result in sales, improvements in your products, or other benefits. Copy e-mail exchanges, list server postings (see Chapter 9), or newsgroup messages (see Chapter 10) that reflect positively on your online efforts. Then describe how additional investment can yield more benefits.

As with any other company effort that involves significant expenditures, you need to plan your online effort. The plan should include the sections described in this chapter, such as assessing your current marketing effort, matching your customer base to the online community, and assessing the competition's efforts. The process of creating a written plan from these elements is described in the next section.

The beauty of the online world is that can change your place in the continuum of online innovation quickly. As you read through this book, or gain experience of your own, and learn more about what it takes to create a strong online presence, you may decide to scale back your effort a bit, or focus only on one particular area. Conversely, you may decide to up the ante to match competitors' successes online. And you can never forget the possibility that your company's stockholders, owners, or top management may suddenly decide that you need fit the online "Innovator" category yesterday!

Unlike printed information, online information can be updated and extended quickly and cheaply. (If you put a typo in a product brochure and print 5,000 of them, you have to scrap all 5,000; if you put a typo on your Web page, you can easily change it after only a few people have seen it.) For larger changes, though, you need a firm grasp of what you're doing and why to make alterations quickly. Doing a careful and professional job of planning your online presence today actually prepares you to be flexible down the road.

Creating the Written Plan

Before investing the time and money to create and maintain your online presence, you need to create at least a brief written plan. Companies vary in how much they depend on such plans; you may be absolutely required to do a highly structured, well-researched plan to justify your project to senior management before you can spend a single dollar, or you may be encouraged to just "throw something up on the Internet and see what sticks." If possible, take a middle course, and write a relatively brief plan that covers at least the following elements:

- ✔ **Marketing assessment.** Quickly describe your current marketing goals and resources and the state of your current online effort relative to how many of your current and potential customers are online. Include any feedback you have gotten about your online presence. This stuff should be lying around your office if you already went through the "Assessing Your Overall Marketing Effort" section in this chapter.

- ✔ **Competitive assessment.** One problem businesspeople have in working with the Internet is that they are often thinking about profit and loss while the Internet types are talking about hits per day and other technical measurements, as described in Chapter 7. A brief competitive assessment translates the online issues into terms that businesspeople can understand — that is, who's ahead and who's behind. If you have already worked through the section "Assessing What Your Competitors Are Doing Online" in this chapter, and created the comparison chart suggested there, you're in business; if not, now's your chance to do so.

- ✔ **Goals.** Specify your goals for your initial online effort, framing them in terms of your customers' needs and competitive comparisons as much as possible. Use concrete terms such as the names of the major sections you plan to develop for your Web site, the specific online service forums you plan to monitor, any newsgroups you plan to create, and so on, as described in this chapter under "Sizing Your Online Marketing Effort."

✔ **Resources.** Even if you are considering doing most or all of the work in-house, get bids from outsiders so you can get a reality check on your internal estimates. Wherever you are using internal resources, make sure to consider what other work will be deferred or not done while employees are busy working on the company Web presence. In many cases, you are best off planning to use external resources, as we describe in the previous section, "Budgeting and resourcing your online effort."

✔ **Budget.** List the budget figures you have developed or create a budget now. Specify that marketing is a crucial enabling factor for your company's sales and relate the proposed Web investment and the number of people it is intended to reach to the rest of your company's marketing efforts. If about 10 percent of your target audience is online, for instance, you can build toward having about 10 percent of your total marketing budget devoted to the online effort. If you need to get into more detail about defending your budget, see *Marketing For Dummies* by Alexander Hiam (IDG Books Worldwide, Inc.)

✔ **Timeframe.** Specify a timeframe for completing your initial online effort. Allow more time than you at first think necessary; the more work you expect to do in-house, the more generous you need to be with your schedule. Stage the effort to allow control by several smaller deadlines, or milestones along the way, rather than just one big one, and allow time for testing before you take the online resources you create public. Consider using a chart developed in a word-processing or spreadsheet program, or specialized project planning software like Microsoft Project, to make deadlines and progress visible.

✔ **Maintenance.** Your online effort doesn't end just because you finish the design and load the pages up to your Web server. As part of your plan, specify what your online presence requires in terms of ongoing maintenance and updates, including responding to e-mail that arrives at your Web site, adding updated content to your Web site, monitoring newsgroups and online service forums, managing and commenting to questions on an automated electronic mailing list like LISTSERV if you have one, and more. Don't be surprised if maintenance of your online presence ends up taking longer than you expected — if you don't prepare, it probably gets done poorly or not at all.

✔ **Next steps.** If someone in your organization is pushing for a much bigger online presence, and that someone wants it fast, they may be disappointed when they see your carefully staged, conservative plan. (In fact, if no one who sees your plan is disappointed in it, it may well be overambitious.) Here's where you can mollify any critics by pointing out what you can do in the future, after you've completed, deployed, and proven the value of your initial online efforts. (Don't be too blue-sky here either, though; you may be called to account for what you write here someday.)

Who owns your online presence?

The answer: Marketing. The computer people may be responsible for running the server and providing you with reports — and you need them on your side, and there's no reason to alienate anyone involved in the overall online effort. But at the end of the day, the marketing department needs to be responsible for the look, feel, content, or other aspects of your online presence. Also, as we recommend throughout this book, you should consider outsourcing tasks like running your Web server anyway; it's much easier to control and reduce costs, and to add and remove services, through an outside vendor than through people in your company.

If your company, division, or product group already has an online presence through the efforts of other departments besides marketing,

then you may have to work with the other departments for now (and slowly bring them around to letting marketing call the shots). This has to be backed up by money, of course, so start planning now how to have marketing pay most of the bills.

Even with marketing running the overall show, others in your company are part of your online presence whether you like it or not. Every e-mail message sent by an employee and (especially) every newsgroup comment made by an employee using a company e-mail account is also a marketing message from your company. See Chapters 8–10 for information on how to get everyone on the same page to support — or at least not undermine — your company online marketing messages.

As you work on the plan, continue gathering information. Keep an eye out for changes in competitive efforts and in customer requests for an online presence. If your online presence is successful, you may receive a great deal of e-mail from potential and current customers — all of whom expect an answer. A smallish company or medium-sized product group may find itself receiving enough e-mail to require a full-time person just to respond to it. See Chapter 8 for information on how to manage the flow of e-mail, and don't put an e-mail address on your Web site until you're ready to respond to the messages you get.

After you create a plan, you have every right to be proud of yourself. You've done a lot of work and set the tone for your company's online presence for years to come. But you still have a few concerns to address:

✔ **Justifying the cost.** Even the senior manager who was initially most enthusiastic about going online may wince when she sees the budget. Marketing expenditures are always hard to justify; after all, they're expenses that don't immediately or measurably increase sales or decrease expenses. You'll be pressured to cut the budget or to do more internally and less with outside resources. Use the competitive assessment to defend the need for your online presence; if someone wants to cut expenditures, show them exactly where your online presence suffers if you do so. To support using outside resources, point out that using experienced, accountable outsiders reduces risk.

➤ **Riskiness.** As the old saying goes, "making predictions is dangerous, especially when they concern the future." Your plan is likely to be more optimistic and have more risk in it than you realize. An online development effort is somewhere between a major documentation effort and a software development effort in terms of the difficulty of predicting completion dates and the possibility of abject failure. (Robert Brooks claimed in *The Mythical Man-Month* that half — yes, half — of all major software projects fail. Not come in late, not go over budget — that's almost routine — but simply fail. The more complex your Web site, the more like a software project it is.)

➤ **"But you said."** A problem that your plan may cause is a phenomenon we call, "But you said," after something that kids like to say to parents. The online efforts that you propose in this plan will likely be taken as firm promises rather than reasonable projections. If you try to modify your goals during the project, people may be disappointed and upset and question your character, integrity, and maybe even ancestry. Use some qualifiers in the plan, such as "expect to," "as resources allow," and "as competitive comparisons indicate," to help manage this problem if it occurs.

When you complete your initial plan, don't show it to anyone. (If a group has worked on it, keep it within the group for a day or two.) Get a good night's sleep, then take another look at the plan. Trim it back. Adjust the plan so that it contains only the core elements needed to meet your customer and competitive goals. Delete or defer everything that's not critical to scoring an early success in the online world. Doing this reduces the amount of money you're asking for, greatly increases your chances of success, and thus increases the odds that management will trust you with more money later to expand your online presence as needed.

Creating an online marketing plan makes more sense if it's done while referring to an overall marketing plan. However, you may not have one, or your overall marketing plan may be out of date. If you need to have all your ducks in a row before proceeding, create or revise the overall marketing plan first; if it's more important to get going on your online presence, create or revise the overall marketing plan after the online marketing plan is done.

Implementing Your Online Marketing Plan

If you've done most or all of the steps we suggest in this chapter to this point, congratulations! You're much better prepared to succeed online than many others who've just rushed in, spending time or money without a clear plan or goals.

Should you start an Internet-based business?

In your planning process, or at the end when you show your plans to others who haven't worked on them, you may be asked whether selling online will be a part of your project. This is the wave of the future, but it's not really a marketing issue, even though one could say that online selling is best built on a base of successful online marketing. The *mindshare* (meaning basically, awareness) you build with your online marketing effort can be converted into *market share* for your online sales work.

Plan your online sales effort as a separate business with income, expenses, and (hopefully) a profit. See *Selling Online For Dummies* by Leslie Lundquist (IDG Books Worldwide, Inc.) to get started with online sales.

The rest of this book shows you the nuts and bolts you need to implement each part of your online marketing plan — designing and building your business Web site, using e-mail and LISTSERV applications (automated e-mail mailing lists), developing a presence on online services, and more. Use this book and, if needed, other resources that focus on each element of your online presence.

If you're working with others to implement your online marketing presence, ask them regularly for progress reports and for demonstrations of progress. (The squeaky wheel gets the grease, and the colleague or customer who's asking about a project regularly is the one who gets more time and effort devoted to it.) Return the favor for them: Track your own and others' progress to quickly identify any elements that are going over the time or money allotted to them.

As you implement your online marketing plan, keep a record of departures you make from it. You may find that the Web site, for instance, needs to be larger than expected; or the first time you actually see the prototype running on a Web browser, you may decide that the look needs revamping, thereby adding expense. You may also decide to cut back elsewhere to stay within budget. Keep a brief record of decisions you make, the reasons for them, and their impact on your schedule and budget. Such a record helps a great deal when you assess the overall success of your project and when you plan to revise your online presence later. (The only thing constant in the online world is change!)

Part II
Marketing on the World Wide Web

The 5th Wave   By Rich Tennant

Cleopatra Carpet Cleaners

"So far our Web presence has been pretty good. We've gotten some orders, a few inquiries, and nine guys who want to date our logo."

In this part . . .

World Wide Web hype has reached such dizzying levels that it obscures the Web as perhaps the single most important new marketing tool since the advent of television. In this part, we cut through the technical jargon and show you exactly how to create an easy-to-find, effective Web presence, whether you're doing all the work yourself or working with others.

Chapter 4

Mastering Your Domain

. . . .

. . . .

This chapter is about the one piece of the online marketing puzzle that most companies, and individuals working for companies, give little thought to — and yet it may affect your online presence more than anything else. It can be as memorable as www.dummies.com, where you can find more information about *...For Dummies* books, or as forgettable as gold.website. net/users2/webhosting/mybusiness/accounts24/my2342 (which one are you more likely to remember?). This thing is your *domain name*.

People use your domain name to reach you on various Internet services — e-mail, ftp, and the Web, all described briefly in Chapter 1. Future Internet services are likely to use your domain name as well. A domain name is your identifier in Cyberspace — kind of a cross between a company name, a business address, and a CB radio handle, if you're old enough to remember the song "Convoy" ("We got a great big convoy, rolling through the night. . . .") Getting the right domain name is extremely important. The good news: You can register the domain name that you want quickly and for a small fee, as we describe later in this chapter. The bad news: Someone else may beat you to your ideal domain name, as we also explain later in this chapter.

If you're working in a company, or thinking of starting a company, that doesn't have a domain name yet, cancel your appointments, take your phone off the hook, and read this chapter right away; the online presence that you save may be your own. If your company or other organization already has a domain name, read this chapter anyway — you may need to change your domain name, including your e-mail addresses and Web URL, to a better one, or establish a new domain name for a product or service that you're working on. Thousands of new domain names are established every day; time is of the essence.

But along with choosing a domain name, you may want to take a few extra minutes to think about who should provide the online access needed for your online marketing efforts. Do you want to stick with your current access provider, or should you switch to someone better able to handle domain name registration, Web hosting, and more? The next section gives you the inside scoop.

Choosing an ISP for Online Marketing

You probably already have Internet access in one form or another. You may use an Internet Service Provider (ISP), such as MindSpring or Netcom, or an online service like America Online. Online services provide a lot of proprietary content that you can't get access to any other way, and a fair amount of hand-holding; ISPs provide a basic package of software and services, but little content of their own.

Choosing an Internet Service Provider or online service for online *access* is quite a bit different than choosing one for online *marketing*. Your needs for online access are much less. All you need for Websurfing and newsgroup access is a reliable connection to the Internet. If your ISP gets sold or goes out of business, you can just change to another one.

However, for online marketing, your needs are much greater. You need to choose a business that can do some or all of the following:

 ✔ **Register your domain name.** If you want to register your domain name yourself, see "Discovering How Domain Names Work," later in this chapter. If you want your ISP to do it for you, pick an ISP that you can trust to do it right.

 If you register your domain name through an ISP or online service, make absolutely sure that you end up as the legal owner of the domain name. Some unscrupulous ISPs register the domain name to themselves and then charge you whatever they can get for full ownership later, putting you at a real disadvantage in regard to this important piece of virtual real estate. You can use the Whois service described in the "Choosing a company domain name" section in this chapter to determine who the registered owner of any domain name is.

 ✔ **Receive and forward your e-mail.** You need an ISP or online service that can quickly and reliably receive and send your e-mail. (Your ISP receives all e-mail sent to you and then routes it to you.) Occasional misroutings are inevitable, but regular blackouts, crashes, and wholesale losses of mail aren't.

 ✔ **Support you on the road.** When you and others in your company travel, you need access to local access numbers in as many places as possible to keep costs down.

✔ **Provide you access to newsgroups.** Your Internet Service Provider must provide you access to all the thousands of newsgroups on the Internet — for more on newsgroup access see Chapter 10.

✔ **Host your Web site.** Your Internet Service Provider needs to be able to host your Web site at reasonable rates. Carefully compare basic charges for business Web sites, per-hit charges for the number of visitors that you get to your Web site, and disk space charges for storing the content of your Web site. Some providers hide high charges in these rates. You may also want to consider putting your Web site on a specialized hosting service other than your ISP; we describe hosting services in the next chapter.

✔ **Give you support.** Although you can't expect your ISP to manage your online presence for you, you really need to be able to get someone on the phone to help you upgrade your online presence or troubleshoot problems.

✔ **Stay in business.** Given all the things you may be depending on your Internet Service Provider for, the most important thing is that it stays in business. With over 4,000 ISPs in the United States alone and with online services dropping like flies, turnover is a fact of life. The death throes of a failing ISP during its final months may include downtime, billing problems, sudden fee increases, and more. Pick a large national ISP or a large online service, or accept a risk of problems or outright disappearance of your ISP.

Choosing an ISP

Your best choice for online marketing may well be a *standalone ISP*. (Technically, online services are ISPs, too, given that they provide Internet service to people. By standalone ISP, we mean an ISP that's not also an online service.) If you're reasonably comfortable with the Internet and you're willing to search for one of the top standalone ISPs, a standalone ISP may be the right choice for you.

To find an ISP for online marketing, look for a major, nationwide provider that has been in the business long enough to get write-ups in major magazines. Search for those reviews online and compare carefully. One excellent review from *PC Magazine,* including an interactive ISP selector, is on ZDNet at `www.zdnet.com/anchordesk/story/story_460.html`.

For online marketing, you also want an ISP that is technically savvy and thoroughly up to date. Among other things, it should support a broad range of Internet applications and services, not just the Web and e-mail; if you can't get access to Internet Relay Chat (IRC), you sure can't use it for marketing. (Chat is described in some detail in Chapter 7.) A good sign of technical savvy is the availability of ISDN (Integrated Services Digital

Network — a type of digital phone line) support; though ISDN can be costly for consumer use, its high speed makes it a good fit for small businesses and satellite offices of larger businesses.

According to ZDNet, the major national ISPs who support multiple Internet applications, support Windows 3.*x* access (for any older machines you may have not yet upgraded), provide IRC access, support full newsgroup access, and provide ISDN connections are EarthLink Network, GTE Internet Solutions, MindSpring, Netcom, and Whole Earth Networks.

Now (that is, before you start your online marketing effort) is the time to switch to an ISP that can keep up with your Web site. With all the competition out there, you should be able to lock in good rates for a package of services that meets your needs.

MindSpring is one ISP that receives high marks for its strong package of access software and excellent customer service. It's the NetGuide 1997 People's Choice winner and highly recommended by CNET. Check out its Web site at www.mindspring.com, as shown in Figure 4-1, to find out more. Access and sign-up software for MindSpring is on the CD-ROM at the back of this book.

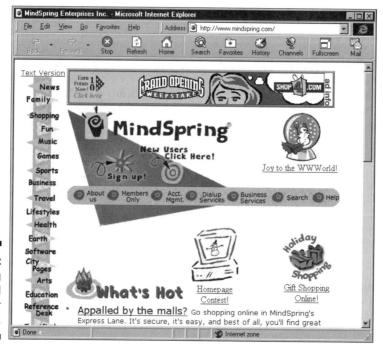

Figure 4-1: MindSpring is a good choice for your ISP.

Though an ISP can be a good choice for hosting your Web site, a specialized Web hosting provider may be a good choice as well. Consider investigating Web hosting services if you expect to get a lot of visitors — hundreds a week or more — to your Web site. And be sure to get your domain name registered to you so you can change where your Web site is hosted any time.

Choosing an online service

If you're really new to the online world and need lots of hand-holding, an online service may be a good choice for hosting your Web presence. The online services tend to have well-staffed phone support lines and lots of people — both paid staff and fellow users — who can give you assistance in a jam.

However, the issue of stability is just as vital for online services as for standalone ISPs (as we discuss in the preceding section). We used to strongly recommend CompuServe, but America Online (AOL) just purchased it; CompuServe's top-rated access network was purchased by WorldCom, just an appetizer preceding its purchase of phone giant MCI (which has its own ISP). So while CompuServe is still a good bet, what it will be like or how independent of AOL it will be in the future is anyone's guess.

The other big online services, Prodigy and the Microsoft Network, have both failed to catch on strongly; while neither is likely to disappear, neither is going gangbusters either.

The only online service worth considering for your online marketing, then, is America Online. (In fact, many small businesses get e-mail for everyone in the company by getting them an AOL account, saving the hassle of setting up their own mail server or ISP-based mail. As the business develops more online marketing savvy, using AOL for Web site hosting, newsgroup access, and more is a natural next step.)

America Online isn't among the top ISPs for online marketing because it lacks important business-related features like ISDN support, access to all newsgroups, IRC support, and so on. In addition, if you want business Web site hosting, you don't actually get it from AOL directly. Instead, you have to do business with AOL's chosen provider of Web hosting services, PrimeHost, as shown in Figure 4-2. Through PrimeHost you can get your own "real" domain name in the form `www.yourdomain.com`, avoiding the unprofessional look of having your domain name include a subdirectory like `www.aol.com/members/fred`. For much more on domain names, see the next section of this chapter.

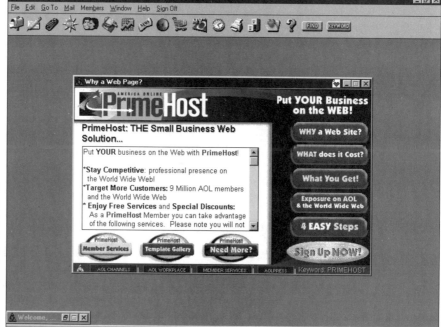

Figure 4-2:
PrimeHost
is the Web
hosting
provider for
America
Online
members.

You can certainly find out a lot about America Online, both for better and for worse, through books, articles in computer magazines, online discussions, and more. To find out the worst things anyone can say about it, look at the famous AOL complaints Web site at www.aolsucks.com. The top page of the Web site is shown in Figure 4-3.

Although AOL is a robust service that has a lot to offer, remember that at the end of the day it's a *consumer* online service. AOL is focused on keeping happy — and making money from — a large group of people whose needs are different from those of a business user, let alone someone doing online marketing. You may be able to find happiness using AOL for your online support, but doing so may require that you "swim upstream."

Consider having an AOL account and logging on occasionally even if you use a standalone ISP for your main online access and online presence support. AOL is home to a lot of smart users who can help with questions about online marketing, and AOL is a pretty savvy online marketer itself. The service can provide you with your own unique, albeit expensive, advertising and marketing opportunities. See Chapter 10 for more about America Online.

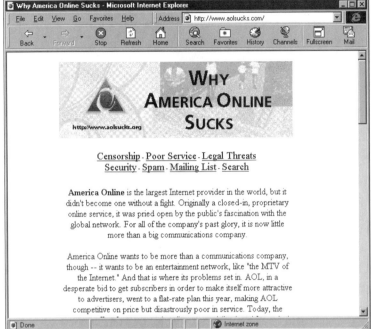

Figure 4-3:
Finding
strong
opinions
about AOL
is easy.

Discovering How Domain Names Work

Few businesspeople understand how domain names work. But understanding how domain names work is like being able to read a map of Cyberspace — with this knowledge, you can put your business, product, or service at a prominent spot on that map.

You're probably familiar with domain names of your regular e-mail correspondents and from Web sites that you frequently visit. But what if you're trying to find a company marketing site on the Web and you're not quite sure of the domain name? Of course, as we point out in Chapter 2, you can search using appropriate keywords. But even better, the right domain name can make a business much easier to find on the Web. A well-chosen domain name can further facilitate marketing communication by making your marketing e-mail address (maybe something like `sales@yourproductsite.com`) much easier for people to remember.

Take a quick look at the Web URL in Figure 4-4 — which is the address of a personal Web page on the GeoCities Web site — and find the domain name in it. The URL has three parts:

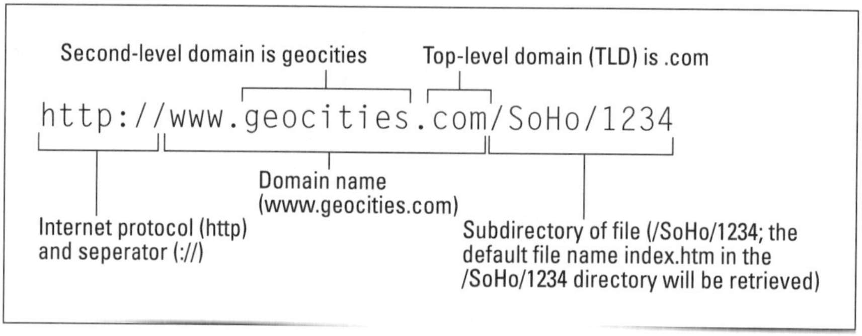

Figure 4-4:
The domain name is in the middle of this URL.

Second-level domain is geocities   Top-level domain (TLD) is .com

`http://www.geocities.com/SoHo/1234`

Internet protocol (http) and seperator (://)

Domain name (www.geocities.com)

Subdirectory of file (/SoHo/1234; the default file name index.htm in the /SoHo/1234 directory will be retrieved)

✔ **Internet protocol name.** Each Internet service has its own special code, or *protocol,* for deciphering its messages. The World Wide Web uses *HyperText Transfer Protocol,* or HTTP, usually seen on the Web as `http`. (Acronyms are usually in capital letters, but Unix people — the originators of the Internet and many other important things in computing — tend to avoid them.) A colon and a double slash are used as separators, so the Internet protocol name always appears within a URL like this: `http://`.

In the recent versions of Microsoft Internet Explorer and Netscape Navigator, you don't have to type in the protocol name to reach a Web site. For example, to reach the *...For Dummies* Web site, you can simply enter `www.dummies.com` in the Address or Netsite text box.

✔ **Domain name.** The domain name identifies a machine or a group of related machines and is supported by a specific Internet server. The part of the domain name that you need to be most concerned about is the period and three-letter code at the end — `.com`, `.edu`, and so on, called the *top-level domain* (TLD) — and the group of letters just before the last period in the domain name, which in Figure 4-4 is `geocities`, called the *second-level domain.*

✔ **Subdirectory and filename.** The subdirectory and filename simply identify the particular file that the user wants. (If no specific filename is used, the Web server usually looks for a file named `index.htm` or `index.html` as the default.) If you've ever used DOS or Unix, you're very familiar with this kind of pathname and filename; on Windows and the Macintosh, folders play the role of subdirectories, and the three-letter extension at the end of the filename is more or less hidden.

Breaking down domain names

The original role of a domain name is as a shared name for a group of machines connected to the Internet. Every machine on the Internet has a specific identifying number called an *IP address,* but people have trouble remembering long numbers. So machines can be assigned names as well; the names and the numbers that go with them are stored on an Internet server called a Domain Name Server, or DNS — initials you may recognize from setting up programs that access the Internet.

Domain names allow an organization to take over the job of naming all of its machines that are connected to the Internet. After an organization receives a domain name of its own, it can assign any name it wants within that domain. For instance, an organization with the domain name mybiz.com can call machines that it owns fred.mybiz.com, bigserver.mybiz.com, and so on.

The confusing thing about domain names is that they're read backward, not forward, with the three-letter top-level domain, or TLD (such as .com) at the right end, the second-level domain just before it, and so on, as shown in Figure 4-4. Only a few top-level domains are currently in use, and they can show you a great deal about what kind of organization or company you're dealing with, as shown in Table 4-1.

Table 4-1	Top-Level Domains (TLDs)
Top-level domain	*Meaning*
.com	Commercial organizations, businesses
.edu	Educational institutions (four-year colleges and universities only)
.org	Nonprofit organizations
.gov	U.S. government agencies (nonmilitary)
.mil	U.S. government military agencies
.net	Organizations responsible for supporting the Internet (considered prestigious)
.int	International organizations formed by treaty or as part of the Internet database infrastructure
.uk, .ca, and so on	Country codes determined by an ISO standards committee. You can find a complete list at www.iana.org/in-notes/iana/assignments/country-codes.

As far as online marketing is concerned, the most important part of a domain name is the second-level domain. This domain is the middle part of a typical Web URL — for example, the computerz component of www.computerz.com. The second-level domain that you choose needs to represent your company and organization as well as possible within a few constraints:

✔ **No special characters.** Your domain name can contain only letters, numbers, and the dash character.

✔ **Not too long.** Your second-level domain can be only 22 characters long. For example, the second-level domain name for the House of Natural Sound (houseofnaturalsound) is 19 characters.

✔ **Not already in use.** This part is tough. The combination of your second-level and top-level domains, such as smallinc.com, bigcollege.edu, or nonprofit.org, has to be new (not already in use). If it is already in use, you either have to induce the current nameholder to give it up or come up with a new name. (More on this later in this chapter.)

The InterNIC online domain name registration service described at the end of this chapter checks any domain name you enter to make sure it fits the above rules in the preceding list.

The second-level domain of your choice, combined with the appropriate top-level domain, is what you register for your use on the Internet. Below the second-level domain, you can do anything you want. For instance, many people use the third-level domain www. to indicate a Web site — but this is just a common practice. Some organizations use third-level domains to indicate departments within the organization; for instance, when Bud Smith worked on the QuickTime VR team at Apple, its domain name was www.qtvr.apple.com. However, this use of third-level and fourth-level domains is fading because people have trouble remembering multilevel domain names. His department eventually started using www.quicktimevr.com instead.

AltaVista's troubles

The AltaVista search engine from Digital Equipment Corp. (DEC) is one way that DEC makes an effort to show that it "gets it" on the Net — but the service doesn't have the right domain name. In order to use AltaVista, you have to go to altavista.digital.com — most people looking for the search engine don't think of the .digital part. If you go to www.altavista.com, the logical place to look for the AltaVista search engine, you get AltaVista Technology, an Internet postcard company whose Web page is shown in Figure 4-5. The postcard company's Web site gets thousands of additional hits because it got the domain name first. Because the domain name altavista.com was already taken, the product managers for the AltaVista search engine probably should have found a different name for it, one with a good domain name choice that wasn't already registered to someone else.

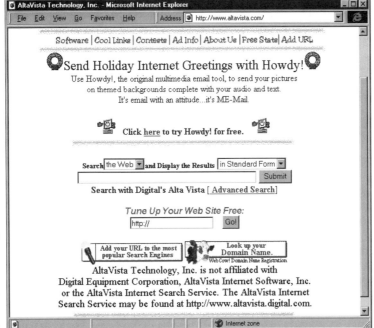

Figure 4-5:
The
AltaVista
Technology
Web site.

The competition for domain names

According to the InterNIC organization, .com is by far the most common top-level domain. Table 4-2 shows top-level domain registrations through mid-1997. Many of these domains have been deleted for nonpayment or nonuse, so the actual number of current domains is substantially less. But, as you can see from Table 4-2, over 80 percent — 1.5 million out of the total 1.7 million — of domain name registrations have been for the .com top-level domain.

Table 4-2   Total Top Level Domains (TLDs) through Mid-1997

Top-level domain	Number of registrations	Percentage
.com	1,538,298	87%
.edu	4,005	< 1%
.org	107,683	6%
.net	118,938	7%
.gov	628	< 1%
other	229	< 1%
Total	**1,769,781**	**100%**

If you're part of a government agency or the military, please check out the policies that apply to your agency before registering a domain name. We don't want to get blamed for someone's tax return getting sent to the wrong e-mail address.

If you want your domain name to specify that your organization is located outside the U.S., you should use the appropriate country designation in your top-level domain (TLD) name. To see country designations look online at `www.iana.org/in-notes/iana/assignments/country-codes`. (Take a minute to look at the notes at the bottom of the page that list changes since late 1989. You can see the breakup of the Soviet Union and other changes in the world reflected in the country code changes.)

Because the `.com` domain is so widely used, many organizations register and use the `.com` version of their domain name as well as the more appropriate version — `.edu`, `.org`, or whatever. If your domain name ends in something besides `.com` and you need to reach many of the non-cyberelite, you should consider registering the `.com` version as well.

A great deal of competition exists for desirable domain names. Figure 4-6 shows the rise in the number of domain names ending in `.com` that are registered by InterNIC. As you can see, the number is doubling every few months. A land rush is going on for prime spots in Cyberspace, and you can't risk not staking your claim.

Why domain names are so important

A business consultant once said that the three keys to starting a business are location, location, and location. Your domain name is the location to which all your e-mail and Web traffic comes. You are likely to print it on business cards, stationery, and print ads, as well as hastily tell it to inquiring people in the elevator.

Typically, when people use the Internet, they're trying to get information quickly. If they've heard of your company in the offline world, they may try to guess your Web URL and enter it in their browsers. If you have the URL that they expect — `www.`[*a reasonable version of your company name*]`.com` — they may find it on the first or second try. If not, you have problems.

Having failed to find you quickly, the Websurfers — also known as the potential (or current) customers, investors, journalists writing stories about your industry, or just people who are curious — can do several things. More often than not, they just go surf somewhere else. Or they may try using a search engine to find you. But even if their search is successful (and especially if it's not), you've frustrated someone important to you.

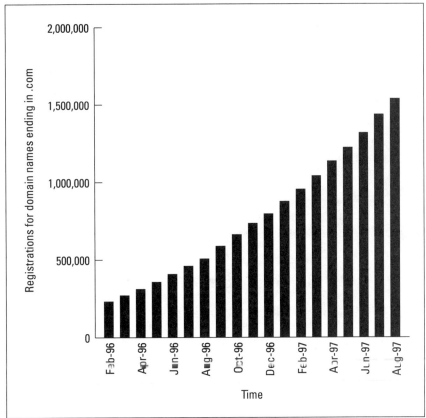

Figure 4-6:
Communism may be dead, but .com is growing like a weed, as these figures from InterNIC (www.internic. com) show.

The first thing to do is to make sure that you get a domain name of your own. Putting your Web page in someone else's domain means that the user has a lot harder time reaching you because your URL looks something like this: http://www.isp.net/yourpoorcompany. People will have a great deal of difficulty finding your poor company and will be irritated with you for your low-rent Web presence when they do. Think of company stationery — you wouldn't buy another company's unused stationery, cross out its letterhead and logo, and then slap a rubber stamp with your contact information over it, yet a low-rent domain name like this one isn't much different.

The second thing to do is to make sure you get a good domain name — one that someone looking for your company online can easily guess. In many cases, figuring out a good domain name is easy; your company name translates into an easy-to-guess second-level domain, the domain name that you want (your desired second-level domain and the appropriate top-level domain, such as .com) is available, and you're in business. Other times, identifying the appropriate unused domain name is much more difficult, especially if only one name is really a good fit, and that name's taken.

The benefits of the right domain name are significant. Every time you advertise your company name or communicate it in any way, you effectively communicate your online location as well.

Imagine a phone book that has a thin front section with some company names alphabetized and a larger section in the middle and back with company names in random order. The front section is orderly and usable; the rest is a mess. Which part would you rather be in? Organizations with the right domain name are in the front of the book; people can go right to them online. Organizations whose Web presence is in a subdirectory of someone else's domain, or who have a poor domain name, are in the rest of the book, hard to find.

For one marketer's aggressive strategies for reserving domain names, see the article, "The Smart Marketer's Strategy for Reserving Domain Names," by Andy Bourland at `www.clickz.com/archives/112897.html`.

Possible new domain names

As this book is being written, a proposal to add new top-level domains (TLDs) to the existing set is being actively considered by various parties on the Web. Proposed additional top-level domains include `.firm` for businesses, `.shop` for online retailers, `.web` for organizations that have activities relating to the World Wide Web, and more. For details of the proposal, see the Global Top Level Domain Memorandum of Understanding Web site at `www.gtld-mou.org`. This site includes pointers to valuable information about the current domain name system as well as the proposed changes.

While the proposals are highly controversial and their implementation has already been held up for over a year, some additions to the existing set of top-level domains may very well be made. What's unknown, however, is whether any new domains will be widely accepted and used. Keep careful track of possible changes to the set of available domains and carefully consider registering any appropriate new domain names that become available as a result of these proposals.

Choosing Your Domain Name(s)

With a little thought as to how people use domain names, you can understand why registering the domain name(s) that you need is so important. Consider registering the following kinds of domain names:

  ✔ **Ideal company domain name.** Figure out the ideal domain name for your organization, as we describe in the following section, and register it if it's still available.

✔ **One or two close alternates.** If reasonable alternate domain names for your company — names that people may try — are available, consider registering them too. You can then set up your Web server to automatically bring up the right Web site for the alternate, too.

✔ **Product domain names.** If you sell a computer product or service or a mass-market product with wide awareness — anything a substantial number of current or future Websurfers may find interesting — register the domain name that's the best fit for it soon, before someone else does. Do the same for products under development.

Unlike some people, we don't recommend that you register every possible alternate domain name for your company, any divisions thereof, all your real products, and potential product names. Registering too many names just exacerbates the problem of too many organizations chasing too few desirable domain names. Be reasonable in deciding how many domain names to register and then move quickly to register all the ones that you choose.

Domain name follies

Your domain name is not a chance to rename your company something different online than in the offline world. (If you don't like your company name, change it — and consider what domain names are available as part of the company renaming process.) Neither is it a chance to be cute, funny, interesting, intriguing, or anything else except *easy to guess.*

The ideal domain name is the domain name that a savvy Internet user who knows your company's name would guess first when trying to find your company on the Web. It's simply the closest translation that you can make of your company's name into a single word with no spaces, commas, periods, or other punctuation.

As we mention earlier in this chapter, the only characters allowed in a domain name are letters, numbers, and dashes. However, we suggest avoiding the dash — remembering whether a domain name has a dash in it and where the dash goes can be difficult, and may cause potential visitors to miss your site. Stick to letters and numbers whenever possible.

For some examples, Table 4-3 lists the top 15 most profitable American companies, the best domain names for them, alternates that would probably be worth registering, and their actual domain names.

Table 4-3	Domain Names of the Most Profitable American Companies		
Company name	*Ideal domain*	*Alternates to name*	*Actual domain registered*
General Motors	gm.com	generalmotors.com	gm.com
General Electric	ge.com	generalelectric.com	ge.com
Exxon	exxon.com		exxon.com
Philip Morris Companies	philipmorris.com	phillipmorris.com	kraftfoods.com, miller-brewing.com, **and so on**
IBM	ibm.com		ibm.com
Ford Motor Company	ford.com		ford.com
Intel	intel.com		intel.com
Citicorp	citicorp.com		citicorp.com
Merck	merck.com		merck.com
Du Pont de Nemours	dupont.com		dupont.com
Coca-Cola	cocacola.com	coke.com	cocacola.com, coke.com
Chase Manhattan	chase.com		chase.com
Procter & Gamble	procter&gamble.com	proctergamble.com, pg.com	pg.com
Wal-Mart Stores	walmart.com	wal-mart.com	wal-mart.com
BankAmerica	bankamerica.com	bankofamerica.com	bank-america.com, bofa.com

Looking at Table 4-3 you may think, "Well, those companies are all big, and they no doubt have lots of lawyers working on getting the right domain names and rights." In fact, the number one most profitable U.S. company in 1995, General Motors, was slow to register the domain name `generalmotors.com`. This hesitation left the field wide open, and another group took the Web Uniform Resource Locator (URL) `www.generalmotors.com`. Figure 4-7 shows what you get if you try to reach General Motors by typing in `www.generalmotors.com` in your Web browser.

Besides the big General Motors problem, other problems are evident as well. Several of the large companies in Table 4-3 don't have obvious alternates to their names sewn up. Procter & Gamble doesn't have `procter&gamble.com` or `proctergamble.com`; Wal-Mart doesn't have `walmart.com`, an obvious alternate. BankAmerica Corp., which its customers know as Bank of America or B of A, doesn't have `bankofamerica.com`, but does have `bofa.com`.

Other large organizations have problems, too. Many users looking for Stanford University on the Web try `www.stanford.com` first, being used to typing `.com` in domain names, but that URL gets them the Stanford Management Group and no pointer to the Stanford University Web page.

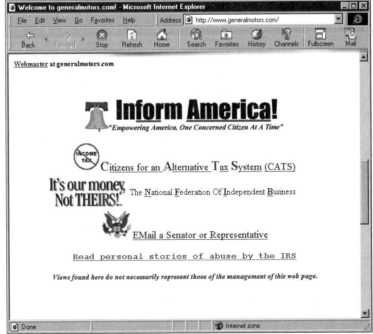

Figure 4-7:
The site at
`www.general motors.com`
isn't what
you may
think.

The Stanford University Web page is at www.stanford.edu — appropriate if you know your domain names well, but not the first choice of a lot of people who are used to seeing the .com designation. For you Ivy Leaguers, www.yale.com gets you Yale Materials Handling Corporation; www.harvard.com gets you an error message.

Government agencies aren't immune to domain name confusion, either. The URL www.dod.com gets you a sound company; www.whitehouse.com gets you a porn site that claims over a million hits a day; however much you may dislike X-rated Internet sites or the misuse of such a hallowed name in America, you have to admit that reserving that domain name was pretty smart marketing. (To reach the White House's Web page, use www.whitehouse.gov.) The U.S. Navy, however, has gotten hip to the scene; the URL www.navy.com gets you to a recruiting-oriented Web site, shown in Figure 4-8, and www.navy.mil (the proper URL for the Navy under the usual domain name rules) gets you the official Web site of the Navy, shown in Figure 4-9. The Navy's approach shows perfect pitch in terms of how to handle Web users: Newer users who are more likely to know only the .com designation get recruited to join up (with a pointer to the official Web site at the bottom of the page); those in the know, who are more likely to try the .mil designation, get the official Web page.

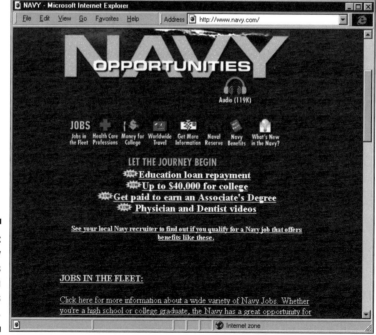

Figure 4-8:
The Navy wants all you .commies on board.

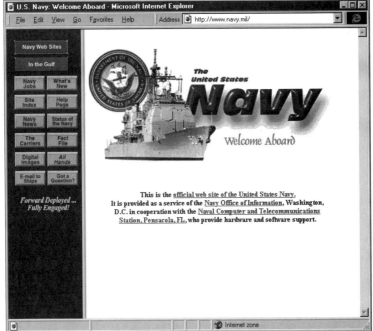

Figure 4-9:
The official
.military
site for
those in
the know.

Good and bad domain names

You can see from the examples in the previous section how to pick the best domain name for your company: Find the word or short phrase, with no spaces or other punctuation, that best represents your company name. You simply translate your company name into a domain name. (The test of whether you have the right domain name is: Can someone who regularly uses the Web guess it on the first try?)

Not all companies come as close to the ideal domain names as most of the Top 15 most profitable companies shown back in Table 4-3. Also, many companies' names are difficult to render into a domain name. Looking at the category *Home Theater* in Yahoo!, you can see some interesting examples of good and not-so-good domain names:

✔ **Adrian's Home Theatre.** URL: `www.aros.net/~adrian`. This small company gives the impression that it wants to stay that way — even though a look at its Web page shows that it has an address and phone number and sells very expensive equipment. The company's Web site is stored in a subdirectory of someone else's domain — which is cheaper than getting your own domain (and looks it). This company should get its own domain name, preferably `adrianshometheatre.com` (`adrian.com` is already taken).

- ✔ **Ambiophonics.** URL: www.ambiophonics.org. This nonprofit group promotes realistic music reproduction. The domain name is easy to remember except for the .org part. This group should also register ambiophonics.com and create a Web page at www.ambiophonics.com that automatically redirects the user to the correct Web page at www.ambiophonics.org.

- ✔ **Audio Design Associates.** URL: www.ada-usa.com. This manufacturer has worked around the fact that its obvious domain name choice, ada.com, was taken by adding a geographic identifier, -usa. This solution is a decent one, but unfortunately no one is likely to guess the URL when searching for the company on the Web. Also, the dash is easy to forget. The company should have gotten audiodesign.com instead, if it was still available, or adausa.com if not.

- ✔ **House of Natural Sound.** URL: www.houseofnaturalsound.com. More and more companies with long names are trying this brave solution: If you have a long company name, just make the whole thing into a domain name. You can use up to 22 characters plus the top-level domain name, which is .com in this case; houseofnaturalsound is 19 characters, close to the limit. The House of Natural Sound Web page is shown in Figure 4-10. In this case the long name works well, given that no shorter alternative that anyone is likely to guess exists. We would suggest that the company also get hons.com as an alternate name, because some users are likely to try the acronym.

Figure 4-10:
Visit the home page of the House of Natural Sound.

- **Martin-Kleiser.** URL: `www.martin-kleiser.com`. Like Wal-Mart, this company has a dash in its name, so it keeps the dash in its URL as well. However, because no other special characters are allowed in domain names, some people may think that the dash isn't allowed either and try the name without the dash. The company should also get `martinkleiser.com` as an alternate name for those who try it without the dash.

- **NAD Electronics Limited.** URL: `www.nad.co.uk`. This domain name is typical for a non-U.S. company that doesn't want to appear multinational.

- **NPR Audio.** URL: `home.aol.com/npraudio`. This company manufactures over 1,800 products, but not only can't be bothered to register its domain name, they put their Web page in a directory of AOL's Web page as well — a good way to get started, but a poor appearance to make in public. Some Internet old-timers hate AOL for bringing newbies to the Net, and some of AOL's own customers detest it for busy signals and other problems. If your domain name is *truly* your Cyberspace location, this one's on the wrong side of the digital tracks.

- **Performance Imaging.** URL: `www.hdtvsystems.com`. Many companies use a URL that refers to the *type* of product they make rather than their company name. We think the company name should be the first and foremost choice. In this case, Performance Imaging registered `www.performanceimaging.com` as well, which is good, but they promote `www.hdtvsystems.com` as their URL, when it should be a secondary point of access.

- **Signature Technologies, Inc.** URL: `www.signaturetech.com`. Not a bad choice for a domain name — *tech* is well-known shorthand for *technology* or *technologies*. And, showing more savvy than some of the Fortune 500, this company can be reached at `www.signaturetechnologies.com` as well. Its Web page is shown in Figure 4-11.

Should you make your product name a domain?

One interesting dilemma is whether you should make your product name a domain name. We don't think that you should use your main product's name as the domain name for the whole company, unless the product is much more well known than the company (in which case you may want to change your company name to match it!). However, you may want to consider registering key product names as domain names in addition to your company name. You may eventually want to have a Web site dedicated to a product, or automatically reference people who enter your product name as a URL to your main company site. (For instance, if you enter `www.kleenex.com`, you'll automatically be redirected to the Web site of Kimberly-Clark Corporation, the makers of Kleenex.)

Figure 4-11:
Signature
Technologies
supports
double
URLs — a
sign of the
times?

Though we picked one very narrow category for these examples, any group of organizations is likely to have a similar range of easy-to-guess and hard-to-guess domain names. Just make sure that yours is in the easy-to-guess group!

Choosing a company domain name

Now is the time to choose your own domain name (or, if you already have one and you don't like it, to choose a new one). Follow these steps to choose a domain name:

1. **Sit down with a piece of paper or a blank document in your word processor, and list all the possible domain names that fit your organization.**

   Use .com as the ending (top-level domain, or TLD for short) for your domain name if it's for a company. If you're part of a nonprofit, educational, government, or military organization, or in a country outside the U.S., use the appropriate TLD (.org, .edu, .gov, .mil, or .uk, for example). Even if your company was unprofitable last quarter, you're still a company and shouldn't register as a nonprofit! However, because the .com ending is so much better known, you may want to consider registering your nonprofit or other organization domain name with .com at the end as well.

2. **Ask several friends and colleagues who use the Web what domain name they think your company should use.**

   Most people encounter domains as part of Web addresses (URLs), so ask some of them what Web address they think you should have. Experienced Web users try to guess Web addresses without consciously thinking about it, so you may want to even ask a few people to sit down in front of their browsers and try typing in the right URL for your company. The results may surprise you!

3. **Shorten your list to a few favorite candidates.**

   Include alternates that aren't the best choice, but that some people may try — for instance, a name with your company's acronym should be kept as an alternate if people usually think of your company by its full name.

4. **Use the InterNIC Whois service to find out if the domain name that you want is taken.**

   Fire up your Web browser and go to `rs.internic.net/cgi-bin/whois`. (You can also get to the Whois service by following links from the main InterNIC Web page at `www.internic.net`.) The Whois Web page is shown in Figure 4-12.

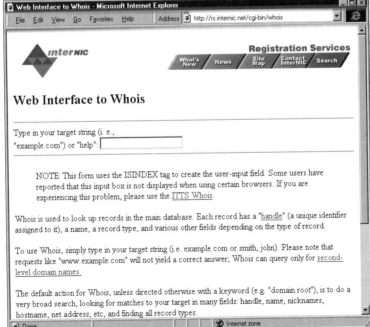

Figure 4-12:
Find out if someone already has your domain name.

5. **Enter the first domain name that you want to check; for instance, as a domain name for this book, we may try** omfd.com.

6. **Press Enter.**

   The Whois service tells you whether someone already has your domain name. If it's still available, you see the message, "No match for yourdomain.com. If it's taken, you see a description of the person or organization who has it. Figure 4-13 shows good news on this front; Figure 4-14, appropriately, shows bad news. (You may be in luck; a near match to your name may be taken, but not the exact name that you want. In this case you see a bad news page, but without your exact desired domain name listed on it.)

7. **Check all the domain names on your list. Even if your first choice is available, check the others in case you want to register them as alternates.**

8. **If your top choice or top few choices are taken, print out or save the contact information that Whois makes available for these choices. (In Windows, you can save the Web page by choosing File⇨Save As. Whois is light on graphics anyway, and saving the page as text gives you greater portability.) Then follow up with the domain name holders and see if any of them are willing to part with their domain name for a reasonable price or even for free.**

9. **For the choices that are taken, try entering the domain name as a URL in your Web browser — add** www. **at the beginning and then the domain name — to see if the domain name is in active use. If not, it may be easier to negotiate getting the domain name for yourself.**

If your first choice of a strong alternate is available, you're ready to take the next step and claim your domain name. If all the reasonable choices for your business are taken, consider using a variant on the name of your business. For example instead of abcplumbing (which is taken as we write this), consider abcplumbers or abcp (which are not). If you're really stuck, try inserting a dash — abc-plumbing, for instance. California Plumbing could use calplumb, calplumbing, californiaplumbing, or other variants.

You can also contact the current holder of the domain that you want to use and see if the folks that own it are willing to give up their rights to it. If the domain name is not in active use and they reserved it to possibly use later or to prevent it from being used for something objectionable, they may be willing to let you have it.

Some domain names are held by domain name brokers, speculators who reserve domain names that they don't need in hopes of selling them to a high bidder later. (Yes, this practice is common, and no, it's not a crime.) If such a person holds your domain name, you may have to pay him or her off, or consider another name.

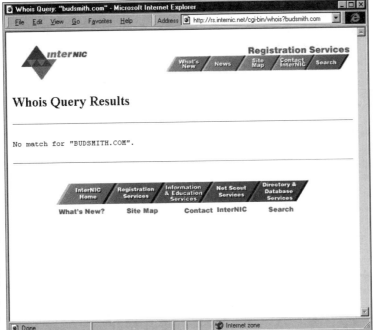

Figure 4-13:
Here's what you see if your domain is still free.

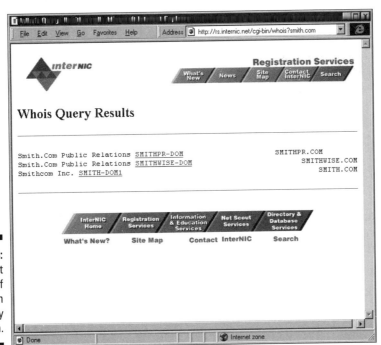

Figure 4-14:
Here's what you see if your domain is already taken.

You can also consider suing the current holder of the name for rights to it. If you have a strong trademark claim to the name and the current holder doesn't, then you may be able to win — but suing is often a long, expensive, and uncertain venture. InterNIC has specific rules for trademark disputes that you can review at `rs.internic.net/domain-info/internic-domain-6.html`. Threatening to sue a domain name broker may drive the price down — or, if the broker believes your claim is weak or is just stubborn, it may drive the price up instead.

If the domain name holder is actively using the domain name for a Web page, you may want to ask the holder for a link from its Web page to yours — just as the Navy's job site and official site link to each other, and just as `whitehouse.com`, the porn site mentioned earlier in this chapter, provides links to other whitehouse sites. One of the authors once did this when the short version of his product's name was in use by a consultant — not wanting to anger the product group, and fearing legal action, he put up the link that same day.

Starting out in a subdirectory

As you get your virtual feet wet in Cyberspace, you may decide to go ahead and start out with a Web site that's in a subdirectory of someone else's domain. Here are a few do's and don'ts:

✔ **Don't use an America Online (AOL) domain.** AOL is the leading online service, and you may find having AOL host your initial Web site tempting. If you do choose AOL and don't pay extra for your own domain name, you end up with a URL like `www.members.aol.com/yourbiz`. This kind of URL is an instant mark against you in your online marketing efforts. AOL in particular has had many well-publicized problems and has somewhat of a bad name in Cyberspace. No sense in associating yourself with someone else's problems.

✔ **Do use an ISP.** Many users consider independent Internet Service Providers (ISPs) to be cooler than big online services like America Online and CompuServe, so start out with an ISP. The ISP included on this book's CD-ROM, MindSpring, offers Web hosting services. Your Web URL would look like this: `www.mindspring.com/yourbiz`.

✔ **Don't publicize your subdirectory URL too widely.** If you do put your Web site in a subdirectory of someone else's site, don't publicize your URL too widely; you'll just be publicizing the fact that you haven't gotten your Web presence just right yet. Also, you're just making life more difficult for yourself later on when you do get your own domain name and need to publicize it.

✔ **Do get your own domain quickly.** Most ISPs help you quickly move your Web site to your own domain name and even register the domain name for you for a small fee. Then you can publicize your Web site freely.

If your business is small, and your desire to be accessible on the Internet is large, you may even consider changing your business name to one that translates well to an available domain name. ABC Tools may become LA Tools (domain name `latools.com`) or Toys Aren't Us (`toysarentus.com`).

After all your efforts you may just be stuck and end up having to use a less desirable name. If so, go ahead and get the less desirable name registered — before someone else takes that one, too! — and take steps to make reaching your Web site by a link or by a search engine easy, as we describe in Chapter 5.

Registering Your Domain Name(s)

After you identify an available domain name that you want, you need to register it. You can approach registering two different ways, each of which has its own benefits and hazards.

Registering your domain name yourself

The first approach is to do it yourself. The good news is that you can register the domain name by filling out a form on the InterNIC Web site at www.internic.net. The cost is only $100, which is prepayment of two years' registration fees at $50 per year.

To complete the process of getting your name registered, however, you need to have access to two machines connected to the Internet and running software that makes them *domain name servers* (often called, redundantly, *DNS servers*), computers that contain lists of Internet machine names and numerical addresses. The domain name servers need to be updated with the name and machine addresses you want to register. If you don't have a couple of DNS servers handy, this isn't a practical option.

Having an ISP or Web hosting service register your domain name for you

The second option is to get an ISP or Web hosting service to register the domain name for you. Reputable ISPs charge about $150 — $100 for the InterNIC two-year registration fee, plus $50 or so for their trouble — and get your forms in right, with no mistakes, and set up their domain name servers with your naming information as well.

However, by trusting an ISP or Web hosting service, you are putting a big responsibility for your online presence — getting your domain name registered — in the hands of someone else. Watch out for some of the following possible pitfalls:

- ✔ **Overcharging you.** Some ISPs charge you a high monthly fee, like $100 a month, for a package of Internet services that includes your own domain name. Shop around for a reasonable price, and try to pay a one-time setup fee for your domain name, and monthly fees for the rest of the service.

- ✔ **Ripping off your name.** Some unscrupulous Web hosting services or ISPs have registered customers' domain names to *themselves,* not the customer. The ISP then becomes a domain name broker, as we describe in the "Choosing a company domain name" section earlier in this chapter, and can then charge you to get your own domain name back if you ever quit using their Web hosting service. Make absolutely sure that you own the exclusive rights to your domain name.

- ✔ **Insufficient backup.** Your ISP or Web hosting service should have backup hosting of your site using a different Internet connection in a different location than the main host. That way, if a problem with the main host arises, support for your site can continue at the backup location while the problem at the main host is resolved.

- ✔ **Using subdirectories.** Some ISPs or Web hosting services with limited technical capabilities host your Web site in a subdirectory of your own domain, as happened for a while to one of the authors (Frank Catalano). His URL was `www.catalanoconsulting.com/catalano`, thereby not making use of the effort spent registering the domain name in the first place. Get an ISP who can give you your Web page in a domain with no subdirectory. (Incidentally, Frank's Web site now happily pops up at `www.catalanoconsulting.com`.)

- ✔ **Going out of business.** You really don't want your ISP or Web hosting service to go out of business — for the online marketer, it's like being a cowhand and having your horse shot out from under you, as you sometimes see in old Westerns. Try to ensure that your ISP will be around for a long time. (We discuss some of the general considerations of choosing an ISP in greater depth in the "Choosing an ISP" section earlier in this chapter.)

- ✔ **Confusing legal language.** You need to be able to clearly understand the terms of any contract that you sign regarding your domain name and rights to it. Make sure that the contract clearly states that you own your domain name and that you can transfer it to another ISP or Web hosting service at any time.

Once you're sure that you own your domain name, and your Web site is up and running, you can relax and go on to other concerns. However, if your bills for Web site hosting start to mount, you can always research competitive services online using the techniques described in Chapter 2. If you find better rates from a provider that seems like a solid company, then either negotiate better rates with your current provider or take your domain name elsewhere.

Chapter 5

Creating a Basic Business Web Site

A basic business Web site is the meat and potatoes of the online marketing world: not too exciting, but satisfying and sustaining. By creating and maintaining a basic business Web site, you can credibly claim to be online, and provide customers, press, and analysts with basic information about your company and products. If the initial effort is successful, your site can lay the groundwork for a larger online marketing effort, possibly including online sales.

You've probably seen a lot of advanced Web technology used in high-profile Web sites — technologies such as Java, Dynamic HTML, and immersive 3-D worlds. These innovations are all good, if used properly, but they have little place in a basic business Web site. Although planning is vital in business, as we describe in Chapter 3, you can create a basic business Web site without too much planning. You can even begin construction of the site while you're also beginning the planning process. The idea here is to get off your duff and jump-start your online presence by getting a competent representation of your company up and running — fast.

In this chapter, we describe how to create your initial site yourself or working with a colleague or consultants.

Although some companies and consultants advertise that they will create a basic business Web site for you for as little as $500, many of these ads are teasers designed to get you to pick up the phone and begin a process that results in big expenditures. Although you can and should use consultants for larger Web efforts, creating and publishing the initial site yourself is sensible. If you get some hands-on experience, you can know what you're paying for when you hire a Web design firm to expand your Web presence from the initial, successful base that you create using the steps in this chapter. If you do hire help for the initial Web site effort, use this chapter to do as much of the work as you can on your own, and to double-check the outsiders' advice so you can make sure that you're getting your money's worth.

Guiding Principles for Simple Business Sites

A basic business Web site is like a simple, glossy brochure that briefly describes your company and products. A basic business Web site reassures people that you're a competent player who will be around for a while and from whom they can buy with confidence. It also lets users move easily from picking up basic information to more active steps such as calling you, writing you, or sending you e-mail. But watch this last option, because it can byte you (excuse the pun); you can receive so much e-mail that you have trouble responding to all of it. See Chapter 8 for details.

Here are the basic principles that should underlie your effort to create a basic business Web site:

- ✔ **Fast construction.** Your initial Web site effort should proceed quickly from initial idea to published online site. If you can do all the work yourself and don't need anyone's approval, you may get it all done in two weeks. If you need to discuss certain aspects of your site in advance and you need approval of the final product at the end, you may need a month or longer to complete the site. Keep the project time as short as possible.

- ✔ **Cheap.** A basic Web site can be created by in-house personnel, with perhaps some outside help on the look and feel, and published on a Web server by an Internet Service Provider (ISP) or Web hosting service for very little cost. Expect to spend a few person-weeks on creating the site and somewhere around $50 a month for an ISP to maintain the site on its server.

- ✔ **Effective.** Any marketing effort needs to support moving a prospective customer along the sales cycle. A basic Web site helps potential customers consider you as a possible supplier, and encourages them to contact you in order to go further. (It gets press people, analysts, and investors to take you seriously, as well.)

✔ **Widely usable.** In Chapter 2, we emphasize that only a small part of the world is currently online. Why exacerbate this deficit by making your Web site unusable by many potential users? A basic Web site needs to be usable by anyone with an Internet connection and a Web browser; it should not contain any advanced Web technology that isn't supported by almost every available browser. That restriction means no frames, no Java, no Dynamic HTML. Graphics and tables are okay, though your site should not rely on graphics for links to other parts of your site so that users who either turn graphics off, or are visually impaired and use screen readers, can still navigate your site. This kind of simplicity makes your Web site easier to design and use.

✔ **Fits in the online world.** Because of its origins among academics and scientists, the Internet has certain standards and practices that you ignore at your peril. (Until early in the 1990s, any commercial use of the Internet was forbidden, and even now some resistance to online commerce remains.) Respect the history of the medium by avoiding hype, overstatement, alarming layouts and graphics, and so on. A conservative approach will serve you well until you develop a good feel for where you can have some fun without seeming out of place.

✔ **Does no harm.** The first words of the doctor's Hippocratic Oath are "First, do no harm," and this dictum should be honored by people doing marketing, as well. Misspellings, poor grammar, and errors in the site's text harm your company's image of competence. Web pages with large graphics that download slowly, or with advanced technologies that not everyone can use, irritate potential customers. Allowing people to send you e-mail that goes unanswered can cause lost sales. Be cautious and avoid problems.

Specifying Your Site Content

A basic business Web site is not something you advertise or market heavily. The site is there for people to find when they're looking for information on the Web. So its contents should be simple and spare, attractive but not exuberant. In baseball terms, the idea is that it's early in the game, and you want to start things on a positive note by hitting a solid single for your team.

A basic Web site fulfills the primary function that any Web site in marketing must fulfill, that of a validator. "Valid" means "worthy," and a Web site functions as a validator by showing that you're worth doing business with. Validators do much of their work on a subconscious level, so the absence of key validators makes people feel uncomfortable, in ways that they find difficult to define but that operate very effectively in steering them clear of you. The powerful role of validators is why, as we mention in the previous section, making your Web site free of errors, technical barriers, and other irritants is important. (Would you send out salespeople who were poorly groomed, ignorant of your products, or unable to speak the same language as their customers? Similar considerations apply to your Web site.)

A basic Web site needs to meet fundamental information needs, but not much more than that. In fact, putting in more information than strictly necessary is more likely to make your site difficult to navigate than to make it more useful. Avoid piling on a lot of content until you can also devote some time and energy to making your Web site easy to navigate.

If some material seems like a good idea, but not strictly necessary, drop it (or, better yet, put it on a list for later). Your final list of contents will vary depending on your company, your industry, and the available information resources you have at hand that can readily be repurposed for the Web. But most sites include the following:

- **Contact information.** This information is really, really important, and many sites — even big ones that cost big bucks to create and maintain — either don't include it at all, or bury it. Provide your company name, address, main phone number, and fax number. (Don't include your e-mail address until after you read Chapter 8.) Make your contact information easily accessible, one link away from your home page. Figure 5-1 shows contact information displayed on a relevant Web site.

- **Where you do business.** If your geographic range is limited, make this fact clear up front. Be subtle and positive. On your home page or contact information page, include a phrase like "San Francisco's leading supplier of electrical services to business" or "Western Europe's most innovative maker of eyeglass holders." Help people who don't need to spend time on your Web site find out quickly and leave happy, rather than angry.

- **Key people.** A brief list of key people, with a paragraph or so of descriptive information, can go far to make people comfortable with your company. (Some companies are reluctant to include this kind of information because they're afraid of attracting executive recruiters, but the benefits to your site's visitors outweigh this risk.) Don't include spouse-and-kids stuff — just name, title, and a brief professional biography.

- **Key customers.** Though some companies are reluctant to include it for fear of attracting competitors, a list of key customers is a very strong validator of your success. List the customers' names and a sentence or two about how they use your product. (Take the time to ask your customers if they mind this inclusion, and ask them if they want you to include a link to their Web site.) If you don't have an impressive list of key customers yet, don't try to include this information.

Figure 5-1:
Online
marketing
heroes are
easy to
contact.

The "where to buy" crisis

Putting even seemingly innocuous information on the Web can have serious offline consequences. Consider "Where to buy" information. One Web site managed by one of the authors included links to all the service companies from which customers could get consulting and customization services for a software product. When we first offered this information, the concept worked very well; companies listed on our Web site received many visitors to their own Web sites via our link to them. But, over time, two problems developed:

✔ **Vociferous demand from service companies for links to our Web site.** Several dozen new companies entered the market, worldwide, in a one-year period. These companies sent e-mail to our overloaded e-mail account requesting a link. When that e-mail got backlogged, their links were slow to appear on our site. Angry e-mail messages (which fell into the e-mail black hole), then phone calls, then personal visits to our offices and to our trade show appearances ensued. This problem was easier to remedy, by catching up on the link backlog, than the following dilemma was.

✔ **Repeated requests from our leading service company for special placement, a larger entry, or other premier status on our Web site.** In a very real sense, our leading service company deserved this favored status; it had at least double the staff and client volume of the competing companies. But if we gave that company extra focus, others would first complain and then want at least proportional representation themselves — which we couldn't do without a lot of work, nor without asking intrusive questions about just exactly how much business each of these small, privately held, often secretive companies did with our product.

The solution to this problem was to enter into a series of newsworthy arrangements with the leading service company that got prominent mention in the news section of our Web site, leading to some well-deserved new business for them. The company still wanted more prominent coverage in the service providers list, but was at least somewhat satisfied by what it got. Of course, all these special deals that generated news irritated our other service companies. . . .

✔ **Company, product, and service validators.** List positive descriptions of your company, people, products, and services from any reputable source, including analyst reports, the general press, the trade press, and individual customers from well-known companies or other organizations. Include any awards you've won. Like your company Web site itself, these validators let people know that your company is worth doing business with.

✔ **Products and services.** Include simple, brief descriptions of your products and services. You can also link to more detailed information, but put the simple descriptions together and make them easy to access; people scan them to learn just enough about your company to decide whether to explore further.

✔ **Price.** Include specific price information if you can. Price can vary by sales channel, by options, or by many other factors, so including specific prices can be difficult, but find some way to communicate the rough price range of your product. Describing the price paid in a few specific instances does nicely. People hate to "turn off" customers, but encouraging people who can't afford your product to contact you (by not letting them know your price range) is not in anyone's interest.

✔ **Where and how to buy.** Tell people who visit your Web site where and how to buy your products and services. You would think that this kind of information was a national security secret from the way it's hidden or absent on all too many Web sites. If you have several sales channels, list each of them, along with a brief description of the advantages of each. Even if you create only a one-page Web site, tell people where — or how to very easily find out where — to buy your product. One option is to set up an interactive area of a Web page that lets people enter their locations and then receive information about nearby sales outlets. But if you're setting up your basic Web site and this feature involves too much work, consider using a toll-free number as a stand-in until you can design and implement an interactive Web capability.

✔ **News.** This area is the most difficult to organize and maintain, so keep it as simple as possible. People search for your Web site when they hear about your company in connection with offline events such as trade shows, product launches, and even that pesky lawsuit that just keeps moving upward toward the Supreme Court. You look clueless if you don't list a few basics: trade show appearances, product launches, press releases, article mentions of your company, and so on. (Oh, you don't do many press releases? Now's the time to start!) Figure 5-2 shows the news section of a well-designed Web site. Construct this section after you've cut your teeth on the others, and then put some real time and energy into getting it right.

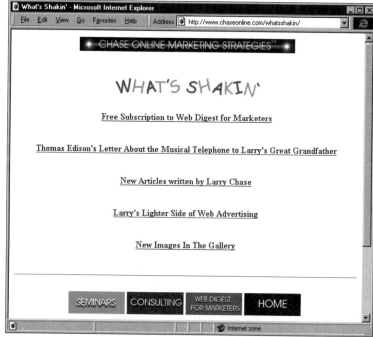

Figure 5-2:
Provide
company,
product,
and
industry
news.

Creating a Look and Feel for Your Site

Most marketing pros are good with words — either in writing, in public speaking, or both — and can create vivid pictures in listeners' minds. However, like many other people, most marketing pros lack graphic design skills.

Graphic design is the art of using visual elements to create a pleasing impression in the viewer's mind, and it's an important element in Web site design — to some of your Web site visitors, the most important element of all.

Graphic design for the Web is a specialized art. Users view a company Web page in different-sized windows, using different-sized screens, with different color capabilities, in all sorts of lighting conditions. Some users have custom settings to override the designer's choice of font, size, and text colors. Large graphics may make a page look strikingly attractive, yet take such a long time to download that they annoy and drive away users.

Unless you have graphic design skills and are willing to learn the details of Web-specific design, you need help in designing the look and feel of your site. Here are a few possible sources of help:

- ✔ **Existing resources.** Your company may already have a "look" based on its logo and printed pieces, such as annual reports. Consider adapting this look for the Web, giving people who are familiar with your company in an offline context a comfortable feeling when they encounter your firm online.

- ✔ **Other well-designed sites.** Stealing the designs of other sites just isn't kosher. Looking at other sites, finding ones you like, and using the same *principles* as they do, however, is fine. (You are also free to avoid the practices of the sites that irritate you!)

- ✔ **Online advice.** Many sources of online advice on all aspects of Web page creation, including graphics, are available. Two good places to start are the World Wide Web Consortium at `w3.org` and the HotWired design advice site at `www.hotwired.com`. Other places include online magazines such as Web Review (`www.webreview.com`).

- ✔ **CD-ROM resources.** CD-ROMs with professionally designed graphics optimized for online use are available. You can pick up a few thousand buttons, backgrounds, icons, and other graphical elements for under $100 in many cases. With a little time and a good CD-ROM art collection, it's amazing what an average schmoe can do.

- ✔ **Printed advice.** Many good books and articles describe how to create and deploy online graphics. Visit online bookstores such as Amazon.com (`www.amazon.com`) and Barnes and Noble (`www.barnesandnoble.com`).

One resource that's always available is outside help. Consider hiring a graphic designer to assist with the look of your Web site. One good way to find a suitable designer is to use the search techniques that we describe in Chapter 2. Graphic designers who advertise on the Web are likely to have designed several sites they can refer you to as examples of their work. An example of one designer's Web presence is shown in Figure 5-3. If you need help finding a designer, one company that specializes in finding suitable professionals is Paladin (`www.paladinstaff.com`).

Hiring a graphic designer is different from hiring a Web design company. A Web design company will construct your entire site for you; a graphic designer will just work on the look. For a basic site, which you want to do quickly and cheaply while learning as much as possible yourself, a graphic designer is preferable. You can get him or her involved early in the game, late, or even after your initial site is up.

Tell the designer who you expect to visit you online, share any existing design that you have, and then let the designer work. Expect to get a couple of alternatives and a quote for updating your site to include the design. (The designer may even offer to update your printed materials as well, improving consistency.)

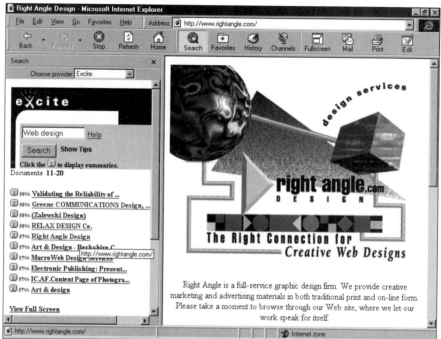

Figure 5-3:
Hire the
best
designer
Excite
can find.

At the end of the job, you should own the designer's work. This arrangement is called *work for hire* and is looked down upon by top professionals doing large jobs, but is a fact of life for smaller jobs and for designers who haven't yet made a name for themselves. Avoid complicated licensing arrangements in which the designer retains some rights to the design.

Creating a Web Page with FrontPage Express

Whether you decide to create your own Web presence, or hire someone to do it, knowing how to create and edit simple Web pages yourself is a good idea. Why? Here are two reasons:

✓ **To demystify the process of Web publishing.** If you know that you can create and edit Web pages yourself, you open up the option of doing your own Web work, and you'll have a better understanding for the amount of work that's really needed if someone else does it for you.

> ✔ **To add information and make changes faster.** In marketing, speed is of the essence, and never more so than on the Web. As soon as you get a business Web site up, you're likely to get many requests for changes, everything from fixing misspellings to adding links to partners' Web sites to posting press releases. If you know enough to do these tasks yourself, you can quickly get them done, instantly updating your Web presence and showing yourself to be a savvy online marketer, indeed.

You can easily create a Web page yourself with any of a number of free Web tools. Two of the best of the free Web tools come with the two leading Web browsers. Microsoft FrontPage Express comes with the Internet Explorer 4.0 Web browser. And Netscape Composer comes with the Netscape Communicator online software suite. (You can try any Netscape Communicator Suite programs for free, but you may be responsible for a licensing fee if you use them on an ongoing basis. Check the Netscape site at www.netscape.com for details.)

Free Web tools are great for beginners and for editing text that the Webmaster can then integrate into your existing Web site. However, for larger sites that need a professional, polished look, you really need to know HTML. Don't be afraid to do some initial work, up to and including building a basic initial Web site, on your own, but be ready to call in the professionals — who use more powerful tools and also work directly in HTML — after that.

In this section we show you how to create a simple Web page by using FrontPage Express, which is a "light" version of the popular Microsoft FrontPage Web page editing program. You can get this program from the Microsoft Internet Explorer 4.0 link on the *Marketing Online For Dummies* CD-ROM (see Appendix A for installation instructions).

Like Netscape Composer, FrontPage Express enables you to create and edit Web pages, including graphics and links to other Web pages, without ever having to see or edit the HTML (HyperText Markup Language) code that underlies Web pages. You can just drag and drop graphics into place and use familiar word-processor-type buttons and menu items to format text and arrange items on the page.

Much of the work of creating any Web page happens outside of the Web page editing program. Many do-it-yourselfers use packages like Corel DRAW and PHOTO-PAINT to add graphics and even some multimedia to their Web sites. Professionals use graphics editing programs, such as Adobe Photoshop, and illustration programs, such as Adobe Illustrator, to create graphical backgrounds and images for your Web page. They also use multimedia programs, such as Macromedia Director, to create animations, video, and sounds to include in the Web site.

You should set aside an hour or so to complete the following steps. Creating Web pages, even simple ones, is often fun, but always time-consuming. The following steps assume that you have access to and are familiar with a couple of different kinds of programs for creating text and graphics. (You can use the Windows Paint and WordPad accessory programs if you have nothing else suitable.) If you get stuck, ask a friend or colleague for help, or skip the step. Otherwise, follow these steps to create a very simple Web page:

1. **Install Microsoft FrontPage Express (part of Internet Explorer 4.0) on your computer using the instructions in Appendix A.**

   You can also use another Web page editor, such as Netscape Composer if you prefer (the details of a few of the steps below will be slightly different, and the screen won't look the same as the screen shots shown for these steps, but the process is fairly similar).

2. **Create a graphic you can use in your Web page.**

   It can be a photograph, a logo, or a background graphic — anything that relates to your business. Save the graphic as a .GIF graphic (if it's computer-generated with relatively few colors), as a .JPEG image (if it's a photograph or other image with hundreds of colors), or as a Windows bitmap (.BMP) file (if you don't have the ability to save a .GIF or a .JPEG from your graphics program).

   Right-click on any Web graphic to save it to your hard disk. (But don't republish it to the world without permission.)

3. **Using a word processor, write some text you can use in your Web page.**

   For instance, you can write a paragraph describing your company history and a paragraph or bulleted list describing your products and services.

   Don't spend too much time on formatting the text; you will probably have to redo the formatting in FrontPage Express.

4. **Also using a word processor, write a brief description of Web sites you use in your work in paragraph or bulleted list form.**

   Just name the site and briefly describe its value.

5. **Start FrontPage Express.**

6. **Copy and paste the text from your word processor into FrontPage Express.**

   Figure 5-4 shows work in progress on a Web page.

7. **Use the text-entry and text-formatting commands in FrontPage to create a first-level header with your business name; a second-level header, About the Company; a paragraph of text describing your company; a second-level header, Our Products and Services (drop one or the other if you don't offer both), and a paragraph or bulleted list describing what you sell.**

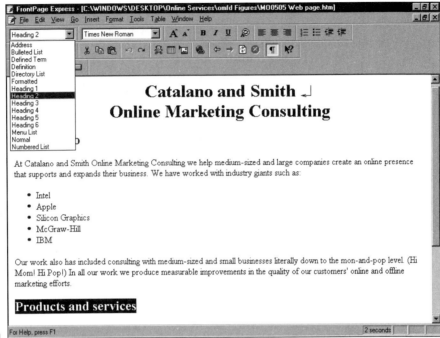

Figure 5-4: FrontPage Express helps rush your page onto the Web.

You can use the following commands:

- **Paragraph format pull-down list.** To assign a header, use the Paragraph format pull-down list, shown in Figure 5-4. Type header text, highlight it, and then pull down the list to select a header level. The text changes to the appropriate header.

- **Paragraph alignment buttons.** The paragraph alignment buttons are Align Left, Center, and Align Right. Highlight the text or graphic that you want to align, and then click the appropriate button. The object realigns.

- **Numbered and bulleted lists.** To make a list of items into a numbered or bulleted list, use the Numbered List and Bulleted List buttons shown in Figure 5-4. Simply highlight the items, and then click on the Numbered List or Bulleted List button once to create a list; click again to undo the list.

- **Bold, italic, and underline.** To add text styles, simply highlight the desired text, and then click on the Bold, Italic, or Underline button. (Use these styles sparingly, or your Web page will look like a hostage ransom note!)

Avoid underlining Web text for emphasis. Underlines are used, along with special colors, to denote Web hypertext links, so using underlines for other purposes may confuse your Websurfers.

8. Add hyperlinks.

In the text that describes Web sites you use, find keywords that describe the site and select them. Then click the Create Hyperlink or the Edit Hyperlink button.

9. In the Create Hyperlink dialog box, type the URL of the Web site to which you want to text to link; then click OK.

The text becomes a hyperlink to the Web URL.

Avoid phrases like, "To see a photo of our building, click here." Using "click here" is a well-known Web no-no, and committing it makes you seem like an amateur (which you may be, but no sense in flaunting it). The best Web designers use hypertext links that fit seamlessly into the flow of text.

However, you also need to avoid putting your links in unclear phrases such as "MyCo just moved to new offices" — the user won't know whether clicking on the link gets them a large, slow-to-download photo of the offices, a brief text description of them, a link to your real estate agent's Web site, or something else. This lack of knowledge may frustrate your Web visitor. Instead, say something like: "Want to know more about our new offices? You can see a photo (50K JPEG image) of the new building or read the press release we sent out about the move."

10. Insert an image in your Web page.

Click on the Insert Image button to bring up the Image dialog box. Click on the Browse button to search your hard disk for the image you want to use. After you select the image you want, click on OK.

The image appears, full-size, in your Web page.

11. Edit the image in your Web page.

Double-click on the image to bring up the Image Properties dialog box, shown in Figure 5-5. Use the Image Properties dialog box to modify the image. You can use these options:

- **Type of image.** You can save graphics in .GIF or .JPEG format. For .GIF files, you can use *transparency,* which erases any single-color border around an image, and *interlacing,* which makes the image appear quickly, but blurry, and then grow sharper as more of the image is downloaded. For .JPEG files, you can lower the quality rating to make the file size smaller at the expense of image quality.

- **Size, spacing, and alignment.** Under the Appearance tab, you can control the alignment of an image and create a border of empty space around it. You can also set the height or width of the image in pixels, or as a percentage of the original image.

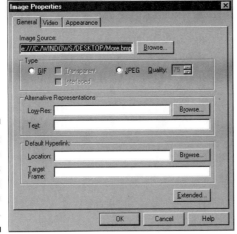

Figure 5-5:
Image
Properties
helps you
change
your image.

12. Continue modifying your Web page until it looks acceptable. Then use the File⇨Save command to save your Web page to your hard disk.

If you want to see what HTML code looks like, choose View⇨HTML. The underlying HTML code for your Web page displays.

You can edit your Web page while viewing the HTML, though the results may be unpredictable and you could possibly make your file unusable.

13. Start your Web browser.

Use the File Open command (File⇨Open or Ctrl+O in either Internet Explorer or Netscape Navigator) to open the file you just created in your Web browser. You can see a fully usable Web page. Try clicking on links to make sure that they actually take you out to the open Web.

The only difference between your local Web page and a true World Wide Web page is that your local Web page isn't available to other Web users until you publish it on a Web server. Even if your machine is connected to the Web, it isn't a Web server unless it's running a program that responds to requests sent via HyperText Transfer Protocol, the http in Web URLs, the communications standard underlying the Web. (HyperText Markup Language, or HTML, is the page layout standard underlying the Web.)

Congratulations! You just created a page that can go on the World Wide Web!

Just creating this Web page is a valuable exercise for learning how Web publishing works and understanding some of its strengths and limitations. If you want to actually publish your page on the World Wide Web, check with your Internet Service Provider to see if they have free disk space for Web pages. You can also use the GeoCities Web site at www.geocities.com to publish noncommercial Web pages for free. When you actually want to use your Web page or Web site for business, GeoCities offers domain name registration and Web site hosting as well. See *Creating Web Pages For Dummies*, 3rd Edition, from IDG Books Worldwide, Inc. for details on how to publish a Web page.

Chapter 6

Marketing on Your Web Site

● ●

In This Chapter

▶ Using your Web site to market products or services

▶ Presenting marketing information on your site

▶ Including business-related news on your site

● ●

*N*ot many people understand yet just how powerful the World Wide Web can be as a marketing vehicle. Because the Web is so new, and still changing, using it effectively is an art that has yet to be perfected. But the same novelty factor that makes the Web difficult to use effectively also means that successful efforts are well-rewarded. You can get a lot of positive attention and feedback if you do a good job of marketing on your Web site.

In this chapter, you roll up your metaphorical sleeves and plunge into the nitty-gritty of the most important ways you can do marketing work on your Web site. If you follow the suggestions in this chapter, you should be able to move quickly to the head of the class in your Web marketing efforts.

Your Web Site as a Marketing Vehicle

Different businesses depend on different ways to get the word out about themselves and their products or services. A consultant may depend on word of mouth and phone calls to business contacts to get new work. For a roadside diner, a billboard on the highway may be the linchpin of marketing. For a used-car dealership, late-night television commercials and newspaper ads may reach the key buyers. Every business has one or more established methods of advertising, and businesses that want to grow are always looking for new techniques to move themselves forward.

The Internet and the Web are going to be the fastest-growing and most important new marketing vehicles for most businesses over the next couple of decades. If you focus now on online marketing, especially marketing over the Web, you'll be well-positioned to benefit from the growth in importance of the online world. If you wait, your competitors will probably benefit from that growth instead of you. Now is the time to decide how to use your Web site as a marketing vehicle in the future.

Coordinating your Web site with your overall marketing plan

Starting your Web marketing effort is easy if you realize that the Web should fit tightly into your more traditional marketing efforts (we refer to traditional, non-online marketing efforts as *offline* marketing in this book). Every advertisement, white paper, mailing, and press release that you create can be used as a resource for your Web site. And every marketing-related event you attend or participate in — each trade show, product launch, or news conference — can be reflected on your Web site as well. Figure 6-1 shows a general idea of the relationship between the offline world and the Web site.

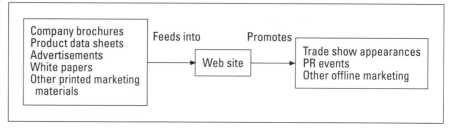

Figure 6-1:
Tie your Web marketing effort into your offline marketing.

The idea behind Figure 6-1 is that your current marketing materials feed into your Web site, and each marketing piece can be adapted for use on your site. Your Web site in turn helps promote other activities, such as trade show appearances and PR (Public Relations) events. After you've been developing and extending your site for a while, arrows pointing in the opposite direction also appear. Marketing events and seminars can be captured and put on your Web site as sound clips, movies, or even just written descriptions. And new content you develop for your Web site can be recast as printed materials to reach people who don't have access to the Web.

Another concern is fitting your Web marketing effort into your company's other online efforts. The way to predict your firm's online future is to realize that nearly every division and department of your company will eventually be reflected online. Marketing goes online first and will be foremost for a long time to come, but customer service and support, sales, hiring, and other company functions will quickly go online as well. Here are some parts of a typical company that may be represented on a Web site:

- **Marketing department.** Marketing should be responsible for the overall Web site and most of its content. Marketing-related concerns and content include the overall look and feel of the Web site, company and contact information, product photographs, descriptions and prices, information about where to buy products, and events the company is involved in.

- **Public relations.** This specialty within the marketing department deserves separate attention. PR should develop an area for press interest — if any group will depend on the Web for its first impression of you, the press will. PR should put press releases on the Web site simultaneously with release over the newswires. PR may also want to put confidential information for long-leadtime press on a password-protected area of your Web site.

- **Sales department.** When your Web site captures visitor interest in your products or services, marketing and sales can work together to help deliver potential customers to the company's various sales channels. (You get a big boost in justifying your online marketing expenditures if you can show that your Web site is generating sales.)

- **Customer service and support.** Post customer service contact info and answers to common questions on the Web site. Online customer service is already very important and growing rapidly; companies reduce expenses by making the customer part of the service and support solution. Use your Web site, automated mailing lists (as we describe in Chapter 9), and other online resources to involve customers in finding solutions to their own problems.

- **Human resources.** Help-wanted ads can be posted on the Web site, with an e-mail address where resumés can be sent. (See Chapter 8 for more information about e-mail contact information.) A good-looking Web site helps your company attract top employees as well as customers. Marketing can help the human resources department get established on the Web site, but updating help-wanted postings is HR's job.

- **Finance.** Finance should put your company's annual report or its equivalent on the Web site, or at least make ordering a copy of your report over the Web easy for interested parties. However, annual reports are required to be honest, and in a bad sales year you may not want to post all the gory details on your Web site.

Out of all these departments, marketing should play the leading role in defining and developing the company World Wide Web site. Other company work may go online as well, but much of this other information appears on *intranets* — employee-only networks that often use Web browsers and servers. An example is employee benefits information that the human resources department puts online for employees only. Intranets aren't a direct concern of marketing, because customers don't access them. (Though one could argue that medium-sized and large companies need to market themselves to their employees as well.)

A more interesting option, from a marketing point of view, is *extranets* — networks that link suppliers and customers. Though extranets may at first be used only for exchanging functional information such as order status, they can grow into marketing tools as well. If your company develops an extranet that includes customers, dealers, or others involved in the sales process, marketing should play a growing role in supplying and maintaining this content.

 Websurfers frequently use bookmarks to return to Web sites and specific pages they like. Encourage your visitors to bookmark your home page and also to bookmark Web pages that have information about specific products and services.

Designing your Web marketing effort

Before you start or expand your Web marketing effort, you should take a few initial steps. These can be formal efforts as part of a design process with storyboards and multiple levels of approvals, or informal checkpoints you keep in mind as you work on your own or with others.

The first step is to decide how you're going to separate company, product line, and product information. Each of your customers, plus suppliers, editors, and even your own employees, sees your company through the lens of those products and services they use the most. This focus doesn't cause any problems for companies with one overwhelmingly important product or a single product line, but if you sell multiple products and services, the result may be a great deal of confusion.

From marketing online to selling online?

Because marketing is partly a sales support activity, you need to be preparing for the day — possibly not too far in the future — when you actually sell products or services over your Web site. By the year 2000, analysts estimate that as much as one percent of the world's commerce will take place online. The percentage will only continue to grow. If you don't get your share of the online-sales pie, someone else will. So start thinking now about how your marketing efforts can be extended into sales efforts in the next few years. And read *Selling Online For Dummies* by Leslie Lundquist (from IDG Books Worldwide, Inc.) if you want to start actively planning and implementing your online selling efforts.

The following are possible ways to handle Web site organization for a company with multiple products and services:

- ✔ **Don't worry about organization.** Simply throw marketing and other information for your products and services on your Web site in a disorganized fashion, with thorough coverage of some and little of others. (This really bad idea actually seems to be the plan followed on too many sites.)

- ✔ **Separate the company and its products.** The home page of your Web site needs to speak for your company and allow for easy access to company-level information. Your company home page should also point to a separate area for products. Websurfers can check out company information, and then *drill down* (link to pages with successively more specific information) to the product they're interested in. This plan is serviceable for a new or newly expanded Web site.

- ✔ **Separate the company's markets.** A more sophisticated approach is to structure your Web site around the different markets your company and its products serve. Because customers think of themselves in terms of their interests, not your products, organizing your Web presence in this way is often the most intuitive for your customers. The Microsoft Web site is a good example of this method in use — it enables access by market, as shown in Figure 6-2. Creating a usable market-segmented Web site is hard to pull off, though, because you must include multiple paths to the same or similar information. Get experienced, professional design help before trying this approach.

- ✔ **Use separate Web sites.** If you have products that have strong constituencies, consider creating separate Web sites for those products. You can still put basic information on the company Web site, but the product site will be the home base for the real diehard users of the product. Creating separate Web sites adds difficulty in design, coordination, and planning, but may considerably increase the effectiveness of your overall Web presence.

One useful way to think of your Web site is as an online trade show or, if you don't do trade shows, a sales call or other customer interaction. Several of the lessons you learn in your person-to-person marketing interactions apply online, as well. For instance, when you meet people in a professional context, you're usually trying to get them to do something: buy a large quantity of your product, write a positive article about your company, or feel good about their relationship with your company to put them in an upbeat frame of mind for a future pitch. Think about how to create these same effects in the minds of people who visit you online. Then identify the marketing materials that you use in various person-to-person situations and place this kind of high-priority information front and center in your Web site.

Link to products

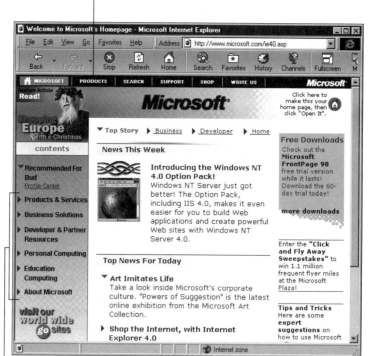

Figure 6-2:
Microsoft
lets you
access its
site by
market (see
the left side
of the
frame) or by
product (the
button
on top).

Links to content serving different markets

After you develop some idea of the overall structure of the marketing parts of your Web site, you're ready to identify some of the resources you can use on it. Follow these general steps:

1. **Make a list of all your marketing resources.**

   List all press releases, data sheets, brochures, ads, annual reports, white papers, and so on that you have available — even old ones. (Old resources may have information and themes you can reuse.)

2. **For each marketing resource on your list, briefly describe what you may need to do to it before putting it on the Web.**

   "Reformat and convert to HTML" is the minimum that you need to do to each document. "Update" is another common notation, because marketing documents need frequent updating — and putting obviously outdated material on your Web site is worse than not putting up any information at all.

3. **Separate your resources into "basic marketing" and "news."**

   Pieces that have a long lifespan, such as product brochures, can be thought of as basic marketing; pieces that have a short lifespan, such as press releases and events, are news. (We describe the difference more clearly in the following section, but take a stab at making the distinction now.)

4. **Give some thought as to what to do first; if your resources are limited, consider putting your company information and in-depth information for one major product online first, and then using the lessons learned to rapidly expand coverage.**

   You're likely to do a better job, and possibly even a faster job overall, by staging your effort than by trying to hit every target at once.

You may want to take this opportunity to review your marketing pieces with one question in mind: What does each piece urge the reader to do? You do have to be subtle and informational with your Web marketing effort; people quickly click away from obvious hype. But each marketing piece needs to impel the reader to take some action they wouldn't have taken otherwise. Hopefully, that action is a step in the direction of buying your product. Double-check your pieces as you ready them for the Web.

Marketing Information on Your Site

In Chapter 5, we describe what to put on a basic business Web site, including descriptive and contact information for your company. Organizing and creating a simple site is easy. As your Web site gets larger and more complicated, information gets harder to organize and update. As your Web site gets more complete, you may spend an increasing amount of your Web-related time thinking about structure and usability, and less about specific pieces of content.

As you expand your Web-based marketing effort, you may also run into some specific concerns about each of the different kinds of information you put online. Based on our experience in both hands-on and consulting roles in this very new medium, we can point out a few of the opportunities and pitfalls to help you be effective right from the start.

Understanding the vital role of press releases

Some people, especially those in the press, look down on press releases. Some online news-gathering services even allow users to filter them out of their daily news updates. What could be worse — or more likely to be misleading and self-serving — than company-written news?

Must Web writing be boring?

Try to avoid being boring, but remember that most writing for the Web does need to be fairly tame. Because of its origins in academia and the military, and because people actively seek Web information themselves rather than passively receiving it, the World Wide Web has a tradition of honesty and directness that makes typical marketing hype seem misplaced. Think of Web writing as describing your company and product to a friend, not as creating an extremely slow-moving television commercial. Adhere closely to the established tone of existing Web writing, at least until you gain enough experience to know when you can bend or break the rules.

Well, a lot of things could be worse. Though a press release that you write is bound to reflect a positive point of view about your products, services, and company, you also have a strong motivation when writing the press release to explain the basic facts that people need to know in as clear, cogent, and understandable a manner as possible. Yes, a bias exists in press release writing, but at least it's a bias the reader expects and can adjust for, unlike some of the more subtle biases and other problems that appear in articles and broadcast stories in the mainstream press.

Many organizations prepare too few press releases. Consider doing a press release for every event of importance, including the following:

- ✔ Field-testing a new product
- ✔ Making a product available for sale
- ✔ Improving a product
- ✔ Launching a service
- ✔ Hosting or participating in an event
- ✔ Entering into a partnership with others
- ✔ Welcoming a new executive

Unit sales, revenue, and other financial milestones are also good press release topics.

Press releases are an underused yet vital tool in marketing in general and especially in marketing on Web sites. The concentrated effort that goes into creating and making sure that all the information is correct in a press release makes it something you can use and reuse online and in the offline world, as well. Follow these rules for using press releases on the Web, and you'll do a better job of getting all your marketing information online:

✔ **When in doubt, do a press release.** An interesting event has happened, and you want to announce it on your Web site. What's the best way? The best and easiest method is to write a press release about the event and send it to newswires as well as posting it on your Web site. That way, you reach far more people.

✔ **Hit the Web instantly.** Press releases should be on your Web site at the same moment that they hit the newswires. People who hear news about your company will immediately check your Web site for information; you look bad if it's not there.

✔ **Make press releases easy to find.** Put a prominent pointer to the new release on your Web site's home page, and then post the press release in an appropriate spot on your Web site. Make sure to send an electronic copy of the press release to people who may want to mention it on their own Web pages or otherwise make it known to others.

✔ **Use Business Wire or PR Wire.** These two popular press release services offer a little-known bonus: any press release that you distribute through them is redistributed to dozens of online databases, from which it is recopied and retransmitted by others, such as the PointCast Industries channel. This is true even for inexpensive regional distribution of your release. So use Business Wire or PR Wire to amplify the offline *and* online audience for your release.

✔ **Link your press releases.** Your press release should include references to key business partners, customers, and others who have a role in the new event, and you can include hyperlinks to their Web sites in the HTML version of your press release. This approach makes you look savvy and is often greatly appreciated by those you link to.

✔ **Do a careful job with the HTML.** Carefully converting a press release to HTML so that it looks good on a Web page takes only a modest amount of time and makes you look organized and professional. See Chapter 6 for information on tools you can use to easily convert a press release, or any word processing document, to HTML for Web publication. Set aside an hour or two to convert and review your press release before the rush to put it on the Web hits.

✔ **Create a text-only version.** You'll want a version of your press release that you can send out by e-mail (see Chapter 8 for instructions); make that version available on your Web site along with the HTML version. Then your Websurfers can e-mail the release to their contacts as well — doing your marketing for you for free.

✔ **Create a .PDF file.** Many people like the look of fully formatted documents. The most popular way to reproduce this look on the Web is with an Adobe Acrobat Portable Document Format (.PDF) document. Figure 6-3 shows a site offering .PDF files, and Figure 6-4 shows an example of a .PDF file in action. Consider creating a .PDF file of your press release and making it available on your Web site.

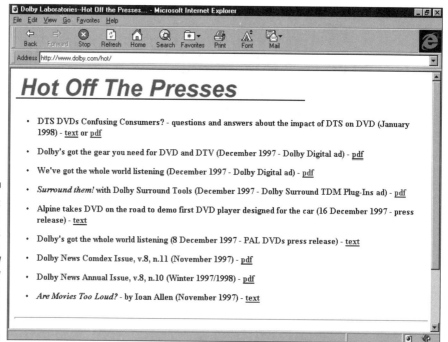

Figure 6-3:
Clicking on
a .PDF link
for the
*Surround
them!*
article calls
up Adobe
Acrobat.

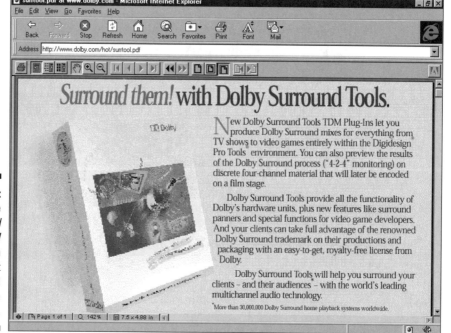

Figure 6-4:
The
*Surround
them!*
article in
.PDF format
displayed
inside the
browser.

✔ **Go beyond the release.** You can include additional information. For example, one easy-to-create and valuable tool is a Frequently Asked Questions document (FAQ), a longstanding tradition for delivering technical information online that has been successfully adapted for online marketing. (FAQs are sometimes called Q&As, for Question and Answer documents, in traditional marketing jargon.) Link to product data sheets, white papers, or any other information you can put online. Or be adventurous and include a sound or video clip from an analyst call or press conference.

✔ **Ask that others' press releases mention you.** After you earn people's gratitude by appropriately including them in your press releases, ask for the same favor in return. When key partners, suppliers, or customers prepare press releases, ask them to acknowledge any role that your company played, and offer to be a source for positive comments on products you like.

Many of the lessons you learn in creating and posting press releases apply to other online efforts as well. Putting information up on your Web site fast; making it easy to find; linking to the Web sites of partners, suppliers, and customers; adding text-only and .PDF versions of files; and asking for mentions and links from others are all vital survival skills for online marketing. If you practice these skills as part of creating and posting press releases, you can go far in the online world.

Putting product information online

Many companies do a fairly good job of marketing their company online, but don't give much detail about the specific products and services that their company sells. Having a robust company presence is great, but the company really only exists to deliver products and services to people — hopefully, most of the time, at a profit. Your Web site isn't finished — well, it's never really *finished*, but it's not even very good — until you provide detailed information about whatever it is that you sell.

Here and elsewhere in the book we use the word *products* to refer to both products and services — partly for our convenience and yours, and partly because you probably need to package your services in product-like fashion to market them effectively over the Web.

Here is some of the information you need to consider providing on your Web site about each product your company sells:

✔ **Product name and functional description.** Don't forget to include a Web page devoted to the product, by name, and a brief functional description of what the product does. If all your previous marketing has been *narrowcast* (sent to a small audience that already understands the topic) via trade-specific publications, industry trade shows, and so on, you may be new to presenting yourself to an audience as diverse as that on the Web. Explain to people, in simple terms, what your product does — even if all the explanation accomplishes is to help them realize that they're not interested.

✔ **Who uses the product.** Describe who uses your product and how. Go into some depth; allow your Websurfers — that is, your well-off, media-savvy, potential customers or influencers — to see themselves or someone they know as part of your customer base. Like the product's functional description, a description of who uses your product also helps your Websurfers know whether they should stick around for more information — or surf on.

✔ **"System requirements."** Most products operate in a specific environment of other products and user activities. You can't run *Doom II* on an original IBM PC XT, and you don't need a copper pot if you don't cook. Communicate, either subtly within other text or in a specific list, what kind of environment your product is used in, what other products need to be present for it to work effectively, and what skills the user needs to have to make it work.

✔ **Market position.** Everyone loves a winner, and if you can identify any customer group in which your product is number one, announce it loudly. "Best-selling veeblefetzer worldwide" is the best market position to have, but "the leading veeblefetzer for the North American forest services industry" is fine, too. The markets in which you're number one are likely to be the most profitable for you anyway, so exploit your leadership position(s) on your Web site.

✔ **Customer information.** List big-name customers (with their permission, of course) or, if the numbers justify the claim, give a blanket customer description like "used by half of the Fortune 500." Let the positive image and success of your customers reflect on you as well. For complicated or expensive products, create success stories that show how a specific customer used your product to solve a problem.

Make sure to get customers' permission before including their names on your site, but don't worry much about being turned down; most customers love the attention. If you exchange links with them to their Web site, everyone gets a boost.

✔ **Awards, accolades, and (positive) reviews.** Let people know that your product is worth considering and is absolutely vital. Provide external validators showing that your product is the best from some independent point of view. Any awards, positive feedback, or positive reviews that you can mention — or, better yet, link to another Web site — go a long way toward helping people choose your product.

Your product doesn't have to finish first in a review in order for that review to be worth mentioning on your Web site. In a so-so review, pull out any positive statement on a substantive aspect of your product and quote it. ("The easiest of the reviewed products to use" is probably worth quoting; "the easiest to remove from its packaging material" probably isn't.) If you do finish first in a review, link to it if it's online, even if it says some bad things about your product. If you finish second or third, consider linking to the review, but surround the link with an explanation of the specific areas in which you're best or information about how you've improved the areas in which the reviewer found fault.

The underlying message in your product description and related information is, "No need to look any further; this veeblefetzer is the one for you." Figure 6-5 shows an effective product description that relies heavily on compelling phrases like "first in" an area of technology and "best-selling."

If visitors to your Web site are looking to buy, be sure your site tells them how. (See the next section for details.) Even if the people reading the information are not looking to buy your type of product today, they may either make a purchase or be called on for a recommendation in the future. A distant recollection that comes out as a recommendation, even a low-key one like, "I heard Acme veeblefetzers are pretty good," can help you clinch a sale. Product information on your Web site can create just this kind of long-lasting positive impression.

The kind of in-depth product information we describe in this chapter may be readily available to you from an existing brochure or print ad, or you may have to develop it from scratch. If you're starting from a blank slate for several products, consider adding one product to your Web site at a time, using the experience and feedback gained from the first to do a better and faster job with the others. And consider how to get the same information into print format so you can deliver it to people who don't see it on the Web.

Don't be afraid to link

Linking strategies are an important part of Web site design. You should link extensively within your Web site, but what about links to other sites — don't they just send Websurfers elsewhere, never to return? Quite possibly, yes, so only link to other sites for a good reason. Web sites you should link to include press or other sites that say good things about your company or product; sites of companies that are part-ners of yours; sites with industry information; or sites with information about products that are used with your own. Not only do these kinds of links help Websurfers find out more about your product in a broad sense, but they also keep Websurfers thinking of your product, as well — increasing the chances that they will return to your site.

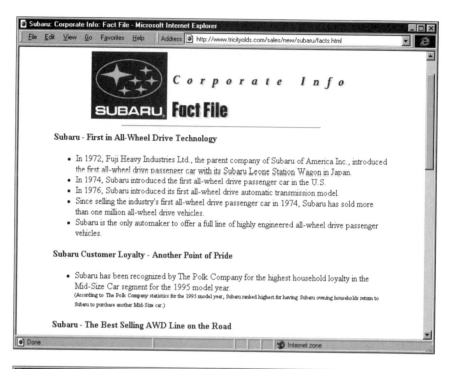

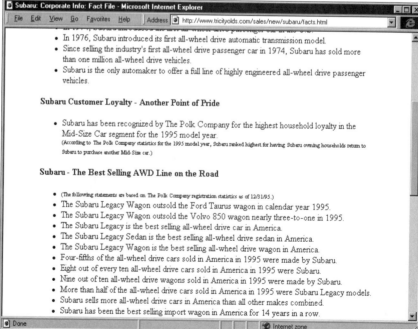

Figure 6-5:
Use attention-grabbing phrases like "first" and "best-selling."

Telling Websurfers where to buy

One of the most important but trickiest issues for marketing on your Web site is telling visitors how to buy your products and services. Because the Web is global, everyone gets the same information at once. However, because of legal restrictions in different places, language barriers, service and support concerns, or for many other reasons, you may not be able to sell the same way — or at all — to everyone who wants to buy.

The first step you can take to prevent problems is to make clear — on your Web site — any restrictions as to who can buy your product and how they can buy. Some limitations will be obvious — if you do interior decoration consulting in Miami, you won't be expected to fly to Moscow to give a quote. But if you sell a product for one price in Green Bay, and a higher price in Germany, you have to think twice before providing pricing and ordering information on your Web site.

Just as an example, consider the issue of price information a bit further. Consider a mythical company that manufactures a high-end stereo system in the Northeastern U.S. and sells it only in the United States and England. This company charges a higher price in England because of shipping costs, lower volumes, and higher margins expected by the English distribution channel. Now if this company puts the U.S. price of its product on the Web, English customers may start trying to get the product for the U.S. price — perhaps by ordering over the phone, perhaps by asking a U.S.-based friend to buy for them and ship it over. English distributors would then become upset by the pointed questions some of their customers would ask them, and the lost business caused by others trying to get around the standard distribution system. This is just one example of the potential problems that can occur when you give pricing information on your Web site. Yet giving customers at least a ballpark idea of your product's price is a necessary part of encouraging them to consider buying it, so what do you do?

To begin solving this problem for your own unique situation, review the kind of pricing information you give in existing marketing and sales materials, and study the ways you've previously handled the problems of pricing differences and availability restrictions. Think about how you can continue to support your current pricing and distribution arrangements — or consider how to change them if needed.

Here are the major options available for giving pricing and distribution information online:

- ✔ **"I know nothing."** One approach is to give no how-to-buy or pricing information on your Web site. This is a sad choice, given the power of the Web to inspire sales, but the best option to use until you've figured out how to avoid threatening existing sales or distribution channels by using one or more of the other approaches described here.

✔ **Give distributor information online.** A classy alternative to omitting how-to-buy information is to simply make your current distributor information available online so as to help your Web visitors reach their local sales outlet for your product. Figure 6-6 shows how one company handles this approach. Giving distributor information online can be tricky; for instance, people based in one country may call another country, shopping for a cheaper price. You may need to consider clever alternatives such as having only information specific to a visitor's country show up in that visitor's browser.

✔ **Give a phone number for distributor information.** You can give a phone number for potential customers to call to find their nearest distributor. (Make sure to hire and train the people in the position before posting the phone number!) This is a nice, low-key way to support your existing sales channels and get the right pricing information to the right customers.

✔ **Give an e-mail address for distributor information.** You can give an e-mail address either in addition to, or instead of, a phone number. With e-mail you have time to think before answering tough questions, and you can re-use the contact information you get from the inquiries.

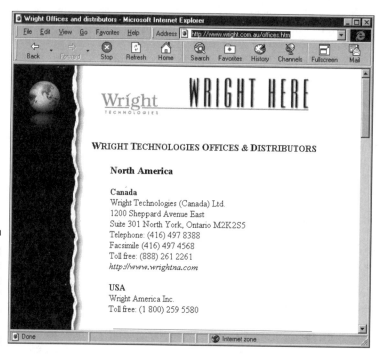

Figure 6-6:
Help Websurfers find your distributors online.

✔ **Give a phone number or fax number for ordering.** "Danger, Will Robinson!" (As the robot used to say in *Lost in Space.*) You can allow people to order directly from you, but don't upset your existing applecart of sales arrangements without a lot of preparation first.

✔ **Support direct online sales.** Online selling is the logical end point of online marketing, but is also a double-edged sword that has the potential to hurt more than it helps by upsetting your existing distribution arrangements. Plan carefully, and see *Selling Online For Dummies* by Leslie Lundquist (IDG Books Worldwide, Inc.) if you plan to take this step anytime soon.

You leave a very bad impression with potential customers if you don't handle phone calls and e-mail messages in a prompt and friendly manner. See Chapter 8 for information on handling volumes of e-mail, and consult other resources for information on how to staff your phone lines.

Don't tick off your distributors

We mention elsewhere in this book that one of the most important rules for marketing online is the first sentence of the Hippocratic Oath: First, do no harm — a crucial principle when you give sales information online. Don't undermine your distributors, direct salespeople, and other sales channels by undercutting them with information about direct phone sales, access to other, cheaper distributors, or secure Web-based sales directly from your site.

But wait, you say: What if the online market is bigger and more profitable than the distribution channels I'm going to undercut? Then stop, take a deep breath, and study the problem carefully. Size the Internet market opportunity coldly and realistically, taking into account the experience of others and actual and potential competition. Remember that only about one percent of world commerce is expected to be online by the end of this century. While the near-term market opportunity for your specific products may be somewhat larger or smaller than that 1 percent, the online market for your products is still likely to be only a small percentage of the total market when you start out. Are you sure that, in going after this small slice, you won't undermine the rest of your sales pie? Review your legal obligations and, just as important, the impression you have left with your distributors, salespeople, and so on as to where they stand with you.

If you plan your move to online-supported or online-based sales carefully, and make it with as little damage as possible to existing sales relationships, you'll be in the best position to come out ahead.

Before you do anything that changes existing sales and distribution relationships, talk to people. Your existing sales channels no doubt know about Web commerce and have some thoughts or even fears about it; ask them what they think and what they would like to see you do. Never surprise your offline sales channels with new developments online; talk to them first, and give them written notice and time to respond before you implement any plans. Even if the only effect of your Web site is to increase overall sales volume, without hurting anybody's interests, people need time to plan and staff for that; if you do take steps that take business away from anyone, or increase sales for one channel but not others, much more time and previous consultation is needed. Moving forward in helping your Web visitors buy is very important, moving carefully is even more important.

News on Your Site

In Wonderland, the Red Queen tells Alice that reality is whatever she says it is. In just the same way, on your Web site, news is whatever you say it is. To be more specific, your Web visitors don't expect "news" in *The Times* of London sense on your Web site; they expect "what's new," in recent events that relate to your company and its products. But the tradition on Web sites is to call this part of the site "news," so you should have a "news" area on your site.

We've heard it said that the most intriguing words in marketing any product are "new" and "free." The Web is already free to use, so you have that base covered. But the word we're concerned with here is "new." We believe that anyone visiting your home page should see some piece of new information right up front, on the first screen of information they access, and that some brand new information should appear there at least once a week. (The Microsoft home page shown in Figure 6-2 earlier in this chapter is one of the many that follow this rule.) Seeing something new makes people stop and click their way into your site, instead of just surfing by, and keeps them coming back regularly.

Figure 6-7 shows an example of news on a Web site. New information appears right on the first screen of the home page and a news section is readily available. Use this approach or suffer from lack of public interest in your Web presence.

So what kind of news should you put on your Web site? Earlier in this chapter we emphasize the vital role of press releases in online marketing, but even we have to admit that not everything that happens relating to your company and products is worth a press release. Here are some of the things that you should put in the news section of your Web site:

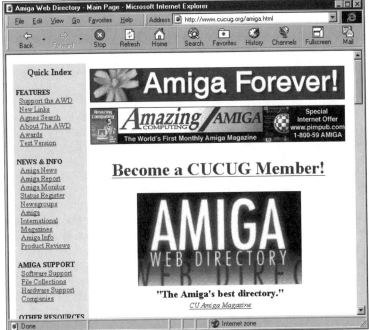

Figure 6-7:
Constantly
give
Websurfers
some-
thing new.

✔ **Product developments.** Have you made any changes in your product —
any at all? Anything "new" or "free" about your product? This is the
place to put minor stuff such as slight revisions in software, new
printings or editions of books, changes to the emission control system
of a riding lawnmower, and so on. Your most devoted customers are
often more interested in this kind of stuff than even your company's
employees.

✔ **Trade shows.** Always let the world know your trade-show schedule well
in advance. A month before the show, give details about what you'll be
doing at the show; a week before, remind people that it's coming right
up. During and after the show, post any news generated on your Web
site.

✔ **Other events.** Any event you participate in — a press conference, a
trade group meeting, a university hiring day — is worth mentioning on
your Web site. (People who see you at these events will check your
Web site to learn more about your company and will be pleased to see
the event mentioned.)

✔ **Sales wins.** Any significant new customers or increases in sales? Give
ammunition to your fans out there — tell them how your business is
growing.

✔ **Distribution changes.** Any new sales channels or new increases in your geographic reach? Other changes in how your products are sold and delivered? Again, even arcane stuff is interesting to somebody. Let people know how your distribution is expanding.

✔ **Executive changes.** Any new hires in the executive suite? Note them in the news section.

This list is hardly exhaustive; many other kinds of events appear in online news listings. Anything that seems significant to you in your work is grist for the mill. Key customers and suppliers may have as big a stake in your company as you do; include them in all the happenings. (But only trumpet the major ones on the first page of your Web site; put the minor ones where your more dedicated Websurfers can find them.)

In each news item, try to include an action item for the reader, and encourage the reader's involvement. Are there changes to a product? Tell people how to get the new one. Is a trade show coming up? Link to the trade show Web site or otherwise tell people how to attend. A big sales win? Remind people how to get your product themselves. You don't have to beat people over the head with your call to action, but do make sure that it's there.

Chapter 7

Getting the Most out of Your Web Site

*I*n Chapters 4 through 6, we show you how to quickly build an affordable and effective Web presence. To reach your goals in online marketing, however, you ultimately have to take your Web site further. As the old navigational charts used to say when showing *Terra Incognita,* or the unknown lands, "Danger! Monsters lurk here!" Wasting time and money is easy to do on wrong-headed Web efforts.

Luckily, you can to build up a winning Web presence that makes your existing customers happy and your prospective customers eager to become existing ones, at reasonable expense and within a relatively short time frame. In this chapter, we highlight how to learn about who visits your site, point out some of the best ways to improve your site for future visitors, and show you how to help people find your Web site.

Gathering Information about Site Visitors

As soon as any new kind of marketing effort gets past the early "gee whiz" stage — imagine the thrill of seeing your company in one of its very first TV ads, for instance — you may start to wonder how to measure the effectiveness of the new medium. The broadcasting industry has the Nielson and Arbitron ratings to help advertisers discover who their ads reach. The Web is developing powerful tools that allow you to know where your visitors go on your Web site, though the numbers gained in this way aren't standardized or comparable across sites the way that broadcasting industry ratings are.

The Web is so important these days that you don't need to go to much effort to justify having at least a low-cost, low-hassle Web presence site for strictly defensive purposes — just a nonembarrassing Web billboard to prevent people from seeing you as road kill on the information superhighway. But as you start to invest more time, energy, and money into your Web site, you need to know something about the kinds of visitors you get.

At the lowest level, the information that's easy to get from your Web server software or Internet Service Provider (ISP) is *hits* — the number of connections made to the Web server to receive HTML files, graphics files, or any other files on your Web site. However, hits are not a good indicator of the number of visitors, because some users surf the Web with graphics turned off for speed; such users generate fewer hits even if they visit the same number of your Web pages. To effectively measure accesses to your Web site, use *page views,* the number of HTML files that have been downloaded. Ask your ISP to provide this information to you, or buy Web server software that can provide it.

Techniques for gathering visitor information

You can use several different techniques for gathering information about your Web site visitors above and beyond hits, each of which may be worth its own chapter in a book on the topic. But just to get you started, here are some methods for learning about your site's visitors:

- **Reading site e-mail.** Just scanning the e-mail that comes into your site gives you some information about who's visiting and what their concerns are. (Of course, you should *answer* the e-mail, too — see Chapter 8 for more information.) Consider printing out a hundred or so e-mails, arranging them by category, writing a brief cover note and summary, and passing the whole stack around to marketing, sales, customer service, and other people in your company who may be interested in what your Web site visitors have to say about the site.

- **Visitor counters.** You can easily install software to count the number of visitors you get to each of your Web pages; your ISP may even offer this service for free or for a small fee. For access to counter software, go to www.yahoo.com/Business_and_Economy/Companies/Computers/Softwware/Internet/World_Wide_Web/Log_Analysis_Tools/Access_Counters. You can use a visible counter if you want others to see how many visitors you've had, or an invisible one if you want to keep the number to yourself. The information that counter software gives you is valuable feedback as to the amount of traffic you're getting on your Web site and what parts of your Web site draw the most attention. You can compare the number of hits and the cost of your site to the cost per thousand impressions that you pay for magazine ads to get a rough idea of whether your Web site pulls its weight.

Any time you see a long URL from the Yahoo! site, you can access the Web page without typing in the URL. Just go to the Yahoo! home page at `www.yahoo.com` and choose the category links that match each folder name in the URL. For instance, to follow your way to the URL in the previous bullet item, choose the `Business and Economy` link, then `Companies`, then `Computers`, and so on through the parts of the URL until you reach the Access Counters page.

✔ **Log analysis.** To get a better idea of who's coming to your site, whether they arrived there from an external link, a search engine, or a book-mark, how long they stay on your site, and the path they take through your site, you need a sophisticated logging capability in your Web server software and both software and human expertise to analyze the data. The results can help you understand what users value most on your Web site and see if navigational problems make navigating your site difficult.

✔ **On-site registration.** One good way to gather information about your Web site visitors is to ask them to register on your site. If you ask them for their registration information, though, you need to give them something in return — an industry survey of some sort, entry in a drawing for prizes, or regular e-mail updates on changes in your Web site. (Different rewards get different kinds of people to register; try to get people who are current or likely customers.) Registration info is useful, but you have to remember that it's biased toward whatever kind of person takes the time to register.

People are rightly becoming concerned about what happens to registra-tion information that they enter on a Web site — they don't want it to be used to make them the target of e-mail spam (as we describe in Chapter 8), junk mail in their mailboxes, or phone solicitations. The GVU study we describe in Chapter 1 reports that many users give false information when registering, perhaps to avoid being the target of solicitors. Reassure your visitors by telling them that you will never rent or sell their information to anyone else. Figure 7-1 shows an example of this kind of reassurance on the Thunder Lizard Productions Web site.

✔ **Surveys.** You can do on-site or e-mail surveys of visitors to your Web site. This is much like registration, but with no ongoing relationship implied, so cash or its equivalent is a good reward. (The GVU survey described in Chapter 1 offered people an entry in a drawing for a cash prize in return for filling out the form.) You can map survey data against log analysis data to get a pretty good idea who's coming to visit your site. If you only want some people to respond to the survey — say, people within a certain geographic area — limit the reward or prize opportunity to people who qualify. Everyone likes cash, so there may be less bias in the results of surveys with cash rewards than with other forms of information gathering.

Figure 7-1:
The
Thunder
Lizard
reassures its
registrants.

Programs that can be used for gathering these types of data include WebTrends Corporation WebTrends and Marketwave HitList, and others exist on the market as well. However, unless you have a large online marketing group at your company already, you may want to consider choosing an Internet Service Provider or consultant who can provide some or all of these information-gathering services for you. Implementing and analyzing these measurement techniques can be technically challenging, and you may need to find someone with lots of online experience, a degree in statistics, or both, who can help you determine who's coming to see you.

Uses for visitor data

At some point in the process of planning and implementing your data-gathering effort, you need to ask yourself what you're going to do with the information you acquire. For example, if your Web site is giving you more impressions per dollar than magazine advertising, and the impressions on the Web are reaching the same kind of people as the magazine, you may want to put more of your advertising and marketing budget into the Web site.

A new kind of opportunity for Web marketing is the ability to actually use the Web to maintain and improve your relationship with a specific customer — this trend is often referred to as *one-to-one* marketing. One way to do this involves using a *cookie,* a data file stored on the site visitor's machine that records the visitor's activities on each visit to your Web site.

With a cookie file, you can access information about customer visits and track their online habits. (Users can turn off cookie capability, but the majority don't do so. You may want to ask users before creating the cookie file the first time.) Going further, you can actually modify the information you present to each of your Web visitors to fit that particular visitor's interests and habits. For example, imagine a home page of a pet store that shows three pictures, each a hyperlink: one of a dog, one of a cat, and one of a rat. Depending on which link the visitor clicks, you can offer information that interests the particular pet owner — clicking on the dog, for example, may bring up an article on dog dental health. In addition, the site can include an ad for dog food alongside the dental health article, and an Internet coupon for a dollar off the next visit to the pet store. In this way, the site can offer useful information that keeps visitors coming to the site, offer visitor-specific marketing information, as well as create visitor profiles that can be analyzed by marketing to better assess who visits. If you're interested in fine-tuning your Web marketing effort in this way, ask your ISP, Web hosting provider, or a consultant to help.

Cookies are only the beginning of the possibilities for building relationships with your customers through your Web site. For an interesting InfoWorld article about advanced software tools for Web interaction with customers, see www.infoworld.com/cgi-bin/displayStory.pl?/features/980112webmarketing.htm

Improving Your Site

Early in the existence of the Web, many people pulled out all the stops, creating large, attractive, highly interactive sites that cost huge amounts of money but did little to advance a company's interests in any measurable way.

This led, naturally enough, to a backlash. Many companies stopped investing in their Web sites altogether, and the Internet is littered with many thousands of these "dead" or barely breathing sites — they're rarely updated, uninteresting, and looking more and more stale with the passage of time.

Now, however, many people are starting to see real results from their Web investments. Companies that sell online report increased business; Web-based marketing and PR efforts are gathering steam and having impact in the offline world as well as simply making companies famous in cyberspace.

As your own Web efforts start to have an impact, you want to consider ways to improve your Web site — partly to meet or beat your competitors' improvements in their online presence, and partly to move toward more Web marketing or an initial effort at Web commerce.

Developing and improving your site into something really interesting and attractive brings in more visitors and results in a more effective online marketing push. Here are some of the techniques you can use to get there:

- ✔ **Improve navigation.** One of the most neglected and most important concerns for your site is improving visitors' ability to navigate it. A clickable graphic with major site areas listed at the top or bottom of each Web page is one starting point. More advanced navigation approaches include a site map, HTML frames with table of contents information, and a search capability for users to find specific things on your site.

- ✔ **Streamline graphics.** The single biggest irritant for many users of the Web is the slow speed with which pages load, mainly because of large graphics files. Reducing the size of the graphics files while maintaining or improving the attractiveness of the Web site is an ongoing challenge. Consider using advanced tools like Adobe Photoshop to help you reduce the size of graphics files, or find a graphic designer with Web experience to help.

- ✔ **Create valuable content.** Creating evolving content that users want to keep coming back for is a long-term win for your Web site. One approach is to maintain and update information for your industry area, which can be as simple as a good page of links to industry-related Web sites, or as complex as an ongoing survey of customer attitudes. (Give away the top-line summaries, but keep the details for yourself!) Providing information for your industry segment sends the message that you're the leader.

- ✔ **Use other Internet services.** Too much online marketing starts and stops with the Web. Use other online services described in this book to create a comprehensive online marketing effort that makes your customers and potential customers feel part of your team. Use the information on e-mail (Chapter 8), automated mailing lists (Chapter 9), newsgroups and online forums (Chapter 10) to enhance and extend the customer relationship you start with your Web site.

✔ **Add multimedia.** When you add multimedia to your Web site, you also open yourself up to tech support questions from users who have trouble running it, and to complaints from users if a multimedia file takes a long time to load. So set modest goals initially and make multimedia additions interesting and appropriate — a brief video clip of your CEO speaking, a 3-D model or virtual reality object photograph of a product to show what it really looks like or how it works. Figure 7-2 shows an example of effective multimedia use on a Web site.

✔ **Make it interactive.** Many Web sites are adding interactivity. One popular technique is to add a guest book that allows people to comment on your site. This can be done with text and *CGI scripts* that run on the Web server and don't risk causing problems on the user's machine (check with your ISP for details and whether they offer this type of service). Many other sites create more ambitious interactive effects such as taking over the whole screen to display information, often through Java programs. You can make using your Web site much more engaging this way, but you also make it more expensive to design, maintain, and support; and many users object to having Web-based programs seemingly "take over" their computer. Define your goals carefully and identify your resources before going too far in this direction.

Figure 7-2:
Multimedia
jazzes
up your
Web site.

✔ **Create a push technology channel.** Push technology keeps your channel subscribers updated with new content from your Web site. It's a great way to build a feeling of community among core users of your products and other fans of your efforts — but remember that the push channel can't just be a commercial, or people won't stay subscribed. Push content that has some value for your subscribers along with your promotional and marketing material. (See *Push Technology For Dummies* by Bud Smith, and *Web Channel Development For Dummies* by Damon Dean — both from IDG Books Worldwide, Inc. — to get started with the nuts and bolts.)

✔ **Add online sales.** The ultimate goal for many Web sites is to make money through direct online sales. If this is an option for you, start planning now for when and how to get there. And see *Selling Online For Dummies* by Leslie Lundquist (IDG Books Worldwide, Inc.) to help you in your planning.

Getting Found with Search Engines

Your Web site doesn't do you any good if people can't find it. The single most important tool you have to make sure people can find your site is to get a domain name that matches your company name as closely as possible, as described in Chapter 4. That way, anyone who knows your company name can easily guess your Web URL and visit your site.

However, you also want people to find your site when they only know a product name, or maybe just the kind of product or company they're looking for. Bringing these potential customers to your site is actually cheap, easy to accomplish, and easy to check up on. Web users who look for certain kinds of sites almost invariably use search engines — over 80 percent of Web users do so, according to the GVU survey we describe in Chapter 1, and search engine sites are among the most visited sites on the Web.

To understand how to use the search engines to your advantage, you need to know that there are basically two kinds of Web search engines. Each kind may borrow tricks from the other, but all search engines rely on one of two basic strategies: *passive* and *active*. Passive search engines require you to register your site with them; active search engines are constantly combing the Web for new sites, and find and list your site without you knowing about it or asking for it! The strategies for successfully registering for each type of search engine are very different, as the following two sections explain.

Marketing with Chat

Chat is one of the most talked-about features of the Internet, so to speak, in part because it's *real-time* — what's typed by one user is almost instantly seen and can be replied to by others taking part in the chat. As a result, text-based chat is used by a number of companies to enhance their Web sites.

Chat's marketing role can be as part of a special event — a kind of virtual news conference to introduce a product or company development. Or it can be used for ongoing customer service and support — for example, interactive question-and-answer sessions with support technicians. Think of it as a conference call with fingers instead of voices.

Chat is well-suited to fast interactions like technical support calls, but it does have its limitations when used for marketing. If you get more than 20 or so people involved without a firm moderator acting as talk-show host, it becomes difficult to follow who's saying what, and the incoherence level approaches infinity. If you have fewer than five people taking part, you may see long gaps while people think of something to type. As a result, Internet mailing lists are a better option if what's being discussed doesn't demand immediate back-and-forth.

You may find yourself doing online marketing for one of your products in a chat session set up by others. For example, one of us (Bud Smith) was a guest in a chat session to answer questions about and promote one of his books. While seeing the upcoming session publicized was gratifying, the actual chat time wasn't too productive. Only about 10 people participated, and the questions sent weren't overly insightful; after about ten minutes of activity, long stretches of nothingness followed. While many scheduled chats are successful, others aren't.

If you want to control your own online chat sessions, you need to set up chat software. Setting up chat on a Web site requires that your customers have a chat "helper application" or plug-in for their Web browsers, and/or for you to run a chat server program on your Web server. Chat server software ranges in price from a few hundred dollars to thousands of dollars, depending on the number of simultaneous participants it handles and how advanced the controls are for keeping everyone in line. Some chat servers include EmeraldNet ChatBox and its sample version, ChatBox Lite (www.emerald.net), WebMaster ConferenceRoom (www.webmaster.com), and IChat Rooms (www.ichat.com). For a newer approach, Java-based chat, visit Parachat (www.parachat.com). These sites also have examples of working chat features.

Another approach to chat doesn't use the World Wide Web at all. Internet Relay Chat (IRC) is yet another type of Internet service that breaks real-time discussions into *channels,* and you take part in discussions with special chat software. Two resources to find out more about IRC, how to set up an IRC channel, and where to find IRC software are the IRC Help site at www.irchelp.org and the Usenet Hypertext FAQ archive at www.faqs.org/faqs/ — do a search for the FAQ "IRC Undernet Frequently Asked Questions."

Consider spending some time in online chats to get a feel for them and judge whether they may be useful for your online marketing work. In addition to the resources listed here, you can find chats about specific topics by searching through the subject hierarchy in Yahoo!, or try Yahoo!'s own Java-based chat rooms, at www.yahoo.com; see Chapter 2 for more information about using Yahoo!

You can also participate in the chat rooms and conferences on America Online and CompuServe. Though participation is limited to subscribers, the online services are a great place to get a feel for chat without a lot of advance work.

You may come across a variety of free and fee-driven tools and services that offer to register your Web site with many different search engines at once. We suggest that you *not* use these services and instead take the time to register your site — and improve it for easier finding — yourself. You're much more likely to end up in the right categories on the major search engines if you take the time to prepare for each one individually.

Registering for Yahoo!

The category of passive search engines — search engines for which you have to register your site to get it listed — is now completely dominated by the granddaddy of all the big search sites, the early leader in Web searching, and now the most popular single site on the Internet: Yahoo! at www.yahoo.com.

Yahoo! first asks you to register your site with them and suggest an appropriate category for your site within the Yahoo! hierarchy. A Yahoo! employee, called a *Yahoo! Surfer,* then reviews your registration form and your site and assigns your site to a main category. He or she — the only thing you can be certain of is that this person probably has more fun at work than you do — also cross-references the site to other, related categories.

Register for Yahoo! early. Yahoo! gets *thousands* of site listing suggestions a day, and getting to yours may take some time. Remember, however, to have at least your basic content up and running before submitting, or the Yahoo! Surfer who checks your site won't find it and therefore won't list it.

The better job you do of deciding on the correct initial category for your site, the easier time the Yahoo! Surfer has categorizing it. Your effort puts the Yahoo! Surfer in a good mood and gives you a better chance that this happy person cross-indexes your site thoughtfully and carefully to the appropriate (hopefully large) number of additional categories. Follow these steps to register with Yahoo!:

1. **Search for your Web site on Yahoo! at** www.yahoo.com **to see if you've already been Yahoo!'d. (See Chapter 2 if you need hints on searching.)**

   Your site may already have been added. If so, check the listing to see if it's categorized properly and whether the listing is up to date and complete. If you need to make changes to your listing, fill out a Yahoo! change form at www.yahoo.com/docs/info/include.html.

   To see Yahoo!'s description of how to register your site, start at add.yahoo.com.

2. Decide on the right Yahoo! category and subcategory for your site.

Surf around Yahoo! to find the right category for your Web site. Use the Search capability for terms associated with your business and see what kind of hits come up. Look for companies and products that compete with yours and see where they're listed to get a good idea of what would be appropriate for your own company.

The most commonly used high-level category for a company site is likely to be in the Business and Economy:Companies category. Your site may be cross-referenced in other areas of Yahoo!, but the main listing will go under Business and Economy:Companies. If you operate only in a specific region — in a U.S. state or a non-U.S. country — your listing should go in the Regional category. Write down the full name of any categories and subcategories that seem appropriate for a cross-reference listing.

3. Surf to the category you want to be in.

Go deep into the category listings. For instance, if you sell several kinds of jewelry, but 80 percent of your business is wedding rings, surf down into the Wedding Rings subcategory.

4. From within the correct category, click the Add URL button, as shown in Figure 7-3.

The first Web page for the Suggest a Site process appears.

5. Click on the Proceed to Step One button.

The Suggest a Site: Step 1 of 4 Web page appears. Part of the Web page is shown in Figure 7-4.

6. Enter the Title, URL, and Description of your Web site in the appropriate fields.

- Enter your business name as the Title field.

- Carefully enter the URL (Web address) of your home page and a description of up to 25 words.

Yahoo! may take several weeks to process requests to add a site or change information about a site. Do a careful job of entering your information so that it will be right the first time and you won't have to enter a change request and wait for it to go through.

Take some time to create a useful description, and keep it under the 25 word limit — if your entry goes over 25 words, Yahoo! may edit it with results you may not like. Include key descriptors and phrases in the Description field. For example, in the figure we use the phrase "online marketing and real-world marketing," rather than tying it together as "online and real-world marketing." Why? Because if someone searches for the phrase "online marketing," in quotes, you want to make sure your site shows up high on the list of hits.

The Add URL button

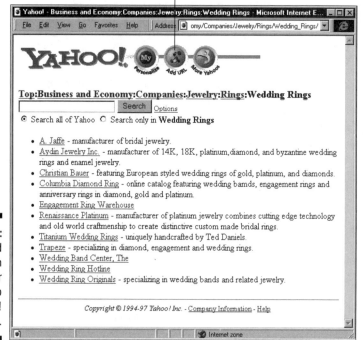

Figure 7-3:
Use the Add
URL button
to add your
Web site to
the Yahoo!
listings.

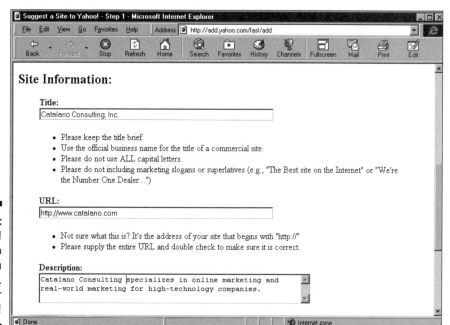

Figure 7-4:
Yahoo!
wants to
know just a
few things.
Answer
carefully!

7. **Click the Proceed to Step Two button.**

   The Suggest a Site: Step 2 of 4 Web page appears.

8. **Enter additional categories in which you think your site should be cross-referenced — here's where you use those full category names you wrote down in Step 2. You may also want to enter any new categories you think are needed for your site.**

9. **Click the Proceed to Step Three button.**

   The Suggest a Site: Step 3 of 4 Web page appears.

10. **Enter a contact person's name, e-mail address, and company information in the appropriate text boxes. When you're done, click on the Proceed to Step Four button.**

    The Suggest a Site: Step 4 of 4 Web page appears.

11. **Provide any applicable information about starting and ending dates for your site and any final comments in the appropriate text boxes, and then click the Submit button.**

    A Yahoo! Surfer checks out your site and compares it to what you suggested in your submission, then categorizes it appropriately.

Congratulations! Your site will soon be listed on the most important search directory on the Web.

Wait for your site listing to appear on Yahoo!, then check that your site listing is accurate and positioned where you want it. Try searching for it using different terms related to your business. Make sure your site comes up at least as often as the sites of competing businesses. If it doesn't, or if at any time in the future you need to update to your Yahoo! listing, use the Yahoo! change form at www.yahoo.com/docs/info/include.html. The Yahoo! change form enables you to make changes to the Description field and a variety of other aspects of your listing, as well as suggest a new category for your site.

Getting found by active search engines

Most search engines on the Web, and for other Internet services as well, are *active* search engines. Active search engines use programs called *Web spiders* or *infobots*. These programs open a Web page, read the contents, index them according to various criteria, store the results in a database, then go on to the next Web page. The result is an indexed database of millions of Web pages.

When you query an active search engine to do a search, the engine doesn't go out and start searching the Web — that would be way too slow. Instead, the engine accesses its database and provides you with the indexed sites that match your query.

If the information in the search engine database has become outdated since the last time the Web spider checked a site, you may get a different-than-expected Web page or an error message when you go to that Web site. Given the sheer size of the Web and other online resources, the database can easily get behind — one popular Web search engine says it needs two to four weeks to index a new site. However, the information that the search engine provides is accurate most of the time, and the search engines are very useful.

Most active search engines enable you to register your site with them by simply entering your URL and e-mail address. The staff of the search site then points its spider your way so that it indexes your site sooner than if you were to wait for it to find you at random. The good news is that you don't *have* to register — the spider finds your site eventually.

Either way, with most active search engines, the Web spider finds the keywords for your site and creates that entry in the search engine database. This is in contrast to how, with Yahoo!, you decide the appropriate description for your site. And Web spiders, like real spiders, don't have much in the way of brains — they simply go out on the Web and index all the words in every Web page they find without knowing which words on a given Web page are the important ones. Some engines simply treat the first words they encounter as the most important; others use different weighting criteria. Your job: to make those first words count so that your site appears high on the "hits list" when a search engine user enters keywords appropriate to your Web page.

The following steps suggest that you make some small changes to the HTML tags in your Web page. You can do this work yourself, if you know HTML or are willing to get your hands dirty (the changes are really pretty simple, and you can use a simple text editor like Windows Notepad or Macintosh SimpleText to make them), or you can find a colleague or consultant who knows how to use HTML to make the changes for you. For an introduction to common HTML commands, see *Creating Web Pages For Dummies* by Bud Smith or *HTML 4 For Dummies,* by Ed Tittel and Stephen James, both from IDG Books Worldwide, Inc.

Here's how to make it easier for Web search engines to bring the right kinds of users to your Web page.

   1. Modify your home page's summary for "findability."

   Every Web page can have a summary that is not displayed to the Web page viewer, but allows search engines and other Web tools to find appropriate Web pages. This summary should mention your company name, area of business, product names, and any keywords by which you would like to be found.

2. Add `<META>` **tags to your home page for "findability."**

The `<META>` tag is an HTML command that allows search engines to more easily find your site. Add the following `<META>` tags between the `<HEAD>` and `</HEAD>` tags of your Web pages, with your own information inside the quotation marks in the `content=` areas:

```
<META name="description" content="Dummies Consulting
does marketing consulting for high-technology
companies.">

<META name="keywords" content="online marketing,
online, marketing, high technology, Web, Internet,
dummies, geniuses, veeblefetzer">
```

Most of the HTML editing software available includes features for adding `<META>` tags. See the documentation for your Web page editing tool to learn how to add HTML tags directly.

A Web page, shown in Source mode with a summary and `<META>` tags useful for searchability, is shown in Figure 7-5. You can view the source HTML document in Netscape Navigator by choosing View⇨Document Source. You can do the same in Internet Explorer by choosing View⇨Source.

Some companies have gone to extremes in their META tag content and have used rival company and product names as keywords. The idea is that someone searching for a specific product will be directed by a search engine to the Web site for the competing product instead. This is not only bad business, but it may incur legal liability as well; at least two lawsuits have been filed over this issue.

Always include one odd, new word in the META tag for keywords so you can test whether each search engine has added your updated Web page yet. In this example we use the word "veeblefetzer."

3. Upload your modified page to your Web server so that it is available on the Web.

4. Go to the major search engines and tell them whatever they need to know to list or reexamine your Web site. Here are the URLs for submitting your site with some of the most important search engines:

Alta Vista: `altavista.digital.com/av/content/addurl.htm`

Excite: `www.excite.com/Info/add_url.html`

HotBot: `www.hotbot.com/addurl.html`

Infoseek. `www.infoseek.com/AddUrl`

Lycos: `www.lycos.com/addasite.html`

Many, many additional search engines, some of which are less-used or outdated: `www.the-vault.com/easy-submit`.

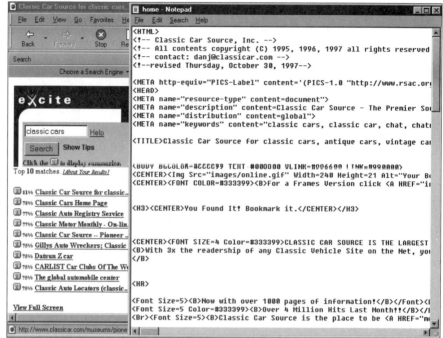

Figure 7-5:
A search
for "classic
cars" finds
a Web
page with
"classic
cars" all
over it.

As you add your URL, check the search site for information on how long the search engine takes to index new sites. Expect not to see your site listed for at least one, and up to four weeks.

5. **Use your test keyword to test each search engine weekly and see if your site has been added yet.**

   As soon as your page shows up, test that search engine with several different kinds of search terms that customers are likely to use to find Web pages like yours. See if your Web page shows up in the listings. If it's among the top 10 hits for crucial keywords that relate to your business, good job! If not, modify your ⟨META⟩ tags, adding the needed keywords, and try again.

   If your Web page doesn't show up near the top, use the View Source command in your Web browser to inspect the Web pages that do show up first. Take a look at the ⟨META⟩ tags in those pages and see what keywords to use to make your own site rise to the top.

6. **When you're happy with the performance of the search engines on your Web pages, ask some colleagues and customers to try searching for businesses and products like yours — and tell you the results.**

This whole process is a lot of work, but it's some of the most important work you need to do for your online marketing presence. Your Web site is most likely the cornerstone of your entire online presence, and it's vital that people who are interested in companies and products like yours be able to find your site.

If you really want to make yourself accessible, consider listing the specific Web pages for each of your key products and services with Yahoo! and the various active search engines. That way people go straight to the exact Web page they need to get the product or service they want — from you, not from someone else.

Many people test out a new Web site by uploading it to their Web server and making it available on the Web and simply not telling more than a few people where it is. This kind of testing allows you to see how features like CGI scripts (if your Webmaster uses them) work under "live" conditions and allows you to test how long your Web pages take to download across the Internet. This works well, but only for a few days, because if there are any links to the page, active search engines find it. (Yes, people have stumbled across valuable secrets by following links from active search engines.) To protect your test site or secret site, don't link to it, take it down after a couple of days, password-protect it, or move it frequently to different Web page addresses.

Publicizing Your Site

One of the most talked-about topics in Web publishing is publicizing your Web site. There's a difference, though, between publicizing your Web site to people who are looking for it and putting the word out to vast masses of Web servers through banner ads, aggressive linking campaigns, and spam. You *do* want to get the word out to your customers and potential customers, which means that you want to include your URL on business cards and press releases and also make your site easy to find via the various search engines, as we describe earlier in this chapter. However, you *don't* necessarily want to spend a lot of time and money — having your Web banner ad displayed on a popular site can cost thousands of dollars — trying to get random Websurfers to stop by your site. Here are some of the common myths of why you should widely publicize your Web site:

> ✔ **To get more visitors.** Getting more visitors to your Web site sounds okay, but it doesn't do you much good if the people who visit aren't potential customers for your products. Getting randomly selected people to — in most cases, briefly — browse your Web site probably doesn't do them or you much good.

✔ **To show people you're online.** This was a good reason two years ago when being online meant you were technically savvy. However, these days it's news if a company is *not* online, and the online public is not likely to be impressed by the simple fact that you have a Web site.

✔ **To let people know your URL.** How much work does it take to remember the CNET, Netscape, or Yahoo! URL? None at all. If you know the company name, you know the URL. If your company has an easy-to-guess URL, you don't need to help people remember it; if not, turn back to Chapter 4 and go get one.

Developing an effective publicity strategy

Okay, so you should never publicize your Web site, right? No, that would be going too far. Here are the steps to take in deciding how to appropriately publicize your Web site:

1. **Determine what you want from your Web visitors.**

   Web sites are hard to perfect because they must meet the needs of several different groups, including customers, potential customers, press, financial analysts, and even employees. What do you want people in each group to take away from their visit to your Web site? Put the answer in the form, "With my Web site, I want to increase their likelihood to . . ." and include one primary goal for each group. Then analyze your Web site to make sure it accomplishes your stated goal for people from each group.

2. **Develop a Web site you're proud of.**

   Sure, you can start out with a bare-bones, cover-your-assets Web presence for people to find when needed, but that's different than trying to actively bring people to it. Until you've made your Web site really worthwhile, don't make extra efforts to bring it to people's attention.

3. **Figure out where the ducks are.**

   If you're a duck hunter, you don't go to Paris for the start of the duck hunting season — you go to a cold, dark, predawn duck blind on some half-frozen lake somewhere. Same with Web publicity: Don't put a banner ad on CNET for tens of thousands of dollars and attract random Websurfers. Instead, figure out where your potential customers are, and publicize your site there. For instance, if you are selling baked hams online, try to exchange links with food-oriented sites. And consider paying one or more search engine companies a fee to put up a banner ad for you each time someone searches for the word "ham."

4. Do initial publicity to some ducks.

Decide on some initial efforts to draw people from among your targeted groups — your potential customers, trade press from within your trade, and any other group you really want to visit your site. These efforts can include a print mailing, an e-mailing, a targeted press release, or other means.

5. Measure the results.

Carefully compare who visits your site before you make a publicity effort and then again after the blitz using the techniques we describe in the "Gathering Information about Site Visitors" section earlier in this chapter. You can get a quick read on who's seeing your publicity by asking Websurfers in your company if they've seen it. But also do a more detailed analysis of the number of visits you get and whether your desired results — visits by people from certain kinds of companies, viewings of specific Web pages, registrations for information, downloads of specific files — are being achieved.

If you follow this process, you'll do the right kind of publicity and get good results that you can not only be proud of, but that you can cost-justify thoroughly as well.

In the radio industry, the conventional wisdom is to not advertise a new format for a radio station — for example, a change from news to talk, or from rock to rap — until a few weeks after the change. The reason is that radio listeners may sample a changed station once, then not come back unless they really like what they hear — and just after a change, there may still be glitches in the on-air experience for on-air talent and production staff, and therefore for the listeners. In keeping with this guideline, many radio stations make sure they're firing on all cylinders before publicizing their new format. Consider following a similar strategy in publicizing your Web site.

Expanding your publicity efforts

When you've developed a Web site that you're proud of — that is, one that has at least basic company, products, and services information, tells visitors how to buy whatever it is you sell, is easily found by anyone using a major search engine, and is one of the better sites, or even the best site, among your direct competitors — then it's time to milk your Web site for all it's worth. That means doing some real publicity work, both in the offline world and online.

Two factors influence the amount of benefit you get from visits to your Web site. These factors can be expressed as two questions: How impressive is your Web site? And what sales impact do you get out of visits to it?

The more impressive your Web site and the more sales impact you get out of Web site visits, the more publicity you want to do. Figure 7-6 expresses this idea roughly in a conceptual graphic form.

The idea here is that the more impact your Web site has on sales, and the more impressive your site is, the "hotter" it is, and the more deserving of publicity. A really hot site — one that is a first-class, award-winning site, and that drives a significant portion of sales for one or more of your products and services — should get a substantial part of your total company publicity effort. For sites that do somewhat less, publicize somewhat less. Here's how we see the publicity effort:

✔ **Cold:** Your site neither stands out on the Web nor has much impact on sales. (The vast majority of company Web sites live here, and actually, that's okay.) Make your site findable, as described earlier in this chapter. Add your Web site URL to business cards and company stationery to give an impression of being technically up to date and to remind your regular customers to visit you online. Make sure your Web URL is in all e-mail .SIG files, as we describe in Chapter 8.

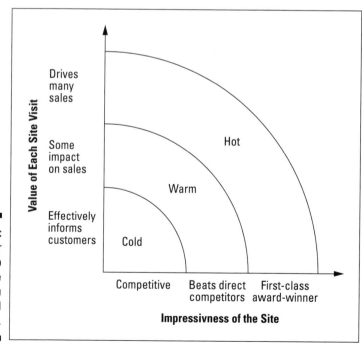

Figure 7-6: The hotter your Web site, the more you should publicize it.

- **Warm:** Your site beats competitors and noticeably increases sales. Push to get the URL on printed company materials and include it in any broadcast ads you do. Do cute things like matchbooks, *tchotchkes* (freebie giveaway trinkets), and so on with your Web URL and a catchy slogan. Start doing press releases when you make major changes to the site or reach visitor or sales milestones related to it.

- **Hot:** Your site is first-class or wins awards and drives many sales. Pay for carefully targeted Web ad banners to pull in traffic; issue regular press releases about awards, sales, and additions; advertise the site directly in the offline world; start developing online sales capability.

You can fine-tune your efforts based on the strengths and weaknesses of your site's impact. For instance, if your site isn't all that impressive, but still drives many sales, put all your effort into targeted publicity among likely buyers, but don't waste money trumpeting your site outside those groups. Or if your site is award-winning, but has little direct impact on sales, advertise it in a low-key way to broad audiences; it's a real plus to your company's image, but not a real plus to revenues.

The important thing for most people to understand is that the vast majority of Web sites live in the "cold" zone and don't merit an active, costly publicity effort. Promotional costs related to this kind of competitive but low-key Web effort should be incidental. Only when you invest more in your Web site and see results from that investment do you need to up the publicity effort

Part III

Marketing with Other Internet Services

The 5th Wave   By Rich Tennant

"Yes, I think we should advertise with America Online. Besides, there is no Vladivostok Online."

In this part . . .

The online world is more than just the Web. The other available Internet services can be cheaper, easier, and more effective in getting out certain kinds of marketing messages, reaching some very desirable groups within the online world, and building a sense of community online. In this part we also give you a glimpse of the future of the Internet.

Chapter 8

Marketing with E-Mail and Listservs

In This Chapter
▶ Using e-mail marketing etiquette
▶ Developing your own e-mail style
▶ Handling high volumes of e-mail
▶ Using mailing lists
▶ Weighing the pros and cons of spam

*A*lthough the most important single element in your online marketing strategy is your World Wide Web site, effective marketing requires going well beyond pretty HTML pages. The Internet offers a wide variety of other marketing vehicles that rely on the decades-old guts of the Internet — plain, unadulterated text.

This Wonderful World of Text includes electronic mail (e-mail), automated mailing lists (commonly called *listservs* after the most popular product, LISTSERV, used to manage them), and public discussion groups known as newsgroups. A convenient way to think of these three text-based Internet services is as a continuum, as shown in Figure 8-1, that starts with one-to-one communication (e-mail), moves to one-to-many information (automated mailing lists, or listservs, described in Chapter 9), and ends with many-to-many discussions (newsgroups), described in Chapter 10. Online services, described in Chapter 11, support e-mail and their own newsgroup-like online forums.

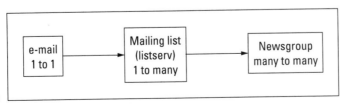

Figure 8-1:
From one
to many.

e-mail
1 to 1

Mailing list
(listserv)
1 to many

Newsgroup
many to many

E-Mail: The Common Denominator

If Helen of Troy had the face that launched a thousand ships, e-mail had the body — body text, that is — that launched a thousand Internet domains. To say that e-mail is *why* the Internet came into being in the first place is not a stretch: ARPANET, the precursor of the Internet as we know it today, was envisioned as a system that would ensure that critical research and military installations could stay in touch with each other, even if parts of the network were destroyed. And the predominant way to stay in touch was with boring, text-based e-mail.

Using e-mail is very straightforward. Basically, you launch your e-mail client software (such as Qualcomm Eudora Pro, Claris Emailer, or the mail components of Microsoft Internet Explorer, Netscape Communicator, or America Online), enter the address of an e-mail recipient, compose your message, and send it off. For more detail on how e-mail works, pick up *E-Mail For Dummies,* 2nd Edition, by John R. Levine, Carol Baroudi, Margaret Levine Young, and Arnold Reinhold from IDG Books Worldwide, Inc.

Ever wonder why the e-mail that someone promised would reach you in seconds may take minutes or hours to reach you? The delay is not necessarily because the sender is slacking off. More likely, the delay resides in Internet mail servers and the route the message has to take. If a mail server at either end is overloaded or shut down for some reason, or if a major Internet backbone is backed up, messages don't move as fast as they theoretically could. So if that promised order or response to a marketing pitch doesn't show up when you expect it, don't blame the sender — it could be that the message is "in the mail."

Although e-mail has been around for a long time (both of the authors have been using it since the mid-1980s), it wasn't very effective for marketing until the early 1990s. Up until that point, many online services with e-mail — such as BIX, Delphi, MCI Mail, Prodigy, and CompuServe — did not directly connect to the Internet or allow a seamless exchange of messages among themselves.

In the early 1990s, *Internet gateways* (methods to translate proprietary online service e-mail address and message formats into Internet-friendly form) finally enabled users of different online services to send text-only e-mail to each other — joining the many who already had Internet e-mail access through an Internet Service Provider, university, company, or other source. With the barrier to text exchange among online services finally eliminated, e-mail has become a critical marketing tool for three reasons:

✔ **E-mail is ubiquitous.** Every online or Internet account subscription includes electronic mail capabilities, whether the subscriber has signed up with an Internet Service Provider (ISP), has Web access through work, or uses a commercial online service, such as America Online (AOL), CompuServe, or the Microsoft Network (MSN). Tens of millions of people have e-mail — many more people than the subscriber base of any single online service or the user base of the World Wide Web. If someone is online, he or she has e-mail. E-mail is the lowest common denominator — it ties everyone on the Internet together with its common, reliable method of transmitting simple text information.

✔ **E-mail is cheap.** As pay-by-the-hour online subscriptions have been replaced by flat-rate, all-you-can-eat digital buffets, composing and delivering an e-mail message costs nothing more than your time. You have no printing or postage cost. On the receiving end, no special equipment is required to read an e-mail message other than e-mail client software — and that software is included in all the online services and in the leading Web browser packages, Netscape Communicator and Microsoft Internet Explorer, the latter of which is shown in Figure 8-2.

✔ **E-mail is easy.** Jotting an e-mail message requires no more skill than that required to type a brief note and click on a Send button. Reading an e-mail message is likewise simple, requiring only an installed base of computer users with literacy skills.

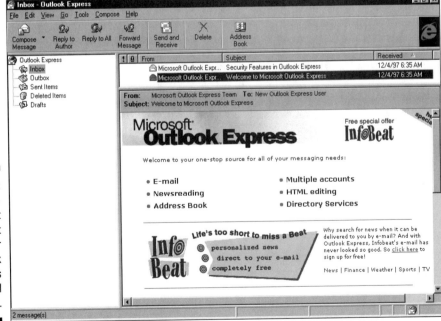

Figure 8-2:
The
Microsoft
Internet
Explorer
Outlook
Express
e-mail
client.

As a result, e-mail — whether as an individual message or as part of an automated mailing list — is the universal "killer app" to reach anyone online.

Basic E-Mail Netiquette

E-mail is a one-to-one medium, meaning that e-mail is inherently personal. In fact, because it arrives directly at a person's computer in their office or home, it seems more personal than printed direct mail. Just as offline marketing vehicles such as direct mail include certain do's and don'ts (do include a call to action; don't deliver it postage due), certain basic rules of Internet etiquette, or *netiquette*, apply to e-mail. (As the term suggests, *netiquette* is a set of unwritten rules for polite and courteous behavior that have become embedded into Internet tradition.)

Flame on!

Flames are, in their own way, an art form. Many denizens of the Internet have spent years perfecting the craft of using text to slam someone up against the wall.

Flames are overtly hostile and in-your-face messages that are commonly sent to those who obviously and repeatedly break rules of netiquette (after what is usually a polite first reminder). Such broken rules include TYPING IN ALL CAPS, posting a message that has nothing to do with the topic of an automated mailing list or newsgroup, or sending the ultimate flame-bait: *spam*, messages that are blatant, and unsolicited, advertisements. (One of our favorite flames is the carefully crafted and lengthy religious tract that a client of one of the authors received after said client made the mistake of sending a spam to every attendee at a trade show. The e-mailed response made an indirect, yet valid point — the client was as interested in reading about someone else's religious beliefs as the initial recipient was interested in reading the client's

unsolicited ad.) Flames also grow out of initially low-key online exchanges.

If you're ever on the receiving end of a flame, the best response is usually none at all. Unless, of course, you enjoy the Internet equivalent of a firefight, the *flame war*. We don't, under any circumstances, recommend you cultivate a taste for getting into such a battle. While it may entertain bystanders, flames almost always reflect badly on you and your company's reputation — no matter how right you may be. If you respond to a flame, be level-headed and offer to deal with any complaint the instigator may have. Ironically, flame wars frequently begin over a simple misunderstanding as opposed to any great disagreement, thanks to text's inability to display nuances that are present in vocal inflection or facial expressions. Many online discussions turn partly or totally into flame wars until the participants either walk away — or their cinders are swept away.

Just because you use the Internet for marketing doesn't mean that you can ignore or sidestep appropriate netiquette — if you do, you run the risk of running headlong into another quaint Internet tradition, the *flame*. Flames are very direct e-mail responses to offensive messages, responses bearing all the subtlety of someone attempting to dispatch a troublesome spider with a nuclear device.

Netiquette applies not just to e-mail, but also to other text-based Internet services (such as automated mailing lists and newsgroups) and even to the text on your Web site. Although using netiquette may seem like a common sense practice, it's amazing how uncommon that practice can be when someone is faced with a new communications medium. Follow these rules as a starting point to becoming netiquette-savvy — you'll find they're basics critical to doing effective online marketing:

- ✔ **KISS (Keep It Short, Silly):** Reading a short message with short paragraphs is still much easier than reading a doctoral dissertation in e-mail. And, with brief, short paragraphs, your marketing message is less likely to get lost in an overabundance of gray text.

- ✔ **Don't type in all capital letters.** Typing in all capital letters is a sure way to communicate that you're new to the Internet. It doesn't matter if all you're trying to do is draw attention to a special offer. IT'S INTERPRETED AS SHOUTING, and no one likes to be yelled at (even if it's well-deserved)

- ✔ **Avoid emoticons.** Marketers should eschew the use of *emoticons,* also called *smileys* :-). Using punctuation to simulate inflection can easily be overdone and come across in business dealings as inappropriately cutesy, unprofessional, or patronizing. If in doubt, don't :-(. Just clearly say what you mean in words.

- ✔ **Be aware of net-savvy abbreviations.** Understand the dense e-mail abbreviations that are a type of keyboard shorthand and include such common acronyms as IMHO (In My Humble Opinion), BTW (By The Way), LOL (Laughing Out Loud), and ROTFL (Rolling On The Floor Laughing). As with emoticons, know them well, but use them sparingly.

The preceding tips are just a few netiquette basics required for good online marketing. For a more exhaustive list of smileys, abbreviations, and other tips, check out *E-Mail For Dummies,* 2nd Edition, by John R. Levine, Carol Baroudi, Margaret Levine Young, and Arnold Reinhold (gasp) from IDG Books Worldwide, Inc.

The Elements of E-Mail Marketing Style

Netiquette's implied rules of online courtesy are, by and large, defensive — the main goal of using netiquette is to not be seen as an idiot. But beyond simple netiquette, you (and the others you work with) have to write e-mail that works for you, not against you. You can take a couple of proactive steps to make sure that all of your company's e-mail is a consistent, positive force for marketing. This advice applies to whether you're responding to an individual e-mail query, or sending e-mail to a large group of people (as covered later in this chapter).

Although we're not great fans of company policy manuals (many of which seem to exist for the sole purpose of providing jobs for company policy manual writers), distributing a list of e-mail guidelines for those handling e-mail from the outside world is a good idea. In this section, we suggest four approaches that can be the basis for your own, more company-specific list.

Write "dressy casual"

Because e-mail is so quick and easy to compose, writers often have a tendency to slip into too much informality and let spelling, grammar, and proper capitalization slide. Don't let your e-mail undermine your personal image and your company's image. Although the style that is used to write an e-mail shouldn't be formal, it shouldn't be sloppy, either — especially now that many e-mail programs, including the Messenger component of Netscape Communicator 4.0 (as shown in Figure 8-3), include integrated spell-checkers.

If you need to aim for a style, consider the handwritten business thank-you note. Such a note is personal without being too informal; brief and to the point.

Be polite

E-mail coming from your company is stamped with a return address — your company's domain name. (If you don't have an easily recognizable domain name and e-mail address that reflects your company name, see the instructions on how to change them in Chapter 4.) If your e-mail message is going to someone who doesn't know much about your company, that person's first impressions about your professionalism and demeanor come from your e-mail text. If you're having a bad day, letting your mood and feelings affect your e-mail to vendors, prospects, customers, or business partners is a bad idea.

So grin while you're writing business e-mail — even if it hurts.

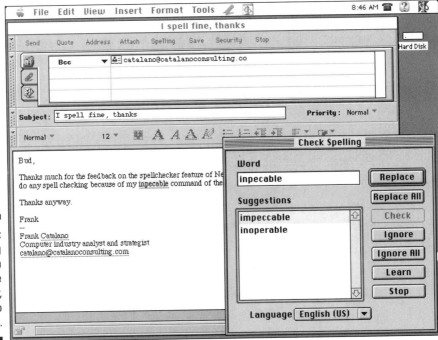

Figure 8-3:
Checking
spelling in
Netscape
Communicator,
just to
be safe.

Don't be afraid to be forwarded

E-mail, unlike paper mail, is easily forwarded.

The upside of easy forwarding is that a useful message can go to anyone and everyone who may benefit from seeing it.

The downside of easy forwarding is that a blistering message — such as your candid opinion of your boss's toupee — can be forwarded to anyone and everyone (including your boss) just as effortlessly — and not just immediately after you send it, but again and again for a long time to come. Some wag may even create a Web site devoted to the e-mail message and immortalize the blunder for posterity.

One of us was graphically reminded of the permanence of e-mail after having published a column observing that America Online was the largest and most successful commercial online service. A reader responded with a copy of an e-mail message — also written by the columnist — complaining about AOL's customer service and wondering how it could possibly stay in business very long. The e-mail was dated October 1989. The column appeared in 1996. As the sender wryly commented, "Guess you didn't buy the stock either, eh?"

Either write your message in such a way that it can be forwarded widely without offending anyone, or include the words "private" or "please don't forward" in the message. Then cross your fingers and hope that such requests are honored.

Create an effective signature

At the end of every e-mail, as with a paper letter, you'd normally sign your name. E-mail has the advantage that it can automate the process — and provide a potent marketing tool — with something called a *sig file* (short for signature file).

A sig file is several lines of text that automatically appear at the end of every e-mail, automated mailing list message, or newsgroup posting you create. Sig files are optional, but they can be powerful reminders of who you are and what your company does. Sig files can range from the whimsical, including favorite quotations and fanciful job titles, to unabashed plugs. Some samples of sig files are shown in Figure 8-4. But the best approach for marketing with a signature file is informational: who you are, what you do, and how people can reach you.

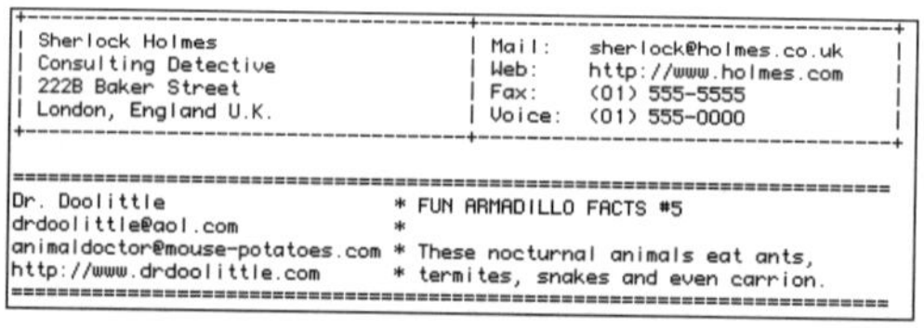

Figure 8-4:
Signature
files range
from the
sublime to
ridiculous.

```
+--------------------------------+--------------------------------+
| Sherlock Holmes                | Mail:   sherlock@holmes.co.uk  |
| Consulting Detective           | Web:    http://www.holmes.com  |
| 222B Baker Street              | Fax:    (01) 555-5555          |
| London, England U.K.           | Voice:  (01) 555-0000          |
+--------------------------------+--------------------------------+
==================================================================
Dr. Doolittle                    * FUN ARMADILLO FACTS #5
drdoolittle@aol.com              *
animaldoctor@mouse-potatoes.com  * These nocturnal animals eat ants,
http://www.drdoolittle.com       * termites, snakes and even carrion.
==================================================================
```

Keep sig files short. A general rule is to make a sig file no more than four to six lines of text. If your sig file is longer than that, your signature may threaten to exceed the length of a message; worse yet, some newsgroups and mailing lists automatically *clip* (reduce the size of) your sig file to keep it within what they consider acceptable limits.

For example, if you run a science fiction bookstore, a good marketing sig file for you might read as follows:

```
Jules Verne
Where No Reader Has Gone Before Books (Seattle, WA)
The biggest science fiction bookstore in the universe.
www.wherenoreaderhasgone.com 206-555-5555
```

You often don't need to include dashes (- - - - - - -) or other separators between your e-mail message and the sig file; many e-mail programs automatically insert them. Try sending a message to yourself to test out your sig file and see whether a separator is necessary.

Signature files can serve one other purpose if you or any of your employees send personal mail, newsgroup postings, or mailing list contributions from a business domain: They can contain a disclaimer if the message is for personal, not work, reasons. ("Any opinions expressed are my own and not that of my employer" is boring, but it does the job. Many such disclaimers are far more creative.)

Creating a sig file is relatively straightforward and can be done for both Microsoft Internet Explorer and Netscape Communicator, as well as for standalone e-mail clients (such as Qualcomm Eudora Pro and Claris Emailer) and newsreaders (such as NewsWatcher). The following sections tell you how to create sig files for the two most popular Web browsers (Microsoft Internet Explorer 4.0 and Netscape Communicator 4.0), both of which come with an e-mail client. The steps in these sections are very similar to those steps that apply to creating sig files for other programs.

Creating a signature file in Microsoft Internet Explorer 4.0

In Microsoft Internet Explorer 4.0, follow these steps to create a sig file for all your e-mail messages:

1. **Launch Internet Explorer.**

2. **Choose Go⇨Mail.**

   The Outlook Express program launches.

3. **In Outlook Express, choose Tools⇨Stationery.**

   A Stationery dialog box with tabs for Mail and News appears.

4. **Click on the Mail tab, and then click on the Signature button.**

   The Signature dialog box appears.

5. **In the Signature dialog box, you have two choices: You can either type your signature in the empty Text field at the top of the dialog box, or you can choose the File option and specify a text-only signature file that you've already created. (For this example, we use the Text option.)**

6. **Type your signature in the Text field; then click on the radio button to the left of the word Text. (The radio button may already be selected, which is fine.)**

7. **Above the Text field, click on the check box to the left of the words Add this signature to all outgoing messages.**

8. **Click on the OK button in the Signature dialog box.**

    The Signature dialog box closes.

9. **Click on the OK button in the Stationery dialog box.**

    The Stationery dialog box closes.

Now, whenever you create an e-mail message in Internet Explorer, the signature you created is automatically appended to it. The preceding steps are similar to those you can use to create a signature file for newsgroup postings.

Creating a signature file in Netscape Communicator 4.0

The steps for creating a signature file in Netscape Communicator 4.0 require you to create the file separately and then tell Communicator where to find it. Follow these steps to create a signature file:

1. **Go into any word processing or text processing program (including Windows Notepad or Macintosh SimpleText).**

2. **Create a new document.**

3. **Type in your signature text as you want to see it, including carriage returns.**

4. **Save the file by giving it the filename sigfile (or any other name — we use sigfile in this example) in text format. Remember the directory in which you saved the file.**

5. **Launch Netscape Communicator.**

6. **Choose Edit⇨Preferences.**

    A Preferences dialog box with a list of options on its left side appears.

7. **Click on the plus sign (Windows) or arrow (Macintosh) adjacent to Mail & Groups on the left side of the dialog box.**

    Additional options appear below Mail & Groups.

8. **Click on Identity when it appears under Mail & Groups.**

    The right side of the dialog box changes to Identity preferences.

9. **Click on the Choose button to the right of the Signature File section.**

10. **Navigate through your hard disk until you find the file that you created and named sigfile in Step 4 (which should appear as sigfile.txt).**

11. **Click on sigfile.txt to select it.**

    The Identity portion of the Preferences dialog box appears again, indicating the file you've chosen as your signature file as shown in Figure 8-5.

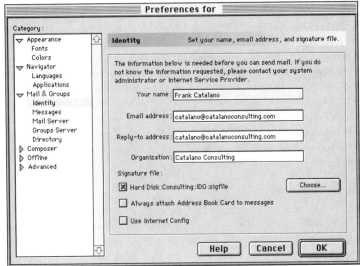

Figure 8-5:
Selecting a
signature
file in
Netscape
Communi-
cator 4.0.

12. Click on the OK button.

The Preferences dialog box disappears.

Now, whenever you create a new mail message or newsgroup posting with Netscape Communicator 4.0, your signature automatically appears at the bottom of the message, separated from the message by a series of dashes.

Processing E-Mail by the Pallet

If you have a company Web site and it includes any e-mail addresses at all, there's no way around it: You're going to get e-mail. E-mail can come to any addresses you have listed on your site, and it may even come addressed to generic e-mail addresses that your customers are used to seeing on *other* sites — addresses like `sales@yourdomain.com`, `info@yourdomain.com`, or `webmaster@yourdomain.com`.

The types of messages you're likely to receive can run the gamut:

- ✔ Inquiries for details about products or services
- ✔ Comments from existing customers about product experiences
- ✔ Requests for customer service or support
- ✔ Resumés from job seekers

Should you put an e-mail address on your site?

Presumably, if you're reading a book called *Marketing Online For Dummies,* you're planning to do some kind of online marketing (or you just have a Renaissance approach to recreational reading). But online marketing can be, when implemented fully, an intensely interactive, two-way process. If a customer knows that you're online, they expect to do more than just read about your products or services on your Web site. They want to get in touch. And the easiest way for them to do that (after they're online) is through e-mail.

The best sites — and the best organizations — realize that e-mail can be a powerful communication tool that can further bond current and potential customers to them. Other sites treat e-mail as more of a problem than an opportunity.

If you have doubts about your ability to handle a large volume of incoming e-mail, a good initial step to gauge the response you may get is to put a single e-mail address on your site. If the response is overwhelming, temporarily remove the address and use the information in this chapter to help you plan how to handle all the mail promptly in a way that your customers, vendors, and business partners — and even the occasional channeler of alien intelligences — can appreciate.

✔ Inquiries from potential business partners about joint ventures or promotions

✔ Complaints about things people in your company did or didn't do

✔ Spam and wacko mail from people in close personal contact with Regulus IV

✔ Orders for your products

No matter how little interest you think that your Web site may generate, it almost always generates more e-mail than you expect.

Planning for the flood

Before blasting your e-mail address or addresses to the Internet world, plan how to channel the potential flood of incoming e-mail into information streams that you can handle. Here are some planning tips:

✔ **Place all contact information on one Web page.** Rather than leaving your visitors guessing who to contact, make finding the right address for a person or department easy by creating an "About Us" or "How to Contact Us" Web page that includes every salient e-mail address in your company, and link to that contact page from every other page on your

Web site. The presence of this page prevents visitors from having to guess addresses and send their messages to the wrong people inside your company, thereby either delaying your firm's response or preventing a customer from ever getting a response at all. Figure 8-6 shows one such contact page for the computer industry trade publication *InfoWorld,* including a link for submitting tidbits to gossip columnist Robert X. Cringely.

✔ **Embed a** `mailto:` **link behind each text e-mail address on a Web page.** A `mailto:` link enables visitors to click directly on the e-mail address. Doing so spawns a new e-mail message, and sends you the mail without requiring them to type your e-mail address. (This assumes, of course, that the visitors have put their e-mail server information in their browser program's preferences, but that situation is something over which you have no control.) The key is to make it easy for visitors to contact you if they're set up to do so. Visitors who don't have their preferences set to take advantage of `mailto:` links can still send you e-mail, they just have to go through a bit more effort. Embedding `mailto:` links into Web pages is supported by many popular Web page creation tools.

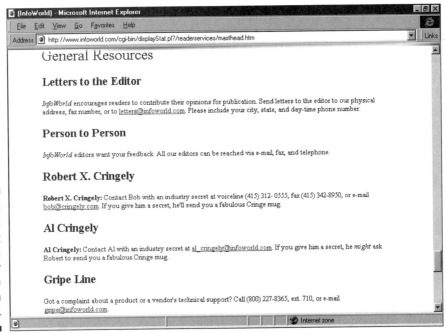

Figure 8-6:
An editorial contact page for the computer trade publication *InfoWorld.*

✔ **Create aliases for departments or functions.** E-mail server software — whether maintained by your ISP or your company — usually allows creation of an *alias* that is, effectively, an e-mail address that points to one or several other e-mail addresses. Thus, the alias of sales@yourdomain.com could point to the sales receptionist who would read each incoming e-mail and either respond to it or forward it to the right person in your organization for a response.

Similarly, custsvc@yourdomain.com could automatically forward mail to the people in your organization who handle customer service inquiries. You can make up aliases for almost any function or even for short-term promotions, such as contest@yourdomain.com.

Most ISPs assist you in setting up aliases. If the mail server resides within your company, your mail server software can be configured to assign aliases.

Make sure that someone in your organization is ultimately responsible for making sure that every e-mail sent to a specific alias is answered or otherwise appropriately dealt with. Because an alias may point to several addresses within an organization, assigning a lead person within that group to ensure that no message falls through the cracks is a good idea.

The 24-hour rule

Pretend that you've just written an old-fashioned paper letter to a company to request information. You've spent time typing the letter, printing it, preparing an envelope, putting a stamp on the envelope, and sticking the envelope into a mailbox. If you get a response in one week, perhaps two, you're satisfied.

Now, pretend that you've called a company's customer service number and left a voice mail message. You've spent the time dialing the number and asking your question. You expect a response the next business day (or perhaps at most in two days). Your expectation is based, in part, on how much effort you put into your end of the communication and, in part, on the speed of the communications mechanism.

Finally, pretend that you've sent your request in an e-mail message. Unlike a paper letter, e-mail is very easy to compose, can be sent with a mouse click, and is usually delivered almost instantaneously. So with e-mail, unlike with either paper letters or voice mail messages, customer expectations for a very prompt response are much higher.

The best rule to follow is to send out at least a brief answer to all e-mail inquiries within one 24-hour business day.

Unanswered e-mail comes with a potentially high cost: You are likely to find yourself with a dissatisfied customer or, at the very least, a customer who questions your commitment to customer service. On the Internet, a dissatisfied customer can quickly spread the word about your perceived shoddy service through online discussion groups (such as newsgroups), automated mailing lists, and individual e-mail messages to friends — the very same vehicles that we're talking about using as marketing tools. And, like other e-mail messages, such negative messages can hang around for years. Unless used with care, the Internet marketing sword can easily become double-edged.

Introducing automatic mail

If you're getting a great amount of e-mail, automating the reply process may be a tempting option. The most common method of automating responses is by using a program known variously as a *mailbot, infobot,* or *autoresponder.*

These programs respond to incoming e-mail by checking the subject line for specific words (for example, "brochure request") or by looking for a specific incoming address or alias (for example, info@yourdomain.com) and shooting off a reply with canned materials, untouched by human hands.

Autoresponder programs and automated mailing lists, or listservs (covered in Chapter 9), can do many of the same things. The major distinction is that autoresponders are designed to evaluate each incoming message according to some criterion such as the subject line or incoming address, and make a predetermined response to the sender. Listserv mailing lists receive messages from the members of that list and then duplicate and send the messages to all members of the list in order to facilitate discussions.

Autoresponder programs reside on the mail server maintained by you or your Internet Service Provider (ISP); ISPs can usually set up such programs for a monthly fee in addition to your normal monthly ISP charge. If you are running your own mail server, you can get an autoresponder program from a variety of sources. One of the better-known shareware programs is Rubberband, available from Dave Central (www.davecentral.com) or CNET's Shareware.com (www.shareware.com). Some mail server and automated mailing list programs, such as Lyris from The Shelby Group (www.lyris.com) and MetaInfo Sendmail (www.metainfo.com), also include autoresponder features.

The Internet has a strong Unix heritage. Despite the progress that Internet tools have made in moving to Windows and Macintosh over the past five years, quite a few of the powerful server programs are designed to work only, or best, on Unix servers. Unless you like getting your hands dirty, have a Unix-based Web server, and are familiar with such arcana as *vi* (short for visual editor, an obtuse Unix text editor), you're better off outsourcing such services as autoresponders to your Internet Service Provider. Who knows? Someone at your ISP may actually like working with Unix.

Using autoresponders autoresponsibly

The bright side of autoresponder programs is that they can make responding to every e-mail within 24 hours brain-dead simple. When an incoming e-mail arrives to an alias, the autoresponder automatically sends a reply.

The dark side of autoresponder programs is that they can become a crutch if overused. The other pitfall is that they automatically send out canned materials — and nothing else — to someone who may actually have a specific, legitimate question that deserves personal attention.

Our advice. Use autoresponders carefully. Make sure that your visitors clearly understand that, when you promote e-mail addresses that are handled by infobots, the response will be automated. (You can, for example, use a `Send an e-mail to brochure@yourdomain.com to receive our product literature automatically` message on your Web site.) In the body text of the automatic response, include a follow-up e-mail address that leads to a mailbox read by a real live human. That way, customers can send an e-mail to the second address if the canned information doesn't answer their questions.

Home of the e-weird

Not every e-mail message you get will be easily classifiable, and some may be, well, downright strange.

Because sending you an e-mail message is so easy, you may get off-the-top-of-the-head questions (or questions designed simply to irritate) that have nothing to do with your products, your business, or even your life. These e-mail messages may take the form of flat statements or questions, such as "When your company was founded, the moon and stars were in perfect alignment" or "What's your company strategy for the unification of Europe?"

Because telling whether the sender is a 12-year-old with too much time on his or her hands or a potential multi-million-dollar client testing your responsiveness is difficult, the safest tack is to take a deep breath, let the query sit for a few minutes, and then do your best with a straightforward, but very brief, response.

Another option is to practice writing the neutral response that puts the offbeat question back in the sender's lap — "We've never actually considered that/thought of it that way. Why do you ask?" — and hope that the response is clearer (or doesn't come at all).

A final approach is the classic one that was used with great effect by Lucy in Charles Schulz's *Peanuts* comic strip. When confronted with deep, philosophical questions by Charlie Brown, she carefully noted, "We had spaghetti at our house three times last week."

If you use an infobot to answer every e-mail promptly, think of your automatic response more as an acknowledgment than as a real response. Tell the sender, "Thank you for your e-mail. We're sending you this automatic confirmation to let you know that we received your message and will respond within 24 hours (or the next business day)." Then live up to that promise.

Delivering E-Mail by the Pallet

At times, you may want to send out e-mail — tons of it. Following are some possible reasons for sending bulk e-mail:

- You're having a sale and want to let preferred customers know about it early.
- You're shipping a new product and need to contact prospects who asked to be notified when it's available.
- You've created an enhancement to a product (or have found a defect) and need to advise current owners immediately.
- You're changing your phone number, location, or even your e-mail address, and your customers, vendors, and business partners have to know.

E-mailing this information one message at a time is not very efficient (or smart). The solution for the bulk e-mail situation is to make and maintain lists of e-mail addresses. Essentially, you're creating different groups of individual e-mail addresses, and you're creating each group of addresses for a specific purpose.

Creating an e-mail mailing list

The most basic way to create simple e-mail lists for a specific, small group of recipients is with your e-mail client software. (Much larger automated mailing lists are covered in Chapter 9.) Netscape Communicator, Microsoft Internet Explorer, America Online, Qualcomm Eudora Pro, and Claris Emailer are just some of the many programs that can handle groups of addresses in their address books, as shown in Figure 8-7.

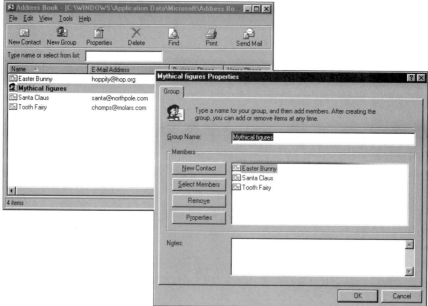

Figure 8-7:
A group in the address book of the Microsoft Internet Explorer 4.0 e-mail client, Outlook Express.

The sources of the e-mail addresses you group can be as varied as the types of information that you plan to send via e-mail:

- ✔ **Existing customer lists.** You may already have these if, at some point, you have asked your customers for an e-mail address in response to mailings, product registration, and the like. (If you don't already collect this kind of information, start now!)
- ✔ **Requests for information generated by visits to your Web site.**
- ✔ **Customer lists from business partners.** For example, a bookstore may get a list of e-mail addresses from a publisher so that the store can announce the publication of a new book. However, this can be tricky, and you should check with your business partner to make sure the potential recipients have given their okay to receive e-mail from a third party.

Creating the right message

The obvious first step in sending e-mail messages to a list of people is to write the message; the second step is to address it; and the third is to hit the Send button. Resist such immediate temptation. The ease with which e-mail can be composed and delivered to dozens (or perhaps hundreds) of recipients doesn't always allow time for the kind of reflection and revision that other marketing materials (such as brochures, direct mail pieces, and print ads) force upon their creators. Make yourself take the time. Before e-mailing anything to a group, step back and do this quick reality check:

> ✔ **Are the tone and style of your message consistent with your image?** The elements of e-mail marketing style noted earlier in this chapter — write "dressy casual," be polite, and keep it short, sender — apply as much to mass e-mailings as they do to individual responses, if not more so. Many of your group e-mail messages may be sent to prospects who are only casually interested in what you have to offer but will quickly note anything offputting about the message's tone or content.

> ✔ **Do you tell enough?** If the message is likely to be seen by people who aren't intimately familiar with your company or product, you need to provide enough background information to satisfy them. Don't forget basics, such as your company name, product or service name, and contact information. (Even those who should know better make this mistake: We've seen at least one e-mail news release that was sent out by a public relations agency to promote a new software product to the press — but neglected to reveal who the software's publisher was.)

> ✔ **Do you sell enough?** No matter what the purpose of your mass e-mail, it should contain a call to action. If your message is designed to announce a new product, say where it can be ordered. If the message is designed to advise that your phone number has changed, remind the recipients to update their address books. Do it without undue hype — e-mail, remember, is a personal medium — but definitely do it.

> ✔ **Is the message strict ASCII text?** Some e-mail client software (including the America Online mail client, Qualcomm Eudora Pro, and browsers that support HTML mail) enable users to send electronic mail with colored text, varied fonts, and underlining. Unfortunately, those features aren't readable by most e-mail clients, which display only plain text and carriage returns. Refrain from using bells and whistles that may look cool to you but could cause your message to frustrate and confuse your recipients.

> ✔ **Do you make it easy to get off of the list?** Even though people may have at one time asked to be notified about new products or other company information, they may at some point change their mind. The first sentence in any bulk e-mailing should provide clear, straightforward instructions on how a recipient can keep from getting any further messages from your business. These "remove" instructions should require no more effort than sending an e-mail back to you — and should be honored immediately.

✔ **Are you sending blind carbon copies?** Unless your message is only going to a handful of people, you probably don't want everyone who gets the message to see the names and e-mail addresses of everyone else who gets the message. To avoid this, use the blind carbon copy (or bcc) option in your e-mail software. Here's how: Instead of choosing To or Cc when addressing the message to the list, choose Bcc in order to suppress the visibility of the complete address list. The recipients who don't have to scroll through a long list of names before getting to the body of the message will likely appreciate your thoughtfulness.

✔ **Have you been the guinea pig?** Before opening the floodgates, trickle one copy of the message to yourself (preferably sent from one e-mail address at one domain to a second, different e-mail address at a different domain). This type of dress rehearsal identifies any weird formatting problems that could irritate those who receive your message and also gives you one last look at the message's content.

✔ **Does your message really need to be communicated by e-mail?** Although this advice may sound heretical in a book about marketing online, not every communication needs to be sent as an e-mail message. If your message is complex, detailed, or controversial, consider another delivery vehicle, such as direct mail or a personal phone call. The same e-mail message that you can send in an instant can be returned just as quickly, with new red-hot commentary, if what you're trying to say is not clear or if your message is seen as insulting.

HTML Mail: Temptation and trap

Both Netscape Communicator 4.0 and Microsoft Internet Explorer 4.0 have integrated a feature, known as *HTML Mail,* into their e-mail capabilities. (Netscape created HTML Mail first, if you're keeping score.) Just as HyperText Markup Language (HTML) enables Web browsers to display graphics, HTML Mail enables you to embed graphics, Web page links, and stylized text (among other things) in e-mail messages.

You may be tempted to jazz up a dull text e-mail message with HTML Mail features. Our advice: Don't, unless you're absolutely sure that everyone who is receiving the message (or is likely to be forwarded it) can read HTML-formatted mail.

If not, you fall into the trap of sending a perfectly good message that is virtually unreadable by a strictly text e-mail program, as shown in Figure 8-8. What your recipient sees: plain text, infested by ugly HTML tags.

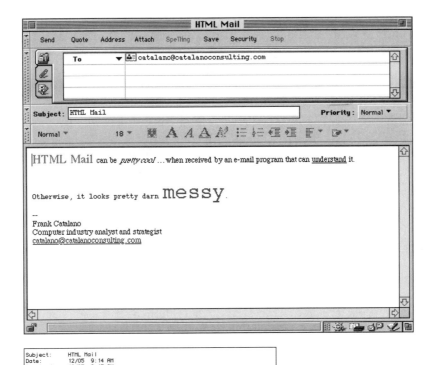

Figure 8-0:
HTML-
formatted
mail, before
and after.

Spam: Pros and (mostly) cons

As certain as summer turns to fall, wine turns to vinegar, and a solitary clothes hanger turns into dozens when not watched, new online marketers turn to thoughts of sending e-mail en masse to prospects who have never even contacted their company. The word for such a Net byproduct is *spam*. (Other words come to mind, too, but we can't print them here.)

The appeal of this automated e-mail equivalent to the cold call is seductive. After all, if a company is already sending out e-mail to large lists of its own contacts, why not just buy an e-mail list from a third party and see how many e-mail recipients on the list bite? Sending a few hundred — or a few thousand — more e-mail messages has little incremental cost.

Unfortunately, cost isn't always measured in dollars. Cost is also measured in goodwill and legal uncertainty. Most Internet Service Providers and commercial online services, such as America Online, Netcom, Earthlink, MindSpring, and many, many others, have strict policies forbidding their subscribers from sending spam. The penalty is usually a warning and/or suspension of service on first offense — and termination of service on the second offense.

In addition, several large ISPs and online services have been aggressive in filing lawsuits against spammers who they believe have fraudulently sent e-mail to their subscribers or misappropriated their e-mail services.

So take any inclination to spam with a grain of salt. Perhaps even an entire lick.

A brief history of spam

On the Internet, the word *spam* is not shorthand for "shoulder pork and ham." The apocryphal story about the word's origin in the online world is that *spam* is an acronym for "self-propelled advertising material." Other Internet lore credits the classic Monty Python sketch set in a restaurant in which every menu item (emphasized by a group of Vikings chanting "spam spam spam spam" in the background) is some variation of the luncheon meat. And to most users of the Internet, the electronic version is not nearly as tasty as the Hormel version.

The more modern version of spam gained widespread notoriety in early 1994, when the law firm of Canter & Siegel, run by a husband-and-wife team, posted a message (to Internet discussion groups known as *newsgroups* — the subject of Chapter 10) advertising Green Card services for immigrants. The team didn't pick one, or two, or a dozen appropriate newsgroups. The same message was posted to thousands of newsgroups, whether the newsgroup topic was cooking or cave art. This novel action was a real shock to many Internet users because online commerce over the Internet, let alone this kind of in-your-face assault, was just getting started.

The backlash was immediate and loud. Tens of thousands of hostile responses (or *flames*) inundated the originators, overloading their Internet Service Provider, costing the duo its Internet access, and reportedly leading to the ISP and Canter & Siegel threatening to sue each other over the matter.

Since then, *spam* has commonly come to mean any unsolicited commercial message indiscriminately sent via e-mail, distributed through a mailing list, or posted to a newsgroup. An example is shown in Figure 8-9.

Spam is also commonly known as *unsolicited commercial e-mail, bulk e-mail,* and *junk e-mail.* But as Shakespeare once noted about a rose by any other name, spam still smells — and tastes — the same.

```
Subject:    $7,000 LOAN--NO PAYBACK EVER!!!!!!!
Date:       11/24/97 10:49 PM
To:         spammaillist@nowhere.com

Look First: Trash Later

I look forward to getting home in the evenings and checking my mailbox so that I can count the
amount of money I have received for the day. You can be in my position too,by counting as much as
$200-$400 each day. This is real and I am a real person on a mission to achieve financial freedom.
Do not give up on this and do not throw this aside because I tell you without reservations, that
this does work!! I am glad that I did not throw this away when I received it because I am now
going to the bank to make deposits instead of withdrawals! Join me and the others by gaining your
own financial freedom and continuing this process by sharing it with whomever you come in contact
with because the more you share, the  more money you make.

You may have an interest in receiving an INTEREST FREE LOAN, even if you have had CREDIT PROBLEMS
IN THE PAST. Well, read on because this one can really bring the CASH FAST! And it only costs a
minimum.

$7,000 LOAN--NO PAYBACK EVER!!!!!!!

Time: 12-30 days

Interested? Read on.


WOULD YOU LIKE A $7,000 LOAN THAT NEVER HAS TO BE REPAID?

You can definitely get up to $7000 within a few weeks and you willnot have to pay it back. This
program is designed to raise money fast.It is VERY inexpensive to participate in because it's been
designed to be run totally online, there are no postage or name list expenses! Read this over and
carefully follow the instructions. It has worked very well for me each time that I have used it.
```

Figure 8-9:
A typical
spam
message,
modified to
protect the
guilty.

If you're uncertain whether your mass e-mail message will be viewed as spam, think of your message as a fax. Would you spend the personal time and effort to send this person a fax with the same information? If so, your e-mail message probably won't be regarded by the recipient as spam.

Spam I am?

Not all e-mail trying to sell something is spam. Before sending mass e-mail, consider these three questions:

- ✔ **Did the recipient request the information?** If someone wants information from you, it's not unsolicited — the recipient is likely to be more upset if you *don't* provide the information. Do note in your message that it is in response to the recipient's query.

- ✔ **Do you have an existing business relationship with the recipient?** If the recipient is a past or current customer, vendor, or business partner of yours, your mass e-mail message is probably not spam.

- ✔ **Are you acting on behalf of a business partner who has the customer relationship?** This situation is a bit more tricky. For example, if you own a bookstore and are using a book publisher's e-mail list to let someone know that you're carrying that publisher's book, you're a step removed from the process by which the e-mail list was created. You're trusting that the publisher's e-mail list is clean and not *harvested* by a third-party from e-mail addresses in newsgroup messages or America Online profiles. You also need to explain clearly to the recipient why you're sending an e-mail message to your business partner's customer.

Generally, if you can answer *yes* to any one of these questions, then congratulations — your e-mail passes the anti-spam sniff test and isn't likely to offend any recipients.

Why spam offends

Most businesses new to online marketing don't intuitively understand why spam generates such a vehement response among those who receive it. With flat-fee Internet access having largely supplanted pay-by-the-hour service, concluding that no one should object (because receiving e-mail is now effectively free) is easy. But rightly or wrongly, spam is seen as an intrusion that steals time, an intrusion much more odious than paper junk mail. Why? Here are some possible reasons:

✔ **Too easy.** For regular mail, the costs of creating effective copy, printing it, and spending money for postage erect an effective "barrier to entry" to amateurish offers that appear more at home on hand-lettered yard signs than in mailboxes. (When was the last time you were sent direct mail for illegal cable television descrambler boxes, miracle vitamin cures, or instant weight loss products?) Spam is much easier to create and send.

✔ **Too confusing.** It's hard to tell from the subject line of an e-mail message — much more so than the design, text, and graphics on a printed return envelope — whether a message contains an unwanted commercial offer.

✔ **Too personal.** The rejection of mass e-mail messages may simply result from the fact that e-mail is considered highly personal by recipients because e-mail is a far more informal method of communicating than paper mail, arrives inside their homes or directly to their work computer, and thus seems to be a violation of that personal space.

No matter what the reason, increasing numbers of spam messages seem to be crowding out other messages in many e-mail boxes as more Internet-unsavvy businesses discover the Internet and users gain experience in freely handing out their e-mail addresses. Flat-fee account or not, an all-you-can-eat buffet isn't very tasty when most of the serving plates contain the same unwanted dish.

Chapter 9

Marketing with Internet Mailing Lists

*1*f you spend any time creating and maintaining lists of individual e-mail addresses for publicity, product information, or other marketing purposes, you may eventually wonder — after you add and delete a few dozen people to your lists and spent time forwarding interesting replies back and forth among different people — if you can automate the entire process. You can, thanks to Internet mailing lists.

In this chapter, we show you how to use automated mailing lists to market your business, from finding the right mailings lists for your interest or industry, to discovering how to create and promote your own mailing list.

Oh yeah — don't forget about the Directory portion of this book (the yellow pages) when you can find the addresses and instructions for a number of online marketing-related mailing lists.

What's a Mailing List?

Although the meaning of *mailing list* is crystal-clear to long-time Internet users, the term can confuse many marketers because of how people use it in the nonvirtual world. An Internet mailing list, unlike a direct mail mailing list, is *not* a collection of e-mail addresses you buy or rent to subsequently blast them with advertising (though collections of e-mail addresses are sometimes offered for sale on CD-ROM, usually through offers that make you wonder if they ship in a brown paper bag). Blast an Internet mailing list with advertising, and you may likely earn a place of honor on someone's publicly posted blacklist.

An Internet mailing list is a self-selecting community of online users who choose to either receive information (such as newsletters) or discuss specific topics completely by e-mail. These two types of Internet mailing lists are referred to, respectively, as *broadcast lists* and *discussion lists*. Internet mailing lists differ from mailing lists you create in your e-mail software (see Chapter 8) because they're largely automated — participants can add or remove themselves from the broadcast or discussion list, and, in the case of discussion lists, e-mails sent to a single e-mail address are automatically distributed to everyone else on the list, as shown in Figure 9-1.

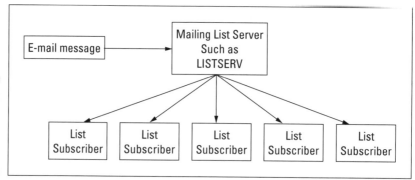

Figure 9-1: A single message, relayed to many users.

Internet mailing lists predate just about everything that's well known about the online world, including the World Wide Web, America Online, and spam. The first Internet mailing lists were distributed in the mid-1980s over Bitnet, a worldwide network that connected academic and research institutions. Mailing lists now provide newsletters and discussions for almost every conceivable interest — everything from computer product debates, to how to breed Golden Retrievers, to Internet marketing. And because they're so specific to an interest or industry, they are an excellent marketing resource and tool.

Subscribing to a mailing list

At the heart of every Internet mailing list is a *list server,* the software program that keeps the list running smoothly. Several list server products exist, of which LISTSERV from L-Soft International is the most popular — all of them respond to subscription commands sent by e-mail.

So the only thing you need to participate in a mailing list is the ability to send and receive e-mail. That's the beauty of mailing lists: Unlike newsgroups (see Chapter 10), you don't have to seek out the discussions; once you sign up for a mailing list, e-mail messages arrive in your e-mail box for you to peruse at your leisure.

LISTSERV vs. listservs

Few things beat being first in marketing. Just ask Kleenex, Fiberglas, or Xerox. Their names, much to their trademark attorneys' dismay, have become nearly synonymous with their product category.

The first automated mailing list program widely used for electronic discussions was developed in 1986. LISTSERV was originally only available for IBM mainframe computers — what mainframe junkies like to call "big iron" and personal computer users like to call "dinosaurs" — but has spawned more than

15,000 public mailing lists, versions for Unix, VM, VMS, Windows NT and Windows 95, and several competitors. The most prominent competitors are Majordomo and ListProc, both found on Unix.

Yet because LISTSERV was the first mailing list software product, its name has forever been linked to automated mailing lists. You may frequently hear mailing lists referred to simply as "listservs." It may give lawyers heartburn, but that kind of generic fame is priceless in marketing.

One mailing list works pretty much the same way as another when it comes to subscribing, no matter which mailing list program runs them. To get on a mailing list, for example, you generally do the following:

1. **Find the name, topic, and e-mail address of an interesting mailing list and send an e-mail to the list administrative address, which is typically** `listserver@host.domain`.

   (See "Finding the right list" later in this chapter on how to identify an interesting list.)

2. **In the body of the e-mail type the word subscribe, followed by the name of the list you want to subscribe to, such as:**

   subscribe listname

   The various mailing list servers may require a different subscription routine, such as typing **subscribe listname** in the subject field, or some other similar wording. Be sure to pay careful attention to the instructions for the specific list you want to join.

   Some list servers then send back a confirming e-mail message, asking whether the person at the submitted address really wants to subscribe. (This confirmation prevents the electronic equivalent of the fun-filled prank, which many people perfected in high school, of sending in magazine subscription cards with the names and addresses of unsuspecting victims.)

As soon as the list server receives the confirming e-mail back from you, you become a subscriber to the list. Your first message from the list is likely to be a welcome message that includes salient details such as the list description, list do's and don'ts, how to send an e-mail to all list members, and a command reference — including how to unsubscribe from the list.

From then on, you get every message sent to the list, until you send an **unsubscribe listname** command to the list administrative address.

If you're tempted to delete a mailing list's welcome message, resist. The most important item in that e-mail is the command reference — and the administrative address to send list commands to.

Almost all mailing lists maintain two separate e-mail addresses: the *list address,* the one to which you send messages that you want every other list subscriber to see, typically `listname@host.domain`, and the *administrative address,* the one to which you send commands or requests like **subscribe**, **unsubscribe**, **help**, and so on, typically `listserver@host.domain`.

If you nuke the welcome message and don't have a photographic memory, you won't know where to send the **unsubscribe** command when the time comes to leave the list. And other list subscribers find few things more irritating than having to wade through lots of messages demanding "Help! I've fallen on this list and I can't get off! Unsubscribe me!" We know. We've done it.

Some mailing lists also have a Web page so that you can sign up for the list directly from your Web browser, including the Dummies Daily mailing list, shown in Figure 9-2. This type of Web page makes remembering commands and the administrative address less critical, but you still have to remember the site URL if you ever want to make changes. So don't toss the welcome message.

Variations on a mailing list

As you may expect with something automated, mailing lists have variations on their one-message-to-many theme. Internet mailing lists are commonly thought of primarily as discussion lists. But one growing variation is the *broadcast,* or *announce-only,* list for missives like electronic newsletters, such as the Dummies Daily list from IDG Books Worldwide, Inc., AnchorDesk news service from ZDNet, and Dispatch from CNET. Broadcast lists can be huge: L-Soft, the maker of the LISTSERV mailing list software, knows of one such list with nearly three million subscribers who receive computer industry news. That's a lot of e-mail addresses for a single alias to point to, and far more work than you likely want to manage yourself.

Figure 9-2:
Getting
on the
Dummies
Daily
mailing list.

But what discussion and broadcast lists have in common is that they completely rely on e-mail for delivery, and list participants, or subscribers, can easily add or remove themselves from the lists without much trouble. Discussion lists can even be more varied.

Moderated versus free-for-all

On your garden-variety discussion list, you find very little filtering. An e-mail sent to the list address automatically goes to everyone else on the list. A major drawback, however, is that unless list participants police themselves vigorously, these unmoderated lists tend to become overgrown with personal notes, single line "Thanks!" messages, and the occasional inedible spam.

Enter the moderator. On a moderated discussion list, e-mail messages first go to the moderator to be reviewed for appropriateness and then are sent on to everyone else on the list. A moderated discussion list is very much like a Letters to the Editor section where an editor makes sure that the messages are relevant to the topic, don't ramble, and don't endlessly repeat previous comments. Moderators also can throw a wet blanket over *flame wars* and hostile message exchanges (see Chapter 8), and that alone is worth the selection of a moderated list over an unmoderated one.

Individual messages versus digest

When a discussion mailing list gets popular, or its participants get really enthused or cranky, the number of messages that arrive in your e-mail box can quickly become overwhelming. Many lists have a digest mode to help manage this kind of list traffic.

Digests are simply compilations of messages that arrive either once a day or after a certain number of messages are processed, as shown in Figure 9-3. The upside of choosing a digest mode is that you get far fewer e-mail messages from a list, and following how separate discussions develop can be much easier. The downside is that the messages won't be as timely. Unless you need to make snap business decisions based on a list discussion, the downside probably won't pose a problem.

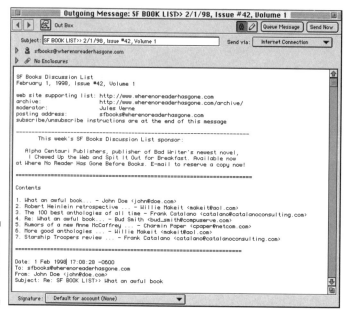

Figure 9-3:
A mailing list in digest mode.

If you're not sure how busy a list is, choose digest mode when you first subscribe. You can always switch to reading messages as they're sent. The instructions on setting your list subscription to digest mode or to individual messages mode are in the initial welcome message — another reason not to delete it.

Finding and Using the Right Mailing Lists

As with e-mail, mailing lists require a light touch if you want to use them to market your products. The guiding principle is that mailing lists are informational, which means typical marketing messages (which often emphasize style at the expense of substance) don't fit in well. But if you can avoid marketing hype and provide solid information, mailing lists can be a valuable part of your overall online marketing mix.

Benefits of participating in a mailing list

Discussion mailing lists make good marketing vehicles for you as a participant for several reasons:

- **Discussion mailing lists are highly targeted.** Discussion mailing lists spring up around specific interests and, if they have a moderator, stay true to those interests.

- **Discussion mailing lists are free.** Almost all mailing lists charge nothing to subscribe and would actually have a hard time charging if they wanted an automated subscription process. Some discussion lists and many broadcast newsletter lists are supported financially by small ads in the messages themselves instead of subscription fees.

- **Discussion mailing lists are communities**. Discussion mailing lists consist of people helping people, whether it's providing solid information on where to find a dog breeder, what the hot new science-fiction books are, or how to troubleshoot software problems. For better or worse, regular list participants become like neighbors. If you can add value to the community, you and your business both become good neighbors.

Participating in discussion lists

The easiest way to gain experience in using mailing lists for marketing is to take part in an existing list (see the section "Marketing to a discussion list" for more on marketing techniques). But first you need to find the right list for your industry or interest and then use the right approach in posting to the list.

Finding the right list

Although tens of thousands of mailing lists are available, they're not neatly organized. Unless a list administrator chooses to publicize the list, it can be virtually invisible to nonsubscribers because all traffic between the administrator and subscribers travels by e-mail.

But several excellent resources routinely scour the Internet for mailing lists and collect what they find in one place. A few examples, most of which overlap in their list selections, are:

- ✔ **Liszt** (www.liszt.com): A huge list of e-mail mailing lists, shown in Figure 9-4, including a search engine to cull through more than 80,000 public and private lists as well as details on how to get more information about each list.

- ✔ **Publicly Accessible Mailing Lists** (www.neosoft.com/internet/paml/): Stephanie da Silva's painstaking monthly compilation of public mailing lists with a search engine and descriptions.

- ✔ **CataList** (www.lsoft.com/lists/listref.html): L-Soft International's searchable database of mailing lists that use the LISTSERV list server.

- ✔ **America Online Internet Mailing List Directory** (ifrit.web.aol.com/mld/production/): A publicly-accessible Web site produced by AOL, the Mailing List Directory has a searchable index of lists and useful tips on list server commands and netiquette.

- ✔ **Yahoo!** (www.yahoo.com): The granddaddy of Internet directories, Yahoo! includes Web site homes of mailing lists and one-line descriptions in a number of categories from entertainment to ice hockey.

You also can find announcements of new mailing lists in the newsgroup news.lists.misc. We cover newsgroups in detail in Chapter 10.

Don't subscribe to a mailing list based on the list name alone; you may be unpleasantly surprised. For example, searching for *golden* in the Liszt database brought up more than 20 lists identified by minor variations on the word *golden* in their list names, including mailing lists for the Golden Key National Honor Society, Golden Age Comics, Golden Oldies, and people whose surnames are Golden. But none for Golden Retrievers — the goal of the search. Before subscribing to a list, use a mailing list search engine, and pay attention to any tips the search engine provides, to make sure that the list name describes what you think it does, or you could be barking up the wrong tree.

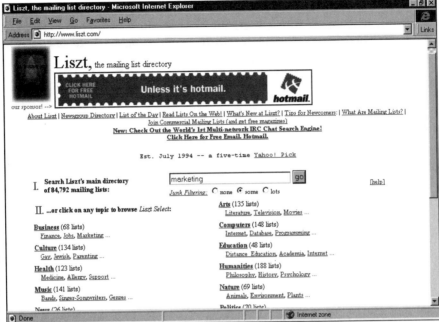

Figure 9-4:
The Liszt list
of lists.

Mailing lists about marketing

Mailing lists can be an online marketing resource as much as a marketing tool. Two of the more lively online marketing lists are the Internet Advertising Discussion List, also known as I-Advertising (www.exposure-usa.com/i-advertising/) with more than 11,000 subscribers, and the Online Advertising Discussion List, also known as Online Ads (www.o-a.com).

Both moderated lists are good examples of Internet resources for online publicity, promotion, advertising, and general marketing, with the occasional warm spam debate tossed in.

And even though it ceased operations in 1996, the Internet Marketing Discussion List is a classic example of how nothing on the Internet ever dies; it just gets archived. Inet-Marketing has left its searchable — and quite valuable — list archives at www.i-m.com.

Finally, don't forget to consult the Directory portion (yellow pages) of this book for a few more online marketing lists worth checking out.

Marketing to a discussion list

After you've found and subscribed to the perfect discussion lists, you're almost ready to dive in with your marketing message. Stay on the side of the pool for a bit longer.

A discussion mailing list is nothing more than a one-to-many exchange of e-mail messages. So all of the rules for e-mail described in Chapter 8 — keep it short, don't type in ALL CAPS, create an effective signature, don't spam, and so on — apply just as much to mailing lists, if not more so.

Before contributing anything, *lurk*. A poorly thought-out e-mail message is read by only one person, but a similarly ill-considered discussion list submission can be read, remembered, and replied to by thousands. So read the mailing list messages for one to two weeks before participating. That way, you get a good feel for the tone of the list, what the current hot topics are, and who the key players happen to be. You also find out whether the mailing list provides Frequently Asked Question (FAQ) documents. FAQs often have details on issues that have been discussed ad infinitum (and even ad nauseum) on the mailing list.

Another consideration for marketing in discussion mailing lists is the fact that most of them are for customer service or for open, honest discussion of an agreed-on interest, and anything that feels like marketing hype within the list will be ignored at best, or cause people to drop the list at worse. You know the feeling when a good friend suddenly starts trying to get a couple of thousand dollars from you so that he can move up in a network marketing scheme? That's how Internet mailing list users will feel if you suddenly start pitching them directly.

After you dive into a discussion list, keep the following do's and don'ts in mind to avoid sinking to the bottom:

> ✔ **Do informational marketing.** Discussions lists are exactly that: discussions. They shouldn't be monologues or chest-beating exercises. Be helpful. If someone is having problems in your company's area of expertise, answer the question directly. If you have a product or service that might help solve a problem, answer the question directly and provide a very brief, casual reference to your product.
>
> One method may be to write, "Several products may be helpful. One is produced by us, (insert product name here). Other similar products are made by (insert competitors' names here)." Your corporate ego may not like having to mention competitors, but the goal is for users to see as a long-term, useful resource. And if your name and company appear in the signature at the end of the message, the reader may likely contact you first.

✔ **Don't cut and paste marketing materials into messages.** Many times the information you want to send to answer a question or elaborate on a thought exists in your current marketing materials — but those are written in an upbeat, cheerful, even inspirational tone usually inappropriate for mailing lists. Take the time to write the facts in a tone appropriate to the mailing list.

✔ **Do stay on topic.** Do you have an annoying acquaintance who somehow manages to bring any conversation around to focus on them every time? If you mention your company or product every time you participate, you risk the same reputation. In moderated lists, you also risk having your messages never appear and getting extra scrutiny from the moderator for any subsequent messages you send.

Equally as odious is forwarding messages containing virus hoaxes, jokes of the day, or pornography if the list doesn't discuss, respectively, computer viruses, humor, or sex. Not only may you have your subscription revoked, some lists take even more drastic measures for off-topic mail. The welcome message for a dog enthusiast list ominously warns that punishment can go as far as "a lifetime flea curse on your dwelling."

✔ **Don't respond in public every time.** You don't need to publicly answer every question posed in a discussion list, especially if your response involves recommending your company or product for a particular situation. Reply directly to the person who sent the message.

✔ **Do be positive.** While wearing your marketing hat, think long and hard before saying anything negative about anyone or anything. It's amazing how far your e-mail message can get forwarded — and anything you say reflects not only on you, but on your company.

✔ **Don't spam.** What you do in the privacy of your individual e-mail account is your business (see Chapter 8). But the fastest way to have your subscription to a discussion list stopped is to send unsolicited commercial e-mail for a product or service to everyone on the list. Not coincidentally, it can also destroy any progress you've made in building your reputation on that list.

✔ **Do a two-pronged approach.** Subscribe to mailing lists that appeal to potential customers and to mailing lists that appeal to your industry peers. If you own a bookstore, this may include some lists for science-fiction enthusiasts and others for independent booksellers. Be equally helpful on both. While one cultivates customers, the other cultivates your reputation within the industry — and few mind being thought of as an industry expert.

Participating in your company's mailing lists

One common scenario that you may find yourself in is as a subscriber and contributor to a mailing list run by someone else in your own company. For example, your company may run a customer support mailing list for a product for which you do the marketing. Such lists commonly wander into broader topics, and if so, the list becomes a good vehicle for the occasional marketing message. Follow these suggestions:

✔ **Read the list.** You should read any mailing list that directly concerns your product, but especially a list from your own company. You can glean quite a bit of useful information from the comments, and you need to be there to respond to flames or cries for help that are marketing rather than customer service oriented.

✔ **Tread lightly.** Remember that someone else is doing the heavy lifting of creating the list and maintaining it. Don't take over the list by posting to it at length or with great frequency.

✔ **Start slowly.** Give brief responses to messages that directly concern you. Watch for responses to your postings that tell you whether your comments are welcome as part of the list.

✔ **Develop relationships.** Send e-mail directly to individuals on the list who bring up topics that the list as a whole doesn't need to know more about. Put people from the mailing list into your own list of people to whom you send key e-mail messages.

✔ **Consider posting press releases.** One of the authors used to post shortened, text-only versions of press releases to his company's customer-service-oriented list, after establishing himself on the list and with apologies for the long, nontechnical message. List members generally appreciated the information because it was positioned as an unusual interruption of the list's normal business and not followed up by further marketing hype.

Creating Your Own Mailing List

Over time, you may find that you don't just want to participate in mailing lists; you want one of your very own. Perhaps other lists aren't specific enough to your or your company's interests, or you have to support a product, or you have certain company information that you think many people would want, or maybe you want to establish yourself as an expert in your field.

In all cases, your own mailing list — discussion or broadcast — could fulfill your needs.

Mailing lists are particularly demanding of one resource: time. Many mailing list moderators put in several hours each *day* reviewing messages, to say nothing of list administration tasks like dealing with misdirected subscription requests or the Psycho Factor (that very small, but very real, percentage of list subscribers whose only role in life, it seems, is to drive the moderator crazy). This estimate doesn't include the time required to physically set up the list server software and hardware — a good reason to outsource the technical aspects, as we describe a little later in this chapter (see "Implementing a simple list server"). Before moving ahead with creating your own list, make sure that you can carve out the time to make it successful.

Benefits of creating a mailing list

Just as you can derive many marketing benefits from participating in mailing lists, you can reap potentially even more benefits in creating one:

- ✔ **Mailing lists are highly targeted.** By creating a list, you define the breadth and depth of the topic area and, in turn, know that people who make the effort to subscribe are actively interested in that topic. The topic can be focused on your products, industry, or related subjects.

- ✔ **Mailing lists are delivered.** What's more compelling: Having someone need to seek out your marketing message by searching for a Web site, or have that message automatically show up in their e-mail? Consider this the definitive example of a rhetorical question.

- ✔ **Mailing lists build communities.** A lively mailing list can create a feeling of shared purpose among subscribers and actually turn more customers into fans of your product or service, especially if they believe they have a say in its direction and if you take an active part in the list as well.

- ✔ **Mailing lists position you as a leader.** Being seen as the source of a good, active list gives both you and your company a reputation as experts in the list's subject matter, especially if the list has a lot of informational value.

Determining which type of list to start

After you decide that a mailing list is a good thing to have, and you give some thought as to the topic of your initial list, you have two flavors of mailing list from which to choose: *discussion list* or *broadcast list*. Here's a more detailed description of the two types of lists:

- ✔ **Discussion lists** are interactive lists that can be used by customers to discuss how best to use your product, by your company and customers for product support, or by anyone in your industry to debate the importance of industry trends. For example, you can create a list moderated by someone in product support for those subscribers interested in learning more about every nuance of your product from you and from other experienced customers. Or you may want to start a list that updates developments in your industry for comment by the list subscribers.

✔ **Broadcast lists** are one-way lists that go from the sender to a group of recipients and don't allow the recipients to reply to the members of the list as a whole. Your company can use broadcast lists to announce new products, weekly specials, or provide industry and company news. For example, you might create a list strictly of news releases for press and analysts, and another list for dedicated customers to give them early notice of sales or special offers. Another approach is to create a regular newsletter for customers and prospects. A simple broadcast list newsletter for a music store, for example, may include new product information and tips from manufacturers and other readers, along with mention of any upcoming sales.

Try balancing *come-on* with *content* in your broadcast lists. Include tips and tricks on using your product and other information that may prove useful even for someone not actively looking to buy. That way, you increase the chances your e-mail message will be opened — and the potential that readers may change their minds about not buying when they scan the specials.

If you're uncertain what topics to focus on in your new discussion or broadcast list, see what others in your industry or related industries have done. Visit one of the several mailing list search engines on the Web (see "Finding the right list" earlier in this chapter) and browse the list descriptions to get some ideas.

Consider creating matched pairs of broadcast and discussion lists as well. While a broadcast list provides one-way information, a related discussion list gives subscribers the opportunity to analyze and comment on the information.

Done properly, a good mailing list or set of lists can

✔ Reward core customers by providing timely information they can't easily get anywhere else.

✔ Replace paper newsletters and catalogs, saving printing and postage costs for mailings to online customers.

✔ Have customers support other customers by answering questions, taking some of the pressure off your customer service, technical support, or sales staff.

Here's how the fictional Where No Reader Has Gone Before science-fiction bookstore uses Internet mailing lists:

- ✔ **New release broadcast list,** updated as often as daily with whatever new book releases have just shown up at the store.

- ✔ **New release discussion list,** where you encourage customers to post their own reviews and debate the merits of new releases.

- ✔ **Author signing broadcast list,** containing news of when book authors come to the store and other events.

- ✔ **Science-fiction convention discussion list,** with news of upcoming science fiction conventions, the bookstore's participation, and subscriber tips on what to expect and who goes.

- ✔ **Futurist discussion list,** a bookstore-sponsored but not bookstore-oriented discussion list on "how to build the future we want."

Even if the purpose of your list is informational, you can advertise in your own marketing vehicle. Consider putting a brief, six-line, text-only "ad" for one of your products at the bottom of your discussion list digest. Just clearly separate it from the discussion list text with dashes (- - - - -) or some other clever punctuation mark :-).

The twilight list

Murphy's Law applies as much to the Internet as it does to every other endeavor in life. Some common pitfalls of maintaining a mailing list yourself:

- ✔ **A weak, or no, moderator.** Make sure that you have a good moderator for any discussion list you sponsor. Nothing looks quite so unprofessional as having a mailing list infested with off-topic posts about alien landings and the occasional "Your company sucks!" message — especially if it's not met with appropriate response. Poor moderation can lead to "topic creep," and if a list loses its focus, it also loses subscribers.

- ✔ **File attachments.** Most lists discourage attaching files to the e-mail messages that make up the list. Do the same. Not only do attachments dramatically slow list download times for subscribers, not all users have either the programs — or the machine — to open every file. You also risk liability should you allow a file attachment to go to subscribers that later turns out to contain a computer virus.

- ✔ **Unsubscribe hell.** Hard to believe, but people toss the welcome message with the unsubscribe instructions. Expect it to happen and for the occasional "unsubscribe me now, [expletive deleted]!" message to be submitted to the list. One ounce of prevention is to automatically attach unsubscribe instructions at the bottom of the digest version of your list, or send out a weekly or monthly reminder message.

Lists also have life cycles:

- **Mailing lists give birth.** Don't be afraid to split off and create a new list from a very busy one if you see a significant amount of message traffic on a particular related subject. If *Cheers* can beget *Frasier,* your creation can have offspring as well.

- **Mailing lists evolve.** The focus of a mailing list can wander to a different take on a subject — from customer support to industry news — or even off to a different subject entirely. You may need to ask someone else to take over a list that wanders too far from your original purpose for it.

- **Mailing lists die.** If list traffic declines to the point where maintaining a discussion proves difficult, then kill the list (after warning the list readers, of course).

Implementing a simple list server

One of the reasons the Internet has grown so fast is that it allows so many different types of communication, from sending and receiving e-mail to creating a Web page. But you still have a "buy versus rent" decision when it comes to running a list server — should you install and run the list server software yourself (buy), or have someone else do it for you (rent)? Here's how the two choices shape up when implementing a mailing list:

- **Renting.** Contact your Internet Service Provider or a third party and ask them to host your mailing list. Many ISPs, developers of list server software, and mail list hosting companies provide this service for as little as $5 to $10 a month. Good starting points for finding hosting services are a search on the words "mailing list" in an Internet search engine or reading the `comp.mail.list-admin.software` newsgroup.

- **Buying.** Find the right list server product and install it on a PC that you can use as a list server. List server products are available for Unix, Windows NT, Windows 95, and Macintosh. Don't forget to factor in the hours you spend installing, figuring out how to use, and running the server.

Another way to think through the "buy versus rent" decision: If your company already maintains its own mail server, then buying makes a lot of sense. If your company already has its domain hosted on an ISP, and uses a dial-up service to get access to it, then having the ISP host the list ("renting") makes more sense.

Unix is no fun. There, we've said it. But many of the most popular, and most powerful, list server packages are available only for Unix, or reserve their most advanced features for their Unix version. Because of this — and the

unexpected challenges involved in setting up any Internet server product —
we strongly suggest letting someone else host your mailing list. Then you
can focus on providing the best content.

Probably the best-known list server product is L-Soft International LISTSERV
(www.lsoft.com), available for VM, VMS, Unix, Windows NT, and Windows 95.
Its major competitors, CREN ListProc (www.cren.net) and Great Circle
Associates Majordomo (www.greatcircle.com), are currently available
only for Unix. A growing number of strictly Windows and Macintosh list
server products are available, but tend to lack the features and automation
of their Unix brethren. Still, for low-traffic or strictly broadcast lists, they
may be an option.

List servers like — and many expect — you to install them on a computer
with a dedicated connection to an Internet mail server. You can install list
server software on a PC that you regularly use to dial in to your ISP, but you
can easily wind up with long mail download times as your list server software transfers waiting messages to and from the mail server.

Whether you host your list server yourself or have someone else do it, it
helps to know in advance the steps involved in configuring a list server.
L-Soft has helpfully released its LISTSERV for Windows 95 product as
shareware; you can find it on the *Marketing Online For Dummies* CD-ROM.
Check out Appendix A for installation instructions.

To set up a simple mailing list with LISTSERV for Windows 95:

1. **Double-click the LISTSERV link on the CD-ROM.**

   The InstallShield Wizard prompts you to install the program in a new
   directory it creates, called C:\LISTSERV\.

2. **If you don't want to install the program in the default directory, click
   Browse and choose another directory.**

3. **When prompted to create the directory, click OK.**

   You're asked to approve creating the Program icon LISTSERV for
   Windows 95.

4. **Click OK.**

   LISTSERV is now installed. You're prompted to configure LISTSERV for
   the first time. Configuring LISTSERV includes providing the following
   information in a series of dialog boxes:

   • **The Internet host name, in the form** nt.xyz.com. This is the
     Internet address of your mail server.

   • **A host name alias, if you have one.**

- **The From: name you want to appear on outgoing mail server messages.** The best choice for this field is either the name you want to give your list, for example, `widgetlist@domainname.com`.

- **A password to protect creation of new mailing lists.** This password keeps other people familiar with using LISTSERV from tampering with your mailing lists.

- **The Internet e-mail address of the person in charge of the list server.**

- **The name of the machine through which Internet mail is delivered.**

- **Whether you want to configure a Web interface to the list archives, and where required files can be found and stored.** Creating such an archive is a good idea — doing so allows you to easily post past discussions from your mailing list to your marketing Web site.

As soon as you enter this information, configuration is complete.

5. Double-click the LISTSERV (Main Program) icon to run LISTSERV.

Starting a list in LISTSERV requires using a text editor like Windows Notepad to make a *List Header.* The List Header has a specific format and standard keywords to which you assign values, which are settings to tell LISTSERV if the list is open, if it sends confirmation messages to subscribers, if it is moderated or not, if it is *announce only,* (this is the term LISTSERV uses to mean *broadcast list,* as we describe in the section "Determining which type of list to start"), and so on. (The details of the various keywords and possible values for the List Header are described in great detail in the LISTSERV Help file included with the program.) The list header is then sent by e-mail to your list server, and you are now the proud owner of a new LISTSERV mailing list.

List management is then done through a text-based, command line interface that opens up in Windows, as shown in Figure 9-5.

Powerful? You bet. Ugly? Better people than ourselves have been known to flee screaming. At least, we expect they have.

Now that you have a taste of what's involved in installing and maintaining a list server, call that mailing list hosting service! Other list server programs may be simpler than LISTSERV, but the learning curve for any such program is still akin to picking up a second language.

Figure 9-5:
LISTSERV:
The good,
the
powerful
and the
ugly.

Promoting Your Mailing List

As soon as your mailing list is up, market it widely to help it get up and
running. (Too many mailing lists die for lack of participation when a little
promotion would have helped build them into a valuable resource.)

Online marketing approaches to consider:

✔ **On your Web site.** Make signing up for your mailing list easy. Include a
link to an online sign-up area, as shown in Figure 9-6. If you don't have
an online form for signing up, include a list description on your site
with the list administrative e-mail address and detailed subscription
instructions.

✔ **In newsgroups.** Post brief announcements about your mailing list in
appropriate industry or interest newsgroups, and in the newsgroup
news.lists.misc (see Chapter 10).

✔ **In mailing list directories.** Submit your list to the America Online
Internet Mailing List Directory (ifrit.web.aol.com/mld/production/),
Liszt (www.liszt.com), Publicly Accessible Mailing Lists (www.neosoft.
com/internet/paml/), and the NEW-LIST mailing list through its Web
site (listserv.nodak.edu/archives/new-list.html).

✔ **In your signature file.** Include the administrative e-mail address for
your mailing list in your signature file, with a comment such as, "E-mail
listserver@host.domain to find out about our newsletter."

✔ **In your mailing list.** For a broadcast list, encourage subscribers to
forward the messages to friends or colleagues they believe would be
interested. Include subscribe and unsubscribe information at the end of
every mailing.

✔ **On other mailing lists.** If related industry or interest mailing lists exist,
politely send them a brief announcement of your new list.

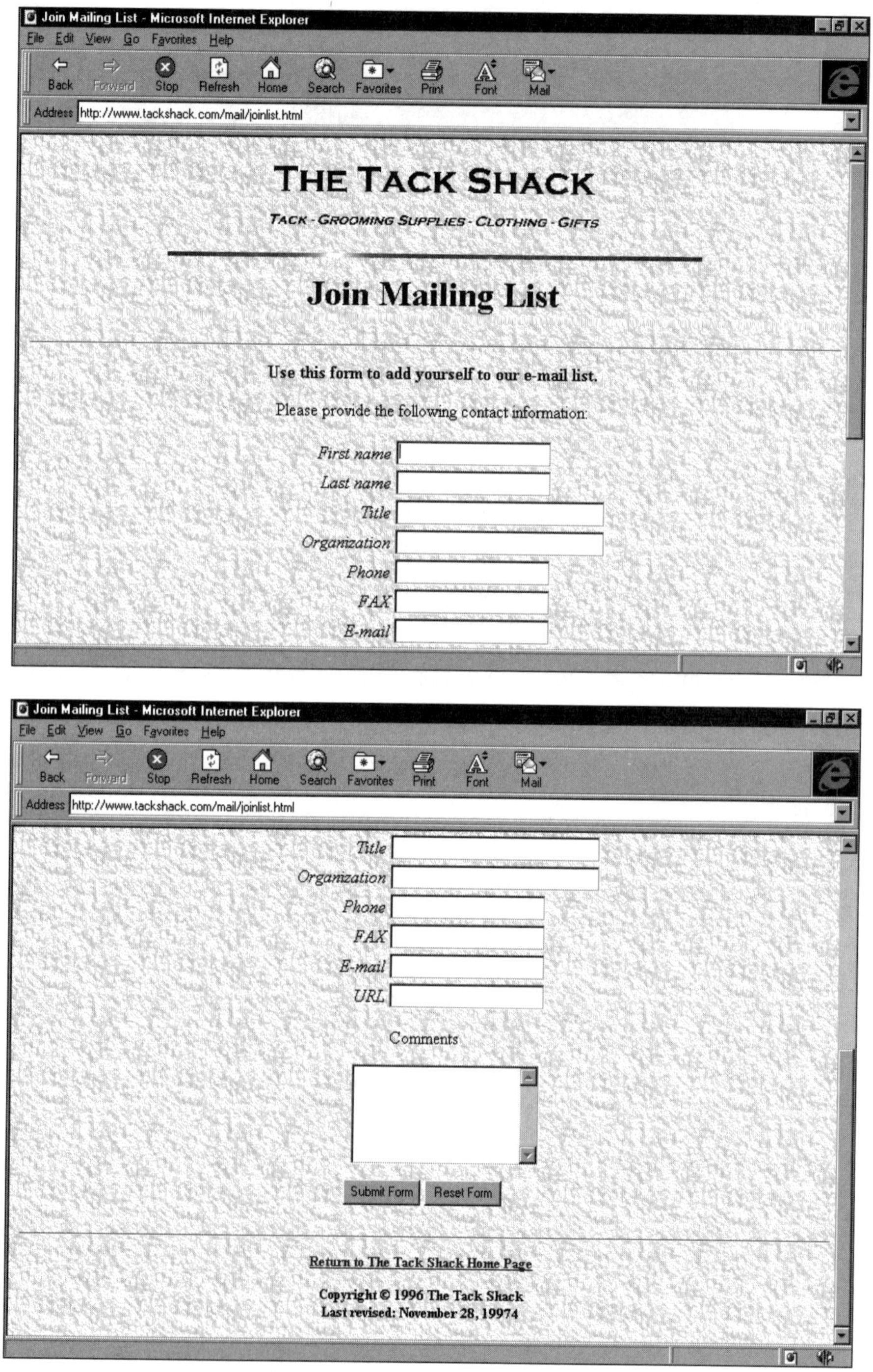

Figure 9-6:
The Tack
Shack
Web site
mailing list
subscription
area.

Tread lightly when promoting your list on someone else's mailing list. The best plan is to first send a private e-mail to the list administrator or moderator asking whether they'd mind such a post before you do it — it is, after all, their list. Treat them as you want people who post to your list to treat you.

As for your offline marketing effort, make sure that you mention your mailing list in brochures, direct mail pieces, and the appropriate ads. When done correctly, an Internet mailing list not only keeps your customer in touch with you, but keeps you in touch with them — even when they don't regularly visit your Web site.

Chapter 10

Marketing with Newsgroups and Online Forums

- -

In This Chapter

▶ Setting up newsreader software

▶ Finding and mining newsgroups for their hidden gems of information

▶ Marketing in newsgroups

▶ Marketing in online service forums

- -

*I*f e-mail is like a private conversation and Internet mailing lists resemble kaffeeklatches, *Usenet newsgroups* are akin to open discussions in the town square. Like any open discussion, Usenet newsgroups have their own tone, regular participants, and unwritten rules of polite conduct.

Newsgroups are similar to mailing lists in that they are formed around common interests, but are different in that, for the most part, they are relatively well organized, are accessible to anyone without special permission, and can be searched. Think of them as public bulletin boards instead of private chain letters. To participate in newsgroups, you use *newsreader* software either on its own or as part of a Web browser.

The power and peril of newsgroups is in their public nature:

▸ **You can't afford to ignore them.** Newsgroups can spread news, good or bad, very fast. In 1994, a posting on the newsgroup `comp.sys.intel` identified a flaw in the floating point unit of the Pentium chip. Intel publicly ignored the problem for weeks, allowing speculation — and anti-Intel sentiment — to ramp up in newsgroups. It eventually spilled over into the mass media, and Intel was forced to offer to exchange the Pentium chips — all thanks to initial newsgroup messages.

▸ **You can't afford to irritate them.** Newsgroups are by far the touchiest online communities when it comes to unsolicited advertising messages, and it's a touchiness earned the hard way. In 1994, the law firm of

> Canter & Siegel posted a message advertising Green Card services for immigrants on thousands of newsgroups that had nothing to do with immigration — and the firm's principals immediately became the poster children for *spam*. Ever since, newsgroups have been hyper-sensitive to inappropriate commercial messages.

Newsgroups also have a close cousin on the commercial online services: forums. Like newsgroups, *online forums* are open discussions of specific areas of interest. Online forums are a strong part of services such as America Online and CompuServe, and give them much of their value and a strong sense of community.

Newsgroups and online forums are many-to-many communications media: Many people can contribute messages, and many can see the messages. Newsgroups and online forums can cause serious headaches, too, if you don't know how to properly use these very public arenas for marketing.

Understanding Usenet Newsgroups

Newsgroups are more properly called *Usenet newsgroups* because Usenet is where newsgroups reside. Usenet itself is short for *user net*work. It started in 1979 as an electronic bulletin board for exchanging public messages between two North Carolina universities. Usenet newsgroups are generally easily accessible by anyone with Internet access.

Each Usenet newsgroup is an ongoing and changing collection of messages, also called *articles* or *postings,* about a particular topic as defined by the founders and sometimes moderators of the newsgroup. More than 15,000 Usenet newsgroups have been formed as part of this volunteer-run, spread-out electronic bulletin board system featuring discussions ranging from favorite actors to flawed microprocessors. Each has its own character — and, not surprisingly, characters.

News over the "back fence"

The name *newsgroup* is in some ways misleading. Although frequently very valuable and sometimes newsworthy information is posted to a newsgroup, the Usenet definition of news isn't the same as the mass media definition — which, from the point of view of one of the authors who's a former reporter, may not be a bad thing.

More typically, the news you find on a newsgroup is of the conversation-over-the-backyard-fence variety between neighbors, back in the days when neighbors actually conversed over back fences. Both have scandalous gossip, strong opinions, helpful tips, and an occasional piece of real "news." These elements of newsgroup discussions can be useful to marketers who are trying to gauge perceptions about their product or industry.

Organized side-to-side and top-down

Newsgroups are carried on *news servers,* which are computers that are maintained by Internet Service Providers, educational institutions, businesses, or other parties that want to be a part of Usenet. When a message is posted to a newsgroup, it first goes to the news server that the sender is connected to. From there, the message is fed to other news servers that carry the newsgroup, which in turn distribute it to still more news servers that carry the newsgroup, as shown in Figure 10-1. The process can take days, which can be aggravating to a marketer trying to follow a discussion — especially when, occasionally, a *response* to a message shows up on a local news server before the initial message does.

Newsgroups are organized in a hierarchical structure that looks impenetrable at first, but it makes logical sense once you get used to it — and makes it significantly easier to figure out where discussions about your product or industry may be taking place.

Figure 10-1:
Newsgroup posts spread from news server to news server.

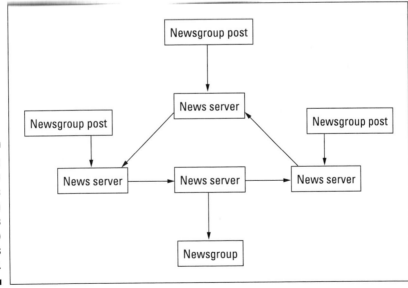

Here are the eight mainstream hierarchies:

- ✔ comp: computer topics
- ✔ humanities: fine arts and the humanities
- ✔ news: issues relating to Usenet newsgroups
- ✔ rec: recreational activities and hobbies
- ✔ sci: science
- ✔ soc: social issues and culture
- ✔ talk: debate of unresolved issues
- ✔ misc: topics that don't fall into the other seven

The alt, or alternative, hierarchy is not considered one of the Big Eight, but in alt newsgroups you find some of the, shall we say, most *creative* and *free-flowing* discussions, including alt.backrubs, alt.revenge, and alt.barney.dinosaur.die.die.die. The alt hierarchy also includes most of the adult content on Usenet. A number of other hierarchies exist, some of which are widespread, others of which are limited to specific news servers or geographic areas. For example, a Seattleite can check out the seattle hierarchy, and many computer companies maintain technical support newsgroups only on their news servers.

The mainstream hierarchies are usually the ones you can count on to be carried in their entirety on every news server. Finding some alt newsgroups and newsgroups in other hierarchies can be more hit-and-miss, depending on what types of groups a news server administrator wants to carry, and how much news server storage space is available.

After you get the hierarchies down, you can easily see how related newsgroups start with the same abbreviated set of letters, and each distinct subtopic is separated by a period. (That period, by the way, is lovingly referred to as a *dot* by newsgroup users, so when you hear someone say, "alt dot barney dot dinosaur dot die dot die dot die," they're talking about the newsgroup devoted to the friendly purple dinosaur.)

Cat lovers (or pet food marketers) who start with the rec newsgroups find that they need to look within the rec hierarchy for rec.pets, and then further into rec.pets.cats where they see a number of cat-related newsgroups such as rec.pets.cats.anecdotes and rec.pets.cats.health+behav, but thankfully no rec.pets.cats.die.die.die. Other newsgroups are structured in the same way.

Why not just a mailing list?

Newsgroups and Internet mailing lists (see Chapter 9) have much in common. People with specific interests contribute text messages and participate in moderated and unmoderated discussions.

Yet there are several important distinctions:

✔ **Newsgroups are sought out, not delivered.** Internet mailing list messages show up automatically in e-mail boxes. You need to have newsreader software to use newsgroups, and you need to actively seek out a newsgroup to find and read it.

✔ **Newsgroups are *threaded*.** Newsreader software can organize messages in a kind of outline format so you only read the specific message exchanges on certain topics, or *threads,* that interest you. A mailing list discussion is linear; that is, you get all the messages in the sequence they're sent, whether you care about all the message topics or not.

✔ **Newsgroups don't require a participant to formally sign up.** Unlike mailing lists, which require a special "subscribe" e-mail to start participating (see Chapter 9), all you need to take part in a newsgroup is newsreader software.

Because of the similarities between them, you can find some Internet mailing lists duplicated as Usenet newsgroups. You can either subscribe to the mailing list or participate in the newsgroup. If timeliness is important to you, the identical mailing list is the better choice because of the time lag involved in newsgroup messages traveling from news server to news server, as described earlier in this section. If timeliness is less critical, you may prefer the organized, threaded format of the equivalent newsgroups to the strict time-received ordering of mailing list messages.

Few of the hierarchies are inherently better than others for use as a marketing resource or tool — you're just as likely to find, for example, a discussion about a specific industry or product in the alt as in the misc or one of the other Big Eight hierarchies, or a particular, useful discussion may be limited to a local newsgroup. In any case, knowing how newsgroups are organized helps you track related discussions.

Setting Up a Newsreader

Before you can take part in newsgroups, you need to set up the newsreader software that lets you find, read, and post newsgroup messages.

Although a number of advanced, standalone newsreaders are available for both Windows and Macintosh, both Netscape Communicator 4.0 and Microsoft Internet Explorer 4.0 include basic, and basically good, newsreader software. You can start with the Collabra software included as part of Communicator, or with the Outlook Express software included with Internet Explorer. Also, popular freeware or shareware newsreader choices include Free Agent by Forte (for Windows) and Yet Another NewsWatcher by Brian Clark (for Macintosh).

If you later decide you need more advanced features — such as filtering out duplicate messages that are posted to more than one newsgroup, automatically monitoring newsgroups at predetermined intervals, or searching among a group of messages by keyword — you can easily switch to another newsreader. Discussions of newsreaders are in the newsgroup news.software.readers.

To set up any newsreader software, you first need to get the name of a news server from your Internet Service Provider. A news server address is usually something like news.host.domain — for instance, if you are a CompuServe user, the news server is named news.compuserve.com.

Then, you do roughly the following no matter which newsreader software you choose:

1. **Launch the newsreader software.**

2. **Indicate the news server name in your newsreader software's preferences.**

3. **Connect to your Internet Service Provider to download all the newsgroup names from the news server.**

4. **Subscribe to the newsgroups that interest you in the newsreader software itself.**

Figure 10-2 displays how the Outlook Express component of Microsoft Internet Explorer handles newsgroup subscriptions.

Newsgroups and Internet mailing lists share the same terminology when you sign up for one or the other — you *subscribe.* A newsgroup subscription is little more than selecting the name of the newsgroup in your newsreader software. You don't get a confirmation e-mail or a welcome message as you often do when you subscribed to a mailing list. You just see a list of newsgroup postings you can choose to read or ignore.

You identify your news server only once, and you subscribe to each newsgroup that interests you only once. After the initial setup, you simply launch the newsreader and scan the latest posts in your subscribed newsgroups. You can work with individual newsgroup messages much as you would e-mail messages, including replying and forwarding.

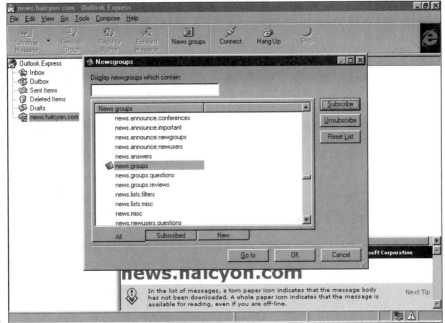

Figure 10-2:
Subscribing
to a
newsgroup
in Microsoft
Internet
Explorer.

A good way to familiarize yourself with newsgroups is to first subscribe to the newsgroup alt.barney.dinosaur.die.die.die (assuming that your news server carries it). It's typical of the odd humor, conspiracy theories, and flames found in many Usenet newsgroups. If you enjoy alt.barney.dinosaur.die.die.die — and the authors do, even though the one with a younger child *likes* The Purple One — you'll like newsgroups.

Other newsgroups can help you familiarize yourself with newsgroups in general: news.newusers.questions, for asking questions about how to use newsgroups, news.announce.newusers, for Frequently Asked Questions documents aimed at new users, and news.answers, for FAQs on a wide variety of newsgroups.

For more information on newsgroups, check out *The Internet For Dummies,* 4th Edition, by John Levine, Carol Baroudi, and Margaret Levine Young from IDG Books Worldwide, Inc.

Participating In and Mining Newsgroups

Even more so than e-mail or Internet mailing lists, newsgroups require a light — even feather-like — marketing touch. Newsgroups are informational marketing to the nth degree — no hype, no sales pitches, and definitely no spamming, unless you enjoy walking around with a target on your virtual back.

Conversely, you can get a lot of information out of newsgroups by reading them as a resource for what others are saying about your company and your competitors.

Searching for newsgroups

Before diving in as a newsgroup participant, get your feet wet to see if your company — or your competitors — is the subject of any newsgroup chatter. If this brings to mind the horrifying possibility of having to peruse every one of the hundreds of messages in each of the thousands of newsgroups on a news server, don't worry: That's why you use Deja News and multipurpose search engines like AltaVista and Hotbot.

- ✔ **Deja News** (www.dejanews.com) bills itself as the "worldwide leader for Internet-based discussion forums," and the reason is pretty clear. Since its founding in 1995, it has grown to the point where today, it gets millions of visitors each month, all searching the contents of Usenet newsgroups.

- ✔ **AltaVista** (www.altavista.digital.com) **and Hotbot** (www.hotbot.com) are general-purpose search engines as we describe in Chapter 2, but they allow choosing either a Web or Usenet search — a useful option. You can also find this option on other popular search engines.

We recommend that you start your searches with Deja News because of its completeness and focus on newsgroups. In fact, several of the other Web search engines rely on Deja News to provide their newsgroup search capabilities, so you may as well go right to the source.

Even if you don't use newsreader software, Deja News allows you to post a new newsgroup message directly from the Deja News site — a handy, and time-saving, shortcut.

Here's how to start your search:

1. **Go to Deja News by launching your Web browser and typing** `www.dejanews.com` **in the Address (Microsoft Internet Explorer) or Netsite (Netscape Communicator) field.**

   The home page for Deja News appears.

2. **In the Find field for a Quick Search, type the keywords or phrase for which you want to search. (If you are searching for a proper name or phrase — like a product or company name — surround it with quotes.)**

3. **Click on Find.**

   A list of specific newsgroup messages that match your search appears on a Web page.

4. **Scan the list of message names and the newsgroups from which they come for any messages that interest you. Click on the message name to read the message.**

   The message appears; an example is shown in Figure 10-3.

5. **Click on View Thread to read the entire newsgroup discussion that led to, or was spawned by, the specific message.**

Figure 10-3: Reading a newsgroup posting on Deja News.

6. **If you are reading a message and you want to find out how prolific the author of the message is — for example, if the person has expressed a strong opinion or an interesting insight about your company or a competitor — click on Author Profile.**

Deja News checks its message database to find any other messages posted from the same e-mail address and provides a summary. Click on the newsgroup name under the author's name to read the individual messages.

You can try variations on this theme: Enter the name of the industry you're in or search the "old" Deja News database instead of the "current" one for messages from more than a few months back — it often provides good historical perspective for discussions and opinions that permeate the current newsgroup database.

You frequently get newsgroup message search matches that have nothing to do with your company, competitors, or industry, but you have the ability to narrow your search with the Power Search or Search Filter options on the left of the Deja News pages.

When you find a newsgroup that shows up repeatedly in your Deja News searches for your company or competitors, make a note of its name. Then the next time you launch your newsreader, subscribe to that group and use it as an ongoing source of information.

Choosing the right newsgroup

Wanting to participate is one thing; knowing *where* to participate is a wholly different consideration. After all, more than 15,000 newsgroups exist, covering every subject from gardening (`rec.gardens`) to game shows (`alt.tv.game-shows`).

A few suggestions on where to start:

- **Ask a coworker or colleague.** Business associates who are already on the Internet may already participate in newsgroups that would be of interest.

- **Ask customers.** In routine contacts with customers — especially those by e-mail — inquire if there are any newsgroups in which your company should participate.

- **Search Deja News.** As we cover in the previous section, searching Deja News for your company, competitors, products, or industry can provide pointers to newsgroups of interest.

✔ **Browse Deja News.** Like Yahoo! does for Web sites, as explained in Chapter 2, Deja News organizes newsgroups by category, such as business, cars, computers, health, hobbies, jobs, politics, sports, and travel. Click on a category to drill down to more detail appropriate to your business.

✔ **Search your newsreader listings.** The newsreaders that come with both Netscape Communicator and Microsoft Internet Explorer let you search for words in the name of the newsgroup. Doing this occasionally may help you find a worthwhile topic. In other cases, the name of a newsgroup may not indicate all the topics it covers (or may even be actively misleading).

✔ **Read** news.announce.newgroups. Announcements of new newsgroups are regularly posted in this newsgroup.

You can add any appropriate newsgroups to your list of subscribed groups in whatever newsreader you use.

Monitoring newsgroups

What, exactly, should you look for when monitoring newsgroups through Deja News or another newsgroup search engine?

✔ **Frequency.** How often are you, or your direct competitors, mentioned in the newsgroups? If competitors are far more prevalent, your company or product may not be as visible online as you think. If none of you are mentioned, you have an opportunity to be first.

✔ **Recency.** How recently have you or your direct competitors been mentioned? A dramatic change over time may signal trouble or a company on the rise — or fall.

✔ **Tone.** Are posts about your company pleasant or hostile? If you encounter a lot newsgroup hostility — especially from customers who are unhappy with your customer service — you may be getting a wake-up call for immediate action. Take special note if someone comes to your defense — or if others join in to help make your firm an online piñata.

✔ **Content.** Do specific topics dominate conversation about your company? The topics of conversation may reflect an area in which your company excels or lags. You get extra points if newsgroups reflect your offline (print, radio, or other marketing channel) marketing messages without your prompting.

✔ **Influencers.** Do any newsgroup message authors routinely write about your company or products? If the posts are positive, the author may be an influencer to carefully cultivate. If posts are negative, you may want to have an honest, private e-mail discussion with the author about the gripes.

The Pentium lesson

Hostility in newsgroups is ignored at your own peril — especially if the hostility has any factual merit. Intel found this out the hard way by not actively monitoring, and promptly responding to, newsgroup discussions.

In 1994, a mathematician discovered that some of his calculations were off and finally narrowed down the cause of the errors to what he believed was a flaw in the first Pentium chip that affected math functions. His findings were posted in messages on a CompuServe forum and in the Usenet newsgroup comp.sys.intel.

Intel did nothing publicly while other newsgroup participants weighed in on comp.sys.intel with their own confirmations of the Pentium flaw. Within days, the controversy spilled into other newsgroups. Yet it took several weeks for Intel president

Andrew Grove to post a message on comp.sys.intel acknowledging that there was a problem. His message did little to encourage participants about a fix. Continued outrage on comp.sys.intel, amplified by other newsgroups and finally in the mass media, forced Intel to offer an exchange program for anyone with the early, flawed version of the Pentium processor.

Intel has learned from this very expensive lesson, both in terms of goodwill and hard costs. When a bug in the Pentium II and Pentium Pro processors was reported on comp.sys.intel in 1997, Intel representatives were quick to respond to concerns posted in the newsgroup. What could have been a major public relations disaster — again — was skillfully and quickly averted. Talk about an early miscalculation.

Make checking Deja News or other newsgroup search engines for mentions of your company and products a monthly routine. Even if you're already regularly reading some newsgroups, your company may suddenly become a hot — even flaming — topic in a newsgroup that you don't monitor. Monitoring what's being said about your company online is a prerequisite to effective marketing online.

Benefits of participating in newsgroups

Given that newsgroups can be very touchy, as evidenced by the Green Card spam we mention at the beginning of this chapter, it may be easy to convince yourself that your company's best strategy is just to sit on the sidelines and watch what's being said, perhaps only stepping in when things get a little out of hand. (This attitude is something like Bill Cosby's classic approach to child rearing: Parents don't want justice, they just want quiet.)

Such a defensive strategy may be comforting or, in some cases, appropriate, but if you follow it, you miss out on the benefits of being proactive in newsgroups:

✔ **Being seen as an expert.** Being helpful on a newsgroup that appeals to your peers, business partners, or customers positions you as an expert in your business area. In addition, being an expert on a newsgroup is a lot less expensive and time-consuming than being an expert in person — traveling to speaking engagements or writing articles for industry magazines — and it makes a very public impact among those you wish to influence who are on the Internet. (Not that you shouldn't still give speeches and write articles.)

✔ **Getting the word out.** Remember the kids' game *Telephone* where you sit in a circle with other kids, quickly whispering the same phrase to each other around the circle until you get to the person who started the phrase and find that the original message is completely garbled? The same holds true for your marketing messages: The farther removed the recipient is from the information source (you), the more likely your corporate actions are subject to being misinterpreted or misunderstood. You can avoid having this happen in newsgroups by making sure that your company's messages come from someone at your company in customer service, marketing, technical support, or another appropriate department. And should you find erroneous statements about your company posted on a newsgroup, quickly identify yourself as an employee of your company and post the truth of the situation so the false impressions can be stopped in their tracks.

✔ **Becoming known for responsiveness.** An active company voice in newsgroups implies that your company is approachable and actually wants to get feedback. Quick response provides a human touch to your online presence, even if it comes, ironically, through a remote, text-only medium.

On top of all this, newsgroups share the Internet mailing list benefits of being highly targeted, free, and a home to online communities, as we discuss in Chapter 9. Newsgroups are also remarkably widely read. The search site Deja News estimates that as of 1997, 24 million people worldwide read the Usenet newsgroups.

Conversely, newsgroups can cause great damage to your company or product reputations if you don't see or respond to negative messages:

✔ **The appearance of flames.** Some of the questions, complaints, and statements directed toward your company and products in newsgroups can be sarcastic, mean-spirited, and cruel. Others — perhaps the worst ones — can be calm, dispassionate, painstakingly researched, and overwhelmingly negative. If not responded to rapidly and respectfully, these well-researched critiques can turn into flames spread by other participants — and grow into a fire.

- ✔ **The persistence of venom.** Some newsgroups maintain their own archives, and many are routinely archived in databases such as Deja News. Anything that has been written about your company — or that you've written in response — lives on in archives long after the controversy dies down.

- ✔ **The "urban legend" effect.** Rumor and misinformation can spread as easily as factual information and take on a life of its own on the Internet as the topic leaps, like a wildfire, from newsgroup to newsgroup. Examples include the long-lived "Good Times Virus" hoax, or the many variations on the "dying boy needs cash/greeting cards/and so on" message.

The fact that your presence can help avoid these problems is an excellent reason to participate in newsgroups — and to be careful about how you participate.

Marketing to Newsgroups

The right way to market to newsgroups recalls the old instructions on porcupine mating habits.

> **Q:** How do you market to newsgroups?

> **A:** Very carefully.

Each newsgroup is a community with its own unique culture, tone, history, and citizens. Violating that culture can make your company as popular among newsgroup participants as a bartender at a temperance rally.

Handle newsgroup marketing with an even softer pair of kid gloves than you use with e-mail or Internet mailing lists. Newsgroup marketing is informational marketing with a vengeance. If a golden rule for newsgroup marketing exists, it's "Help, don't sell." For tips on helping, see Chapter 9.

Everything that applies to e-mail and Internet mailing lists applies to newsgroups: Keep it short, don't type in ALL CAPS, create an effective signature, don't spam, lurk first, stay on topic, don't respond in public every time, be helpful, and be positive. Because of the very public nature of newsgroups, this kind of Scouting Code for Internet participation may apply even more strongly in newsgroups than in private e-mail messages, described in Chapter 8, and automated mailing lists, described in Chapter 9.

Consider these variations on, and additions to, the above themes unique to newsgroups:

✔ **Read the FAQ.** Newsgroups don't have welcome messages like Internet mailing lists to outline tone, topic, and rules. However, they do have Frequently Asked Questions (FAQ) documents that are usually posted regularly. Look for one the first time you scan a newsgroup's messages. A searchable repository of FAQs is on the World Wide Web at `www.faqs.org/faqs/`, as shown in Figure 10-4. FAQs are also found in the newsgroup `news.answers`. And check out the posts in `news.announce.newusers` for useful basic guidelines on newsgroup *netiquette,* how and when to post, and much more.

✔ **Read, then post.** Posting to a newsgroup without first getting a feel for appropriate message tone can be like wearing shorts to a church in North Dakota in the middle of winter. Newsgroup tone varies widely with newsgroup topic — the tone, and what's embarrassing to mention, differs between `alt.sex`, `misc.forsale`, and `sci.physics` newsgroups. And not every newsgroup is in English. Usenet is a worldwide phenomenon. Spend some time reading message threads before contributing your own messages.

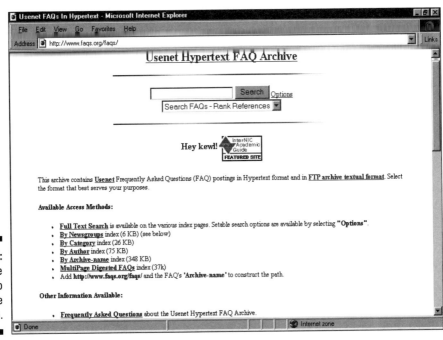

Figure 10-4:
The
newsgroup
FAQ archive
on the Web.

✔ **Craft a clear subject line.** Unlike e-mail and Internet mailing lists, message threading means that the only part of your message a newsgroup reader may ever see is the subject line — a reader has to be motivated to click on the message title to view the entire message. Make the subject line count, without crossing the line into spam-like hype. In an automotive newsgroup, rather than "About cars" when posting a tip, try "Clearly diagnosing carburetor problems." In a book newsgroup, instead of "New release," write "New release by Robert Heinlein." Some newsgroups also use a specific format for the subject line; for example, game newsgroups may include the name of the specific game in all subject lines. Follow the tradition. The more compelling your subject line, the more likely it clicks — and is clicked on.

✔ **Avoid cross-posting.** Cross-posting is the practice of posting the same message to more than one newsgroup. Not only does this confuse participants as to where they should send their responses without duplicating a lot of messages, but cross-posting is a favorite tactic of spammers — not the kind of folks you want to be associated with.

✔ **Don't even think of spamming.** If spamming — posting of identical commercial messages — is bad manners in e-mail and an ejectable offense in Internet mailing lists, it can lead to the equivalent of capital punishment in newsgroups. Imagine your e-mail account — and Internet Service Provider — being overloaded and shut down by *mailbombs,* rapid-fire return junk mail that sends thousands of messages in quick succession until the receiving server chokes. Imagine *cancelbots,* automatic programs that erase messages, unleashed to seek out every newsgroup posting you've ever made and eliminate it. Imagine the *Usenet Death Penalty,* complete banishment from Usenet newsgroups, happening to your Internet Service Provider because of your indiscretion. These things have all happened because of spam, and the Usenet Death Penalty was even applied for a brief time to CompuServe and UUNet, two of the largest Internet Service Providers, because of spams sent out by their subscribers. The bottom line: Just *don't* do it.

Now that you're ready to swear off salty luncheon meat forever — and newsgroups along with it — remember that newsgroups have power because of their reach and easy accessibility to Internet users. If you keep your postings on-topic, helpful, hype-free, and appropriate, you can go a long way to increasing awareness of, and good feelings toward, your company.

Creating your own newsgroup

You've got a newsreader. You've got a topic. Why not start your own Usenet newsgroup? As tempting as it sounds, it's not a trivial task.

Complete details on what it takes to create a Usenet newsgroup are in FAQs posted in the newsgroups `news.announce.newgroups` or `news.groups` for the mainstream hierarchies, and `alt.config` for the alt groups. But suffice it to say, creating a new newsgroup requires that you first come up with a newsgroup idea that doesn't duplicate an existing group, then submit a proposal, and then wait three to five weeks for the results of a public vote. The alt, or alternative, newsgroups require no vote, but a proposal is highly recommended to encourage news server administrators to look favorably upon your group so they'll carry it; then again, the reality is alt newsgroups aren't as widely carried as the mainstream hierarchies.

You also need to sweet-talk a current Usenet site into getting the group going. Or, you need to have a computer to use as a news server with enough storage space to hold a whole bunch of other newsgroups. One FAQ suggests a serious Usenet server requires a Unix system with at least 64MB RAM and 8GB of hard disk storage. Oh, and don't forget to track down an existing Usenet site to feed your news server news postings.

If your discussion doesn't have to be distributed throughout Usenet, one alternative is to create a private newsgroup on your news server, as many software companies have done. But that requires a fair amount of technical knowledge, a computer to use as a news server, and news server software.

A better idea: If you want the control and focus that running a finely crafted newsgroup implies, but don't want to go through the difficulties of creating one, read Chapter 9 and consider starting a mailing list instead.

Marketing to Online Service Forums

After you've gotten your feet wet with Usenet newsgroups, consider an important variation on the discussion group theme embodied by newsgroups: forums on commercial online services, also known as online forums, *message boards, bulletin boards, roundtables* or *Special Interest Groups* (SIGs).

Like Usenet newsgroups, online forums are industry- or interest-specific discussions. Unlike newsgroups, they're run from the top-down: The commercial online service sets the rules for forum discussions, and the forum *moderators,* people who actually monitor the forum, strictly enforce them.

Online forums are only open to paying members of online services. Despite the millions of members that services like America Online and CompuServe attract, they are only a subset of the tens of millions of people on the

Internet. Plus, all the major commercial online services make Internet content available to their subscribers, extending the reach of your existing Web site, Internet mailing list, or newsgroup efforts. So if your marketing resources are limited, starting with — and emphasizing — Usenet newsgroups over online service forums can allow for getting to the broadest possible audience.

Pros and cons of online service marketing

Online service marketing isn't for every business. But marketing on the major, and possibly on the minor, commercial services has its benefits:

- ✔ **Eyeballs.** America Online has more than 10 million members; CompuServe, more than five million. That's a lot of people concentrated in one place, funneled through a single service — rather than being dispersed over the entire Internet and its many entry points. And these services can promote certain online forums to their members to drive traffic to the forums and related features, using a level of promotion not easily reached on the Web.

- ✔ **Community.** Online forums, and the regulars who participate, are the greatest asset of many services. CompuServe is by far and away the leader in forums: A number of CompuServe's more than 1,000 forums have been around for at least a decade, and their leaders are influencers in their areas of expertise.

- ✔ **Focus.** Online services each have a slightly different personality. America Online is aimed more at home users and offers breadth of information. CompuServe is aimed more at professional and business users and offers depth of information. Quite a few smaller, even more focused, proprietary services exist as well. In all cases, online services may make targeting specific customer segments easier than is possible with Usenet newsgroups.

Marketing on online services has a number of drawbacks as well:

- ✔ **Reach.** Commercial online services, even combining them all, don't equal the total number of people with access to the Internet and Internet services, such as the World Wide Web and e-mail. At best, they're a subset of the Internet, and most, if not all, online service members can get to Internet resources through gateways provided by their online services.

- ✔ **Cost.** Expect to pay monthly fees ranging from $20 to $25 for each commercial online service to which you subscribe, in addition to whatever monthly fees you already pay your Internet Service Provider.

✔ **Fortunes.** A hot online service may not be hot forever. At one time, Prodigy was seen as a leading commercial online service, but it has since faded. The Microsoft Network, too, has gone through several gyrations affecting its emphasis and content. CompuServe was recently bought by America Online and its future as a separate entity is uncertain. If you tie your business too closely to a single commercial online service, and the service begins to sink, your marketing efforts may go along with it.

The best approach to online forums may be the simplest: Use the skills you've already gained in newsgroups and consider commercial online services a supplement to, not a replacement for, Usenet newsgroup marketing.

Choosing the right online service for your marketing effort

The most cost-effective marketing vehicles on the commercial online services are the online forums, the online service equivalent of newsgroups. And the two most prominent commercial online services are America Online and CompuServe. To find out where you should start on either service, you can begin on the World Wide Web:

✔ **AOL.** The America Online Web site at www.aol.com contains descriptions of AOL *channels*, shown in Figure 10-5 — essentially topic areas such as news, sports, entertainment, families, health, personal finance, computing, and so on. Within many of the AOL channels are forums, and the AOL Web site briefly describes some of them.

✔ **CompuServe.** The CompuServe Web site at world.compuserve.com features a searchable Forum Directory, listing all of the thousand-plus CompuServe forums and providing a detailed description of each.

If either America Online or CompuServe looks promising, both routinely have free trial offers that waive the first month's subscription fee so that you can sign up and explore the service further with little risk. Find the offers on the America Online and CompuServe Web sites.

As soon as you're on a commercial online service's forums, do the smart thing — re-read the earlier parts of this chapter for Usenet newsgroups and apply the same marketing techniques: Lurk first, be helpful, craft a clear subject line, don't cross-post, don't spam. Commercial online services may have different communities than Usenet, but they're communities nonetheless.

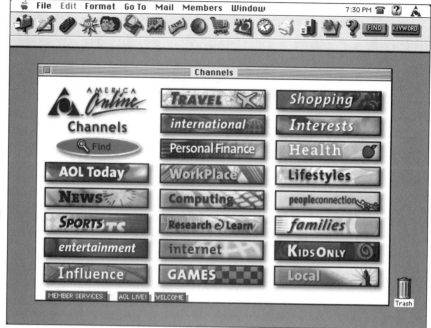

Figure 10-5:
America Online is organized into channels.

Other marketing with commercial online services

We can hear you thinking: If America Online and CompuServe attract all those eyeballs, certainly you can do other kinds of marketing with them. You can — but be ready to open your wallet.

Companies with the reputation and resources used to be able to establish their own online areas as *content providers* — and even share in the hourly fee revenue that such a forum generated for the service. But now that flat-fee memberships to the online services have largely supplanted hourly charges, the trend is going the other way.

AOL and other services have started to levy fees from some forum organizers for having a forum on the service. The logic apparently is that because the services control so many eyeballs, the resulting exposure for the company should be considered a marketing cost.

At the very least, you'll be quizzed as to how your forum proposal will generate revenue and how you'll market the new online area to draw customers to the service.

More information about being a content provider for America Online is found on AOL itself using the keyword "Information Provider." CompuServe has content provider information on its Web site.

More traditional advertising and sponsorships are also available. AOL, for example, offers ad banners, chat room ads, event sponsorships, branded or themed areas, or online store space. Ad banners start at $1,000 per week; sponsorships, at $50,000; custom areas, at $300,000.

Upon reflection, forget opening your wallet. Open your bank.

Chapter 11

The Future of Business Online

In This Chapter
▶ Mixing and matching your online efforts
▶ Growing with the Internet in the U.S.
▶ Growing with the Internet abroad
▶ Driving business online

*I*n writing this book, we've made every effort to explain how to work both the main thoroughfares and some of the more important secondary roads of the online world. The road system is not yet complete and is filled with potholes, but the growth of the online world is a great challenge and opportunity for every organization. How well you cope with and take advantage of the changes it brings does much to determine the future of your business.

We hope that this book is helping you establish a competent presence in the online world and that we've helped you not only to do it well, but also to have fun in doing so. If you're enjoying yourself, you do your best work, and you can find an awful lot in the online world that's new, exciting, and fun.

Now is the time to sum up what you can expect from your initial online efforts and, if we may reuse a metaphor, look down the road a bit. We can tell you what we expect to happen in the future — although our efforts here are only informed speculation — and help you tie that future to the best interests of your business. The heavy lifting in deciding what you should do in the future is, of course, left to you.

Mixing and Matching Your Online Efforts

In building up your online presence, you can mix and match different online technologies in ways that best suit the needs of your business. Following are some of the strengths of the online technologies that we discuss in this book:

✔ **World Wide Web.** For most businesses, the company Web site is the umbrella for your online presence, as we describe in Chapter 4. Few businesses can go without at least a simple Web presence site to establish credibility. As your online efforts grow to encompass use of multiple technologies, your Web site should serve as an up-to-date central point of access to all your online marketing vehicles. Marketing should take the lead in developing and expanding a company's Web site, as we describe in Chapters 5 through 7.

✔ **E-mail.** The text-based underpinnings of the Internet are best represented by e-mail. E-mail remains the easiest to use, most flexible, and most widely used online technology. You and others in your company are going to use e-mail whether anyone tells you to or not; the trick is to improve your use of e-mail so that it helps you and your company better meet your marketing goals, as we describe in Chapter 8.

✔ **Internet mailing lists, or *listservs*.** Internet mailing lists, often called *listservs* in reference to L-Soft International, Inc. LISTSERV, the most popular application for creating them, help you control the flow of e-mail for broadcasting information as well as interactive discussions. Through the use of *digest mode,* you can better manage the constant trickle of e-mail from a mailing list. A digest combines dozens or even hundreds of messages into one file that's easy for you to scan quickly or read in depth as needed. As we describe in detail in Chapter 9, Internet mailing lists offer many opportunities for marketing, though often a low-key approach is best for taking advantage of them.

✔ **Newsgroups.** Newsgroups, the grand old man of the online world, are getting a bit cranky as the years go by, but Usenet newsgroup discussions are still an important area in which to be active — because if they aren't helping you, they may be hurting you. Get involved with newsgroups, as we describe in Chapter 10, so that you harness the energy and activity in them to your advantage.

✔ **Online services.** In some cases, you may find that most of the people you're targeting with a product are on one specific online service; the AutoCAD drafting software package, for example, has long had much of its official and unofficial product support delivered via CompuServe, so that's a good place to look for AutoCAD users. But for most products, you should market on the Internet services that we list in the preceding bullets first, and on online service forums and other areas second. Online service forums work much like newsgroups only they are limited to the members of the particular online service; you can also market through expensive special content areas and advertising arrangements, as we describe in Chapter 10.

For your business, using some online technologies and not others may make sense. The needs of sole proprietors vary widely. Some sole proprietors, including many of those who work under their own name and who have little trouble finding clients, may have a minimal Web site, or none at all, but nevertheless use e-mail to do business, and actively participate in newsgroups to stay informed and to convey an impression of expertise to others. On the other hand, a sole proprietor who uses a business name, hires others to help as needed, and is often looking for new clients may benefit from a basic Web presence as an umbrella for a larger overall online presence.

A small business operating locally may have a Web site presence to establish credibility with customers and local press. Some small businesses may start by mining a pocket of potential customers on an online service and then grow from there. A larger business that operates at a national level in the United States or a small business that operates largely or primarily on the Internet may use all the available online technologies.

Review your current online presence one online technology at a time. First, give attention to those areas where you're already active. Ask yourself how you can improve your presence with a moderate effort. You may have content within your company — for example, advertising, public-relations, and sales-support materials — that isn't on your Web site yet. Adding these materials to your Web site is likely to require a moderate effort, yet one that yields great benefits by making the materials available to people who may never have found you anywhere else.

Or say that you've already put all the materials that make sense onto your Web site. Now's the time to start two efforts: In the short term, analyze hits on your Web site to see which areas people use most. Reorganize your Web site to make those areas more easily accessible. For the long term, start developing new content that not only adds interest to your Web site, but that's useful in the offline world as well.

After your Web site's on the way to being an active marketing asset for your company, examine how you use other online technologies. Automated mailing lists, although text-heavy and a fair amount of work to maintain, are wonderful tools for keeping core users updated and for building a sense of community around your company and products. Also look at new and emerging technologies, such as push technology, to find ways that you can inexpensively extend your online presence more deeply into your customers' online lives. And integrate all these technologies into your Web site, the hub for your online marketing vehicles.

Ford versus GM online

One of the oldest and fiercest competitive battles in American business is that fought between Ford and General Motors. Ford took the early lead in Web marketing with a series of online forms that enable users to pick and choose options and, in effect, assemble a desired car online. The buying process still needs to be completed at a dealer, but the user can learn a lot about the desired car and its available options before ever talking to a salesperson. (One of the authors leased a Ford Windstar after using this service to check out and price different combinations of options.)

Recently GM has matched this capability on the Web and also made the same capability available through a toll-free 800 number. The marketing program, called *GM BuyPower,* uses a barrage of radio ads — some aimed at online users, some at people who fear or simply don't use the Internet. By combining a phone presence, accessible to more than 90 percent of people, with an online presence, accessible to a much smaller audience that includes many desirable customers, GM gets the best of both worlds. (At this writing, however, the company hasn't completely closed the loop. The home page of the GM Web site hasn't yet been updated during the campaign to reflect the GM BuyPower tagline. The figure shows the otherwise excellent GM home page.)

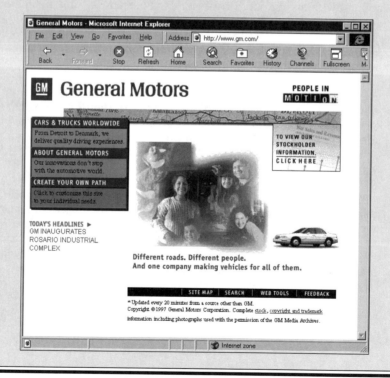

The areas of the online world that you most enjoy using and the type of work that you find the most fun are likely to be the areas where you do your best work. Map out the overall strategy for your online presence and then divide the work up with others so that everyone involved is working with a technology and type of content that they enjoy. Not only does the work seem easier, but the quality of work and interactions that you do online benefit as well.

Growing with the Internet

Guesstimating the growth of the Internet is a growth industry in its own right. In the near term, the experts expect Internet growth to be very rapid, with the most significant growth in the United States. Overseas growth should follow, probably exploding on the sharpest part of its upward curve in a few years, about the time growth begins to level off in the U.S.

Growing with the U.S. online boom

According to the market research firm Intelliquest (www.intelliquest.com), 56 million U.S. adults — about 27 percent of the U.S. population older than 16 — were online as of late 1997. Intelliquest also projected that the U.S. online population was expected to double between early 1996 and late 1998 — a period of two and a half years, representing very rapid growth. Not only were people getting online quickly, but the average amount of time they were spending online was growing to about 10 hours a week, making the Internet a big part of user lives. This information is very promising for marketing efforts that depend on getting a piece of users' online time.

However — also according to Intelliquest — not all is well in cyberspace. More than 10 million people are estimated to have been online and then discontinued Internet use. Although some people reported changed circumstances as the reason for no longer being online, such as leaving school or changing jobs; others reported lack of interest or usefulness. Figure 11-1 shows the Intelliquest estimates and projections of U.S. Internet use through the end of 1997.

By about 2001, the Internet will have gone from nearly nowhere to a major U.S. mass medium in nearly a decade, an amazing and exciting change for Americans in general and for marketing professionals in particular.

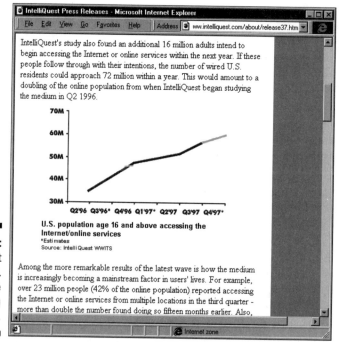

Figure 11-1:
Intelliquest
sees U.S.
Internet use
growing
steadily.

However, the current and short-term future rapid growth is based on the fact that tens of millions of existing computer users have already joined, and continue to join the online world. When these users upgrade to a new computer, they are likely to find that it already has a built-in modem and online service software and a browser already installed on the hard drive. Such users just have to go through a simple signup process and be willing and able to pay the $20 a month or so for all the Internet time they want; other users get hooked up at work by their employers with no effort on their part at all. After most existing U.S. computer users get online, the number of online users will likely grow more slowly because additional new online users must then come largely from among the non-computer-using public who must buy a computer for the first time. Because these new users must first buy, and then get comfortable with computer technology before even considering going online, they are less likely to contribute to the kind of growth the Internet experienced, and in part, continues to experience, with the early influx of established computer users.

The 10 million people who are already *former* Internet users also represent a problem for future growth. We doubt that you'd find nearly as many former TV, radio, or telephone users in the early days of those media. The fact that so many people who've used the Internet find themselves willing and able to live without it is another indication that the Internet use is likely to grow in fits and starts.

From a marketer's point of view, the Internet is certain to become a huge, rich, and impossible-to-ignore market. (We understand that *you* aren't ignoring the Internet even now, but your colleagues who currently have their heads in the sand will be forced to pull them out and take a look around.) By the year 2001, the Internet may well serve about half the U.S. adult population — and the better-educated and better-off half at that. Relatively few companies with more than a few employees can survive at that point without a significant online presence. Online marketing is sure to become a major part of any marketer's skill set and a full-time job for many; expect integrating online and offline efforts to become the biggest single test of skill for marketing.

The growth of the Internet in the U.S. may not all be good news, however. Online pornography, gambling, and privacy are already major online concerns that tie into broader social issues. Concern about social justice may also increase as the Internet continues to disproportionately include those with higher incomes, men, and whites, leaving out large numbers of lower-income people, women, and minorities. (Women, for example, tend to have lower incomes than men.) These issues may cause some degree of backlash against the Internet that would reduce its attractiveness to marketers, and make some companies want to dissociate themselves with the online world. On a more positive note, this trend may (we hope) inspire a wider effort to broaden access.

Efforts to increase accessibility may become more urgent, with assistance from the government and possibly even legal requirements placed on Internet-related companies to broaden access. (Remember that a big reason the telephone company was, for so long, allowed to be a monopoly — and that the U.S. Postal Service still is — was to guarantee access to all.) Increasing access to those who'd otherwise be frozen out is one way in which some companies will "do well by doing good."

Waiting for the boom's echo overseas

According to the WWW User Surveys from the Georgia Institute of Technology's Graphics, Visualization and Usability Center, which we refer to liberally in Chapter 1, about 80 percent of respondents were from the U.S., with almost 10 percent more from Canada and Mexico, for a total of nearly 90 percent of frequent Internet users from North America. Though this result may have been influenced by the survey not appearing in all languages and in all the "hangouts" popular with non-English-speaking Web users, it meshes well with other surveys and our own experience of the online world. Leaving specific percentages aside, the real question is: When can you expect non-U.S. Internet use to take off?

Though Internet use outside the U.S. is generally expected to grow rapidly, it will be a few years before Internet use in many other countries is on par with the current U.S level of 20 percent of all adult consumers. Many of the most desirable consumers from other countries are, in fact, already online: young people who are either well-off, or in college and presumably about to become well-off, and having at least a passing knowledge of English (which online content providers depend on to avoid translation complications and expenses). But to expect most foreign markets to catch up with the U.S. in Internet penetration and usage anytime soon is a mistake. The growth of Internet usage in other countries faces many barriers, including the following:

✔ **Low use of English.** Most Internet content is in English, and you find a classic chicken-and-egg problem here: The majority of content providers don't translate to other languages until many non-English speakers come online, and non-English speakers see little reason to come online until they can find content in their own languages. (Some content providers have already started translating their online information, as you can see in Figure 11-2.) The fact that some of the most desirable consumers in each country speak at least some English further postpones the need for content providers to translate their content. (Newsgroups, as we describe in Chapter 10, are different because *users* are the content providers! Many Usenet newsgroups, therefore, are conducted in other languages.)

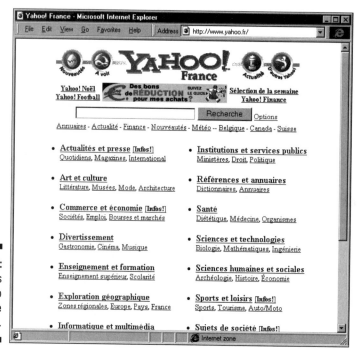

Figure 11-2:
Yahoo! is
ready to
serve the
French.

✔ **Poor telecommunications infrastructure.** Many countries have poor telephone service, and almost no other country has the cable-television infrastructure of the U.S. Computer hardware and software are almost nowhere as cheap as in the U.S., and many consumers in the world simply can't afford the high local cost of computer and telecommunications goods. Expect the barriers to entry for Internet access in these countries continue to remain high until advanced technologies such as wireless transmission become cheap enough to be broadly affordable.

✔ **Low PC penetration.** Internet use grows fastest if millions of PCs are in homes and offices, needing little more than a wire to get online. Yet few countries have the degree of PC penetration of the U.S. Even Japan, one of the major PC sales markets outside the U.S., has relatively few PCs in the workplace — and they're split among different platforms to a greater degree than in the U.S. In addition to Japan, other healthy PC markets include Canada, Germany, France, the United Kingdom, so these countries may be among the markets to most closely follow the U.S. online.

✔ **Legal barriers.** As complex as the legal situation for online content providers in the U.S. has been, featuring proposals such as the Clipper Chip for government-mediated privacy and the Telecommunications Decency Act, now struck down, the legal situation in many other countries is even more complicated. Laws are sometimes vague or subject to rapid change, and penalties can seem draconian. Germany has been notable for its strict laws against certain kinds of speech, and France discourages the use of any language but French. For some countries, developing clear, understandable policies and precedents that content providers can rely when publishing local content may take years.

✔ **Lack of money.** The U.S. economy, starting from a strong base, has grown more rapidly than many other countries for years, making it an even richer target for marketers. Other countries generally have either many fewer consumers or less disposable income per consumer.

These problems don't mean that the Internet isn't going to grow rapidly overseas; it is, and the near-Internet-mania seen in countries such as Japan is sure to be duplicated elsewhere. But the base of users is currently so small that years of rapid growth rates is going to be needed before a significant percentage of the population is online. You can expect the U.S. to lead in every stage of Internet development, from novelty to business necessity to mass medium. Expect other countries to be one or two stages behind the U.S. in Internet development; as the Internet reaches mass-medium status in the U.S. at the turn of the century, for example, it's still going to be a novelty in most countries and a business necessity in others but not a true mass medium anywhere but the U.S.

If you use the Internet in your overseas marketing efforts, you need to realize that it has high visibility and cachet but low penetration. Universities, government offices, computer professionals, and the military are the markets that you can reach over the Internet in almost any country. However, in operating outside North America or outside the English-speaking elite in other countries, don't count on reaching people other than computer professionals, much less large numbers of other mid- to high-income consumers, in the current millennium.

Hoping to buy bandwidth

Many computer prognosticators gaze into their crystal balls and predict fast Internet access for tens of millions of people two to three years out. (Fast Internet access has been two to three years out for five or seven years now.) However, there is finally good reason to hope that faster Internet access will occur. The first step is for the 56 Kbps standard for modem communications, currently split into the *56K* and *K56flex* camps, to be unified into a single standard. As soon as the standard is unified, more people will buy these modems, which over time will cause a near-doubling of the speed with which most people access the Internet.

Even better news, however, is in the offing. Leading PC companies Compaq, Intel, and Microsoft are joining with leading phone companies to develop standards for DSL (Direct Subscriber Line) technology, which can access the Internet more than 10 times faster than current modems at a price that should eventually drop to near modem levels — $100-$200 per machine. This effort offers real hope for everyone who's wanted to access the Internet faster, and for everyone who's wanted to put multimedia on their Web site.

Even with DSL on the way, it will be a few years before many people have it. For now, don't plan on greatly increasing your use of bandwidth-hogging multimedia Web sites or live video in the expectation that quality is going to come anywhere close to even black-and-white television in the near future. (Online multimedia works now only because so few people use it; if online multimedia usage were to spike upward anytime soon, the Internet would choke on all the chunks of data.) Plan conservatively regarding your expectations of future Internet bandwidth and expect the Internet to remain a mostly text and graphics medium for the next few years.

Driving Business Online

Because profitability is growing in importance as the single biggest measure of business success, the most important tools for improving the success of a business are those that help increase revenues or decrease expenses (and thus create more profit). Most online marketing activities are, at least initially, expenses that don't contribute measurably to sales. And in the long term, marketing activities that don't contribute directly to sales are bound to be kept to a small part of your overall company budget.

Yet the demands that your company have a strong and robust presence on the Internet are certain to grow rapidly with time; a few years from now, if you're not a player online, you will risk not being a player anywhere. The only way to meet these demands and be a strong player in cyberspace as well as in the offline world is to start planning now to use your online presence to drive measurable company sales.

You can use your online presence to drive sales in several ways. These efforts may not even pay their own way initially, but investing in and growing them so that you're ready to take advantage of the growth of online commerce is vital. Among the ways you can use your online presence to drive sales are the following:

- **Measuring impressions.** Survey your customers to see which of your marketing efforts they're aware of. Use focus groups or even random one-on-one phone calls to get people's impression of the quality of your online presence. Compare the awareness and effect of your online presence to the awareness of other marketing efforts your company makes. Establish as best you can the degree to which your online presence contributes to awareness — the first step in the sales process — and to other parts of the sales effort.

- **Online lead generation.** Use your online presence to find potential customers. Create an e-mail address where those interested in your products can contact you and publicize it on your Web site, in your automated mailing lists, in your e-mail and newsgroup signature, and in your other online efforts. Carefully track sales activity through this point of contact. (Chapter 8 can help you manage the flow of e-mail into your company.) Then steadily increase your efforts to generate contacts, follow up on them, and close sales through this e-mail address.

✔ **Online sales.** Online sales are the wave of the future, and for some companies, the wave of the present. Start creating your online sales strategy now; see *Selling Online For Dummies,* by Leslie Lundquist (IDG Books Worldwide). Carefully consider and plan how to solve possible problems such as conflicts with your existing channels of distribution. We explain the Web part of this strategy in Chapter 6, but you must develop an online sales strategy that encompasses the specifics of your own online presence.

✔ **Create a new business or division and new products for your online effort.** To fully take advantage of the online opportunity, you may need to repackage your current products and services for better online sales and distribution — or even create entirely new ones. You may want to go to the extent of creating a separate online business. (Make sure that you research a good domain name for this business, as we describe in Chapter 4.) Consider sharing some assets with your current business but running an entirely separate profit and loss statement (P&L) for accountability. Although this course requires a lot of work, you should start brainstorming the idea now; if you don't, your competitors are likely to beat you to it.

Doing business online is still tricky because of the long-entrenched habits of Internet users still accustomed to the old, noncommercial days of the Internet. Although most users accept that more and more Web sites have online sales areas, overt efforts to increase sales through other parts of your online presence, such as with bulk e-mail (or *spam,* as we describe in Chapter 8) or overtly commercial newsgroup postings (see Chapter 10), can get a rough reception. Use the tips and hints in this book to ensure that your efforts to increase business online don't alienate the existing online community.

As you generate first sales leads — and then sales — online, you're better able to calculate a true return on investment (ROI) for your online efforts. Try to separate out pure marketing expenses, such as those for providing company information online, from truly sales-related efforts online; this process helps you better understand both the size of your marketing expenses and the return for the purely sales-related expenses you have.

Part IV
The Marketing Online For Dummies Internet Directory

The 5th Wave   By Rich Tennant

"Games are an important part of my Web site. They cause eye strain."

In this part . . .

Where better to find out more information about online marketing than online? This directory, with its funky yellow pages, gives you a long list of online resources to use for your online marketing effort. We include Web sites, newsgroups, mailing lists — all with a description of what you can expect to find at each address.

The Marketing Online For Dummies Internet Directory

Everyone surfs aimlessly on the Web at one time or another. Sometimes you follow a link just because it's there beckoning. Other times, you begin your search for information, promising yourself not to get side-tracked, but then a few pages down the road, you find yourself in a maze. In this section of the book — set off with the nifty yellow pages — we've put together a collection of sites to help you stay on track and find the information you need.

For each entry you may find one or more mini icons — micons — which provide a quick graphical reference to the site's characteristics. Here is a list of the micons and what each one means.

Chat: Chat rooms are featured on the site.

$ Fee required: This site charges an access fee for some or all services.

Message Board: Interactive bulletin boards are featured on the site.

Sign In: You're required to register here. This usually means no more than providing your name, address, and e-mail address for demographic purposes.

Shopping: The site features online shopping opportunities.

Sound: Site features sound files.

Download: Software is available for downloading at this site.

At the end of each category of sites, we include a section titled "Other Stuff to Check Out." In these sections, you can find lists of URLs for additional sites that contain information related to the particular category.

Advertising

Each day, you are likely bombarded with over a hundred different ad messages some on the Web, some from television, on the sides of buses, billboards, and so on. Some are subtle, and others aren't. Yet like it or not, no business can survive unless it gets its message across to consumers. You have to do it too, so here are a few sites to help you get your message to your potential consumers.

Advertising Media Internet Center

www.amic.com

A look into the world of advertising: This site is for anyone interested in the field of advertising media. The time may come when you consider contracting an agency to handle the advertising campaign for your Web site. This site gives you information on the rates and trends for ad services. The Ad Talk section contains a list of forums and mailing lists dedicated to a variety of marketing- and advertising-related issues. In addition, an on-site Media Guru is ready to answer your media questions.

Advertising on the Web

www.ypn.com/topics/1194.html

List of online advertising agencies: Advertising on the Web is much like conventional advertising: Its main purpose is to attract potential customers. Opening up shop on the Web doesn't guarantee that customers will beat a path to your door. A poorly-designed site coupled with no efforts to target the right customers is akin to not having a store at all. If your personal efforts in advertising have met with little success and you have funds to spend on an advertising campaign, you may want to stop by this site for a list of professional online advertising agencies.

LinkExchange

www.linkexchange.com

Display your company ad banner on Web sites: Maybe your company has one of those ad banners that blink and slide across the top and bottom of your Web page. It's probably very cool, with funky animation, too. But the only people who get to see it are those who stop by your company site, correct? So how do you use it to draw in all those people who have no clue that your oh-so-beautiful site exists? You advertise on LinkExchange. LinkExchange has more than 100,000 members and is the largest advertising network on the Internet. It's like a banner-swapping site, through which your banner is randomly displayed on others' Web sites, and other people's banners are displayed on yours. For every two banners that you display on your Web site, you can display one of your own elsewhere on the Web. LinkExchange is a great way to get exposure and to advertise to people who otherwise wouldn't hear about your company.

Submit It

www.submitit.com

Register your Web site with multiple search engines: You want to give your Web site as much exposure as you possibly can. To do so, you must register your site by sending your company Web site address (URL) to as many search engines as possible. You *could* register your site individually with each of these search engines — a painstaking, though acceptable procedure — or you can do all this registering at the Submit It site in one shot. The site lets you register with 20 search engines for free. You can even selectively register with search engines that may be specific to your product, market, or industry. And if that's not enough, the folks at Submit It offer a variety of fee-based services to promote your Web site.

Other Stuff to Check Out

www.ourbroker.com/media/start.htm
www.commercepark.com/AAAA/

As with everything else, you can either put together a business plan yourself, or pay someone to do it for you. You can hire someone to write those business letters, or you can download them right off the Web. If you're the do-it-yourself kinda person, these are the sites you want to check out.

GreenBook Directory and the Focus Group Directory

www.greenbook.org/green.htm

Online directories of market research firms: The GreenBook and the Focus Group Directory are two distinct research-related directories on one Web site.

GreenBook is an international directory of market-research companies and services. You can use this online version to look up companies and services according to multiple criteria, such as name, market specialties, industry specialties, research services offered, trademarked products and services, computer programs, and geographic location.

The Focus Group Directory, as its name suggests, is a geographical listing of companies that offer focus group facilities and recruiting, moderating, and transcription services.

Office of Minority Enterprise Development

www.sba.gov/MED/

For minority business owners: The federal government gives extensive assistance to businesses owned and operated by minority individuals. This site has information on every aspect of this assistance, including the application process and business-plan requirements. If you're eligible, you may want to cruise on over to claim a slice from this piece of the federal pie. Incidentally, the site carries an explanation of how you can determine whether you are qualified to receive federal assistance.

Service Corps of Retired Executives

www.score.org/

Get counseling via e-mail, and SCORE addresses: The Service Corps of Retired Executives (SCORE) is an organization of retired professionals who volunteer their time in helping small businesses develop into successful companies. SCORE provides extensive expertise and valuable advice. And best of all, this service is free. Why hire a consultant who bills you by the hour when you can have someone who's "been there, done that" at some of the world's most prestigious companies — IBM, Kodak, General Electric — and can tell you how it's done, for free? The SCORE Web site is a wonderful collection of resources. Find a SCORE chapter in your town (see the listing at the site) and make the most of its services.

Seven Myths of Internet Marketing

www.smartbiz.com/sbs/arts/bre2.htm

Useful marketing advice given in a concise manner: This site is a must-read for anyone thinking about starting an online business. It's a frank description of what you can expect from marketing on the Internet. It'll take you no more than five minutes to read, but they'll be the best five minutes you spend when planning your online-marketing strategy. For example, Myth three states, "You can't advertise on the Internet." The author describes why this isn't necessarily the case, and how instead you ought to look at the issue of getting your message across.

Small Business Administration

www.sba.gov

Business plans, software, counseling, and various services for the small business: The United States government created the Small Business Administration (SBA) to assist entrepreneurs in forming successful businesses. You can find out about a variety of SBA programs geared toward getting your business started, like getting loans and keeping your business afloat, using various government-funded organizations like Small Business Development Centers and the Service Corps of Retired Executives (SCORE). You can download software at this site, and also a sample business plan to guide your business. You can even list yourself as a business in the nationwide business card directory, categorized by state. You can also get the addresses of local SBA offices and information on how to get assistance if and when disaster strikes.

Other Stuff to Check Out

www.lowe.org
www.isquare.com

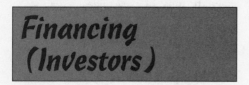

Unless you have a rich uncle who'll gladly lend you the money you need for your business, you'll have to look to banks and venture capitalists for it like the rest of us. The sites in this section provide advice, information, and resources for getting, managing, and investing your finances.

FinanceHub

www.financehub.com

Venture capital, legal, banks, and stock markets discussed here: Don't let the name of this site fool you into thinking that all you'll see here is financial information. It has lots more than that. You can find more than 100 links for venture-capital sources. And get this: The site claims that you will find at least four sources of funds from the venture-capital database. The site has a list of banks sorted into five categories, information sources for entrepreneurs, and even something for those of you wanting to do business overseas.

Money

www.money.com

Helpful resources in making financial decisions: One of the best features of this site is the 150-piece toolbox. It contains worksheets to help you track everything you ever do with your money, from planning for college, to deciding on the size of your mortgage. Additionally, you'll find helpful articles on issues such as investing strategies, limiting your tax liability, and planning your family's finances. You'll also find stock and SEC filing information on companies. Lastly, here's where you'll find the largest collection of bulletin boards — 248 topics — devoted to the discussion of money.

MoneyHunter

www.moneyhunter.com

Find a match for your venture capital needs: Need some money? Who doesn't? If you're looking for someone to fund your business, here's one place you may want to look. No, you won't find a pot of gold, but you'll certainly get some help and advice on where you can go to find a few extra bucks. These folks also produce the Money Hunt Show on PBS. The sole purpose of this Web site is to help entrepreneurs find money to turn their ideas and visions into reality. The Golden Rolodex search feature matches you with investors, based on criteria that you specify when performing the search. You may indicate the amount of money you're looking for, the kind of financing you're looking for, and the market you're in. Conversely, if you have money to spare, MoneyHunter is a good place to find a waiting entrepreneur.

Quicken Financial Network

www.quicken.com

Get financial help, chat online, and post on bulletin boards: This site, by the makers of the best-selling personal finance software, Quicken, is a warehouse of financial information and advice. It includes pages and pages of information on issues such as taxes, investments, borrowing, saving, spending, mortgages, refinancing, stock quotes, a tax tip of the day, and how you can get started on

planning for retirement. You can also create model investment portfolios. The site also hosts online chats with authors and financial advisors. And if you can't make it to the chats, you can always air your views on the many bulletin boards on the site. Finally, the site also maintains a support area providing help with Quicken products.

Venture Capital Sources

www.datamerge.com

Business plans, venture capital sources, advice from venture capitalists, and downloadable finance software: DataMerge Corporation provides a valuable service to all businesses looking for venture capital. The Venture Capitalist Database is a list of sources willing to fund a business. Additionally, you can find information on how to get financing, which kind of financing is right for you, and what you should do to spruce up your loan request to impress lenders.

Other Stuff to Check Out

www.onlineinvestores.com
www.zdii.com
www.bloomberg.com
www.moneynet.com

Government and Law

Many U.S. government departments have Web sites, which are much more convenient to visit than going to a government office in person or trying to get through on the phone. Check out the following low-hassle government resources.

Consumer Information Center

www.pueblo.gsa.gov

Free advice from the Federal Government on health, career, food, travel, hobbies, and more: Remember that ad you used to see on TV telling you about free information from the U.S. government? It ended with the address of the place from which you could request free publications. You never wrote the address down because you thought you'd easily remember it. But two commercials later, it vanished from your memory bank. Well, that place now has a home on the Web, with a variety of information, ranging from auctions for seized property to consumer-related information. Complete text of the publications are posted on the site so you can download or print them and read them at your leisure.

Court TV Legal Help

www.courttv.com/legalhelp/business/

Legal help on a variety of subjects: Don't let the name fool you. The name may sound corny, but the information on the Web site is anything but. The few links that this site offers are extremely useful. For example, the Forms and Model Documents link gets you to an archive of documents for a variety of business transactions and Internet commerce. You can download them and then edit them to suit your specific needs. You can also find helpful hints for dealing with lawyers, a legal research service, and information on intellectual property.

Federal Trade Commission

www.ftc.gov

Describes regulations and issues dealing with trade and business practices: The Federal Trade Commission is responsible for enforcing consumer-protection laws. Head straight for the Consumer Protection and Business Guidance sections, where you can find valuable information on various aspects of running a business, particularly with respect to compliance to federal trade laws, such as the Fair Credit Reporting Act and the labeling of products. You may be surprised at what you thought was legal but isn't. This site also includes information on subjects such as how to avoid Yellow Pages invoice scams.

FindLaw

www.findlaw.com

All your legal information needs are met here: FindLaw is one of the most comprehensive law sites on the Web. This site offers a forum to discuss your legal concerns, law reviews, links to almost every aspect of the law (Constitutional, corporate, commercial law, and contracts), state laws, a legal-news reference, legal forms and software, and mailing-list archives. If you're looking for a legal resource, you can find a link to it here.

Internal Revenue Service

www.irs.ustreas.gov

Tax forms, information for businesses, regulations and recent changes to the tax laws: The IRS has extensive information on its Web site. But don't wait until April 15 to go there — that's when the rest of the U.S. goes there, too, making response from the site fairly slow. Visit this site to find answers to almost all your tax questions, download forms, and keep up with the latest in tax laws related to your business.

International Trade Administration

www.ita.doc.gov/

Find trade statistics, export assistance, import regulations, and information on foreign trade zones: You can take advantage of the Internet's global reach to evaluate and pursue international markets for your products and services. The U.S. Department of Commerce International Trade Center provides a valuable service in this area. The Web site contains information on Export Assistance Centers in the U.S. and around the world, trade statistics, industries served by the organization, and also information on what you should take into account when considering the import of items. If you're involved in international markets, don't miss this site.

U.S. Business Advisor

www.business.gov

One-stop shop for your connection to the U.S. government: The U.S. Business Advisor is where you should go when you have questions related to federal government information, services, and transactions. It carries information on business transactions with the government, international trade, labor employment, and laws and regulations.

Other Stuff to Check Out

www.abanet.org
www.uschamber.org
www.laws.com
www.taxweb.com
www.legal.com

Investor's Resources

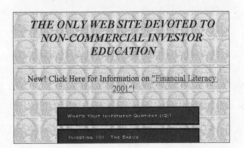

You can never educate yourself too much about investing, and these Web sites are a great educational resource.

Investor Protection Trust

www.investorprotection.org

Think of this site as Investing 101: Investor Protection Trust bills itself as the only Web site devoted to noncommercial investor education. Commercial or not, it's a site filled with information you rarely see elsewhere, like how to pick your stockbroker and how to resolve conflicts and avoid scams. Find out how to protect yourself from CyberFraud, for example. A very good site, especially for anyone who knows next to nothing about investment.

National Fraud Information Center

www.fraud.org

Internet hot-line for reporting and protecting against fraud: Have you ever invested in a deal that sounded too good to be true, only to find out later that it really was — too good to be true? Avoid this situation by visiting the National Fraud Information Center Web site. The site's loaded with information on a variety of fraud — telemarketing fraud, fraud against the elderly, Internet fraud — and what you should do to report a fraud.

Other Stuff to Check Out

www.merrill-lynch.ml.com
www.motleyfool.com
www.etrade.com
www.suretrade.com

A mailing list is an online community of people sharing a common interest via e-mail, as we explain in Chapter 9. To send your message to all the subscribers on a list, you send it to a single e-mail address, which then automatically forwards your message to everybody on the list.

Because a mailing list can have thousands of subscribers, you can easily get inundated with e-mail from mailing lists during the course of a day. To prevent this from happening, you may want to have all messages on a mailing list be sent to you within a single message at the end of the day, called a *digest*. Not all mailing lists offer a digest version — if a mailing lists offers a digest version, it will say so in the introductory message you receive when you first subscribe.

Remember, some of these lists require that you send an e-mail to a particular e-mail address with the word **subscribe** in the subject line or body of your e-mail message. Lists vary — you may need to type **subscribe listname,** or you may need to type **subscribe digest** if you want the digest form. Some mailing lists require that you include **subscribe** in the Subject line, others in the body of the e-mail. Still other mailing lists have gotten a bit more slick and have you subscribe to then via a pleasant Web site interface. Each entry in this section explains how to subscribe to the particular list it describes.

AdPOWER Online

Get tips and ideas for effective ads and newsletters: AdPower Online is an online newsletter published by Drew Eric Whitman, a national advertising trainer, speaker, and consultant. The newsletter is informal but extremely informative. It is aimed at providing tips, ideas, and techniques to increase the response rate from your ads, newsletters, flyers, and whatever mode of communication you use to attract customers. Here's a tidbit from the newsletter: 60 percent of all people who read ads, read the headline and no more. To subscribe, send an e-mail to

adpower@oaknetpub.com

In the body of the message, type **subscribe**

I-Invest

Discuss investment options: Are you wondering what technology stock to buy? Do you have a question about Roth IRAs? For all these questions and more, subscribe to the I-Invest list. It's for those wishing to discuss the ups and downs, and the ins and outs of the investment business. The list is moderated by John Audette, one-time Branch Manager and Vice President with a major stock brokerage firm. You can also browse through archives of the list. To subscribe via a web based subscription form, go to:

www.audettemedia.com/I-Invest/ invest.html

I-Sales

Online sales issues, success stories, and marketing trends discussed here: CNBC described this site as one of the best e-mail discussion lists on the Internet. It focuses on issues relating to online sales. Participants include those who are involved in the online sale of products and services. Examples of topics include order forms, methods of payment for products and services, success stories, and not-so-successful stories too. The I-Sales Digest is sent to subscribers every day. The list has about 8,500 subscribers in over 70 countries. The list is available in digest form only, which means that your mailbox receives only one message a day containing all the posts for that day.

Although subscription to the list is free, a voluntary subscription of $25 gets you a weekly condensed digest in place or in addition to the daily digest. To subscribe via a Web-based subscription form, go to:

www.audettemedia.com/I-Sales/ isales.html

Market-L

Discussions on this list focus on marketing and advertising: The Market-L list is run by the Advertising Media Internet Center. The subscribers would like to portray the list as one with a laid-back atmosphere; one that is ". . . an unmoderated list populated by people whose jobs, fields of study, or hobbies are somehow related to marketing." You can expect to receive upwards of 50 messages a day. Topics may include education, politics, or religion, but with a marketing twist to them. To subscribe, send an e-mail to

listserv@amic.com

In the body of the message, type **subscribe market-l**

The mailing list also maintains a Web site at

www.amic.com.

Mktseg

Find out how to target various market segments: This list focuses on targeting advertising and marketing toward specific market segments based on ethnicity, lifestyles, and other criteria. Topics discussed on the list include advertising material, media issues, research, data base marketing, direct response, promotional issues, and educational material related to market segments. The discussion is among those whose interests lie in ethnic and lifestyle groups from a marketing point of view. What's encouraged is not just a technical discussion of marketing issues, but also one related to things that have been tried and tested. To subscribe, send an e-mail to

listserv@mail.telmar.com

In the body of the message, type **subscribe mktseg**

Other Stuff to Check Out

Asian Internet Marketing

For subscription info, send a blank e-mail to

info@aim.apic.net

Bob's Marketing Tips

To subscribe, send e-mail to

bobstips@pargroup.com

In the Subject line of the e-mail, type **subscribe.**

China Business List

To subscribe, send an e-mail to

cbiv-list-request@valueinfo.com

In the Subject line of the e-mail, type **subscribe.**

Global Interact Network Mailing List (GINLIST)

To subscribe, send an e-mail to

listserv@msu.edu

In the body of your message, type **subscribe ginlist** *your name*.

Inet-Marketing

To subscribe, send an e-mail to

inet-marketing@einet.net

In the body of the message, type **subscribe.**

Internet-Marketing

To subscribe, send an e-mail to

listserv@thevortex.com

In the body of the message, type **subscribe.**

Internet Advertising

To subscribe, send an e-mail to

i-advertising@groupserver.revnet.com

In the body of the message, type **join.**

Internet Marketing University Newsletter

To subscribe, send an e-mail to

progressive@dccserver.com

In the body of the message, type **subscribe.**

Internet Times

To subscribe, send an e-mail to

internet-times@euromktg.com

In the body of the message, type **subscribe.**

Marketing Success

To subscribe, send an e-mail to

leslie@themarketingcoach.com

In the Subject line of the e-mail, type **subscribe marketing success.**

Online Advertising Discussion List

To subscribe, send an e-mail to

majordomo@o-a.com

In the body of the message, type **subscribe online-ads.**

Proposal-L

To subscribe, send an e-mail to

majordomo@ari.net

In the body of the message, type **subscribe proposal-l**.

Acquiring demographic information has never been this painless! The Web was seemingly *made* for storing statistics that you can search and retrieve easily.

American Marketing Association

www.ama.org

$

The world's largest marketing association: The American Marketing Association bills itself as the world's largest professional society of marketers, with over

45,000 members in 92 countries. Membership benefits are many. AMA holds meetings, seminars, and workshops for members to enhance their professional development. It publishes a variety of magazines, such as *Marketing News,* which features new ideas and developments in marketing, *Marketing Management,* a quarterly magazine featuring articles about marketing strategies, and *Marketing Research,* a magazine with articles on research methods and technologies.

The Direct Marketing Association

www.the-dma.org

$

Direct marketing practices, regulations, conferences, and seminars: If you're a direct marketer, this site deals with issues that may be useful to you. The site offers guidelines on ethical business practices, online marketing privacy principles, and marketing by phone; a news and events section; and a government-affairs information section that offers information related to privacy and consumer affairs, tax issues, current initiatives in Congress that affect direct marketing, and key bills in legislatures. A conference calendar highlights upcoming conferences and seminars.

International Data Corporation

www.idc.com

D-14 Marketing

Worldwide market research information on technology issues: International Data Corporation, the world's leading provider of technology data, has operations in more than 40 countries. Its Web site won't let you down. You can find information on the European, Latin American, and Asia Pacific markets, and much of it is available for free. Although the information contained here is related to the world of technology, you can find material on marketing and strategic planning, too. A free e-mail service can even inform you of new research results. A very good site.

The Marketing Resource Center

www.marketingsource.com

One-stop shop for marketing tools, information, assistance, and associations: As its name suggests, this site is truly a resource for marketers, online or otherwise. It has a comprehensive collection of everything marketing: hundreds of articles on topics ranging from Internet and non-Internet advertising to marketing, home-based businesses, Web development, and Internet commerce. The Tools of the Trade section has a database with over 2,000 worldwide marketing associations and a software library from which you can download business-related software. You'll also find a special section about marketing on the Net, and links to government business sources. The Marketing Forum has bulletin boards on which you can share ideas and ask questions. The Eye on Business section carries a listing of business magazine and other news source Web sites. A very professional site.

User Surveys at Georgia Tech

www.cc.gatech.edu/gvu/user_surveys/

Free research results on Internet user demographics: The Graphics, Visualization, and Usability Center at Georgia Tech's College of Computing periodically conducts surveys about the Web and Web users. As a public service, the Center provides the results of this service for free. The topics that these surveys cover include general demographics, advertising, Internet use, transaction security, political opinions, purchasing behavior, data privacy, information gathering, content authoring, opinions of vendors, Webmasters, and service providers. The coolest thing about the folks who put out these results is that they don't charge a cent for them, unlike some of the other folks on the Internet.

Wilson Internet Services

www.wilsonweb.com

Message boards, online marketing newsletter, advice on Web site design, and e-commerce: This Web site, hosted by Wilson Internet Services, has useful information about marketing on the Web. Its Web Marketing Info Center has hundreds of articles covering almost all the questions you are likely to have about Web marketing. You can find information on banner-ad design, push marketing, e-mail marketing, Web-site promotion, Web-traffic analysis, international marketing, and demographics of the Web, as well as a Web-marketing checklist. The E-Commerce Research Room has a wealth of information, too. You may also subscribe, for free, to the *Web Marketing Today* online newsletter. Lastly, at the Web Marketing Forum, you can exchange ideas with other Web marketers like yourself. The Forum has within it 15 subforums, classified by subjects ranging from strategies and trends to demographics, transactions, and ad revenue. Don't miss this site.

Other Stuff to Check Out

etrg.findsvp.com
www.researchinfo.com/
www.teleport.com/~tbchad/stats1.html
www.marketingsource.com/
    marketingforum/marketingforum.shtml
www.focusgroups.com/
www.quirks.com/
www.census.gov
wdfm.com/promo/tenquest2.html
www.wolfbayne.com/library/publish.html
www.worldopinion.com/home.qry
www.marketingtools.com

The world's leading newspapers such as the *New York Times* and the *Wall Street Journal,* and magazines like *Time* and *Forbes* are now available on the Web. You don't need to go to your local library any more to get your hands on them.

Electric Library

www.elibrary.com

$ ↘ ▨

Online versions of printed media like newspapers and magazines: Electric Library is an online library of newspapers, magazines, radio and TV transcripts, and much more. Although the service isn't free, you can try it for 30 days at no cost. You do have to sign up with a credit card, though; you start getting billed after the free trial period ends. You can cancel the free trial subscription at any time if you don't like it, and not get billed.

Inc. Magazine

www.inc.com

▢ ▨ ↘

Beats the printed version of the magazine hands down. This site is the online version of the popular business magazine. You'll be pleasantly surprised if all you expect to see on the site are articles from recent issues. As a matter of fact, magazine articles form only a small amount of what's here. The Peer-to-Peer area is a great forum to share ideas, ask questions, and seek solutions to your dilemmas. It's been categorized into over a half-dozen subforums by topic, including Marketing, Technology Exchange, Networking by Industry, and Ethics. The guides to the Internet, Finance, and Biz Tech explain the fundamentals to the novice, with relevant links and information within each of them. The Virtual Consultant section has interactive worksheets to help you make important decisions about profit margins, inventory, and expenditure. The Guide to Finance section also has a software directory from which you can download software for such things as billing for time and doing a break-even analysis. The International Business section has helpful information on

D-16 Search Engines and Directories

aspects of international business that you may not have considered, like obtaining a carnet. (Don't know what a carnet is? Stop by the site to find out.) Lastly, you can also find information on expos and conferences.

NewsWorks

www.newsworks.com

Read online versions of newspapers and search through news articles for specific information. At NewsWorks, you can search through U.S. newspapers for information that your local newspaper may have missed. The search feature on this site is helpful if you're looking for information on something specific — say, a 401(k) plan — and want differing points of view. The search results pull together all related articles that appeared in the press.

Other Stuff to Check Out

www.forbes.com
www.businessweek.com
www.wsj.com
www.fortune.com

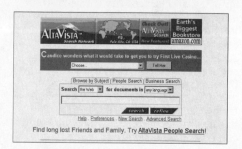

When you search the entire Web for a specific word or phrase, you often end up with hundreds, thousands, or even

millions of sites — most of which are only tangentially related to your search term. Still, with some practice and patience, you can end up with some worthwhile *hits* (successful searches).

Alta Vista

www.altavista.digital.com

Mother of all search engines: Alta Vista is probably the most widely used search engine on the Web. Its searchable index of over 200GB (gigabytes — that's a lot of bytes), on an extremely fast machine called an Alpha server, lets you find what you're looking for on the Web in less time than finding a file on your PC. To make thorough use of the search engine, spend a few minutes with Alta Vista's Help feature and learn the commands that will help you narrow down your search and zoom in on your results. Alta Vista now even offers a translation option, called *babblefish,* with which the contents of a Web site can be translated into your language of preference. It's a very impressive service.

BigYellow

www1.bigyellow.com

Yellow Pages on the Web listing millions of businesses: What you find on this site is a lot more than what you see in your local phone yellow pages directory. For one, BigYellow is a global directory of businesses, not just a local one. It includes over 16 million businesses listed in over 7,000 categories, and 50 states. In addition to business listings, you can look up the e-mail addresses of long-lost pals, their telephone numbers, and residential addresses too. Lastly, BigYellow includes a home office section containing business advice.

Lycos

www.lycos.com

Search engine and personalized e-mail addresses: There was a time when the Lycos site offered little more than a service to search the Web for information. These days it offers a lot more than that. You can sign up for a personalized e-mail address. For example, if you are a doctor, you can get an address like johndoe@doctor.com, or for cat lovers, something like jennifer@catlover.com. Lycos also includes chat rooms on the site devoted to investing, news, sports, art, and entertainment. Lastly, a menu with almost two dozen categories allows you to go directly to links and information on a specific topic.

Yahoo!

www.yahoo.com

Most widely used library of Web site listings: Two graduate students at Stanford University started cruising the Web a few years ago and maintained links on their personal Web sites of all the sites they visited. Before long, this hobby became an obsession. Their graduate studies were put on hold, they became full-time Web cruisers, and they eventually founded Yahoo! Today the Yahoo! Web site maintains one of the most comprehensive lists of sites on the Web. Sites are classified into over a dozen categories and many subcategories. The Business category currently has over 300,000 sites listed within it, split over 35 main categories.

Other Stuff to Check Out

www.excite.com
www.infoseek.com
www.bigfoot.com
www.wp.com/resch/
www.hotbot.com

Whether you're in the market for hardware, software, or just some technical advice, you can find plenty of information online.

CyberSource

www.cybersource.com

Online transaction processing service: If your online store accepts credit cards for purchases, you can concentrate on just selling your goods and let CyberSource handle the monetary transactions for you. CyberSource takes over the handling of credit card transactions so that you don't have to burden yourself with setting up the infrastructure for electronic commerce and worrying about security and other stuff that can keep you up at night.

Fairmarket

www.fairmarket.com

Online auctions of computer hardware: Fairmarket is an electronic auction house for computer hardware. All bidding is

D-18 Technical Services

done online. The auction is primarily for business buyers, so don't go there looking for a single computer or printer — you have to buy at least the minimum quantity specified by Fairmarket. A great place to get computer hardware for your staff.

First Virtual

www.fv.com

Online transaction processing service using e-mail: First Virtual is a company that can help you conduct electronic transactions over the Web. First Virtual uses e-mail as its basis for secure Visa or MasterCard transactions. A user obtains a VirtualPIN number and uses that number, rather than a credit-card number, to make purchases on your Web site. Visit the First Virtual site for details on this service.

Free Software at Freeware.Com

www.download.com

www.freeware.com

Collection of free software and shareware: Corporations think nothing of paying hundreds of dollars for software; however, regular people have to think twice about it. Before driving over to your friendly neighborhood computer retailer and donating a hundred dollars to its livelihood, drop by this site to see whether you can find something that will do what you're looking for. Most of what's on this site is *shareware,* which means that you can try it before you buy it. Shareware is much less expensive than the packaged stuff you buy in stores. In addition to shareware, the site also carries *freeware,* which is — you guessed it — free software. To find all the freeware on the site, do a search for *freeware.*

Hotmail.Com

www.hotmail.com

Get a free e-mail account and check e-mail from anywhere: When the Internet revolution took off, everybody wanted an e-mail address. So everybody got one, and then two, and then three addresses. If you're wondering why anybody would need more than one e-mail address, you probably haven't been hit with junk e-mail yet. Yes, junk e-mail — the kind that fills up your mailbox faster than you can empty it. What you want to do is have one e-mail address for official business and another one for random, potentially frivolous e-mail (because you never know when you might find something useful in all that junk mail). The former you guard carefully, and the latter you hand out freely. Although your ISP probably gives you only one e-mail address for your account, you can get another free e-mail account from Hotmail. And one of the greatest things about this e-mail account at Hotmail is that you can check e-mail from any computer, anywhere, that has access to the Web. You don't need special software for HotMail, like what your ISP gives you. Oh, and here's a little tidbit: Bill Gates also must have thought that Hotmail was a cool service — he bought the company.

HyperMart

www.hypermart.net

Free space for hosting a business Web site: Most hosting services charge about

$20 a month or more, depending on the type of services to which you subscribe. Before you shell out the money, visit the folks at HyperMart. These good people host Web sites for free. Uh-huh, that's right — for free. And they don't give you a measly 2MB of disk space for your site; they give you a full 10MB, which is more than you'll need. You just can't afford to miss this site.

Microsoft Corporation

www.microsoft.com
home.microsoft.com

Free software, technical information, and business resources: Hardly a day goes by that this company or its founder, Bill Gates, is not in the news. The largest software company in the world — with more than its share of millionaire employees — has a wealth of information on its Web site. Getting lost on this site is easy, but around every corner is useful information. Find free software, online technical support, and lots and lots of other goodies for managing a Web site and getting a business rolling. If the response time is slow, that's probably because a new version of some software has been released and a gazillion people are trying to download it at the same time. Don't worry; try again a little later.

TechWeb

www.techweb.com

Technical news, financial data on thousands of companies: If you want to keep abreast of day-to-day events in the computer industry, this site is where it's at, especially if you have time for just one technology site. TechWeb carries technology news, stock quotes, product reviews, career listings, and a collection of profiles and financial data regarding 45,000 high-tech companies. You can subscribe to newsletters that are delivered to your e-mailbox every day and scroll through them to find out the day's top stories and the winners and losers on Wall Street. The site also has a small-business area (www.techweb.com/smallbiz) that contains a bookstore and a Small Biz Answer Desk manned by Dr. Net to answer your small-business questions. If you're interested in technology events, the technology event calendar has a comprehensive listing of worldwide events. You can download software, and if you're a Web developer, visit the TechTools area.

Web Consultants

www.ypn.com/topics/1196.html

Listing of professional consultants: Say you've invented a killer product that you're sure will take the world by storm. You want to use the Web's mighty reach to sell it, but you know nothing about HTML, Web-site creation, and all that jazzy stuff. And frankly speaking, you don't care. All you want to do is get your product on the Web and do it quickly. So where do you turn for help? Well, you seek the services of a professional Web consultant. These days, anyone who's got a personal Web page to his or her name claims to be a Web consultant — your 17-year-old nephew, or your friend's daughter. But if you're looking for someone with a little more experience, this site is where you may find that person or company. Some of the companies listed here may charge you an arm and a leg, considering their track record. But you're sure to find one that suits your budget.

D-20 Miscellaneous

ZDNet

www.zdnet.com

Technical reviews of hardware and software: If you're in the market for a particular piece of hardware or software, visit this site for some recommendations. The folks at *PC Magazine,* which is published by Ziff-Davis, test more hardware and software in a month than any one person can use in a year. Their recommendations are unbiased and usually on the money. So before you spend that hard-earned cash on a computer that breaks down every time the clock chimes 12, check out this site. In addition to hardware and software evaluations, you can also find interesting articles on current trends in the computer industry and technical how-to's about using new technology. You can also browse through the *PC Magazine* archives of previous issues.

Other Stuff to Check Out

www.faxsav.com
www.internic.net
www.crazy-free-stuff.com/
www.onlinesupport.com

Miscellaneous

Here are some research-related sites that either defy categorization or are too general to fit in any of the other categories.

American Express Small Business Exchange

www.americanexpress.com/
smallbusiness

Helpful information bundled with a sales pitch: This site, hosted by American Express, is part sales pitch and part helpful information. In addition to advertising the various services that American Express offers small businesses, the site has quite a good collection of information, including tips for business planning, expert advice handed out by a small-business expert, a business-to-business directory, and online classified ads.

Biz@dvantage

www.biz.n2k.com

Patent and trademark searches, company profiles, newsletters, and financial reports: Wow, what a site! Biz@dvantage is a comprehensive collection of business-related information. This site has it all: patent and trademark information, company profiles, business news, U.S. and international financial reports, industry newsletters, and worldwide research. It's unique in many of its offerings. For example, you can check whether your trademark will hold good in over a dozen European countries.

Business America

www.business-america.com

Download shareware and sample business letters: Ever wonder how to phrase a business letter to get your message across to the reader? Wouldn't a sample letter to start with be nice to have? The Business America site has over 500 sample letters from which to choose. It also has a collection of over 500 business shareware programs related to starting, financing, managing, marketing, and running your business.

Business@Home

www.gohome.com

Get information on starting a home-based business: Business@Home is a site that provides valuable information on going out on your own and working from home. It doesn't drown you in information like most sites these days. Business@Home is mostly a collection of very relevant articles on what you should and should not do if and when you do decide that the corporate rat race is not your calling. You can find information about finances, taxes, marketing, and family matters, along with a collection of home-based business-association links in Australia, Canada, the U.K., and the United States.

EDGAR — Online SEC Information on Corporations

www.edgar-online.com/

Read SEC filings of U.S. companies: Electronic Data Gathering Analysis and Retrieval (EDGAR) is an online service providing information about corporations that file their information with the SEC. The SEC no longer accepts paper filings, so all corporate information is no more than a click of the mouse away — and here's where you find it. The database has information going back to 1994.

Four11

www.four11.com

Find your friends on the Web: Looking for someone's e-mail address has never been easier. Using Four11, you need wonder no more whether that friend of yours has a mailbox on the Internet. The Internet's largest white-page directory lets you look up long-lost pals and business associates. You can find not only e-mail addresses but residential addresses as well. Look up 800 telephone numbers, too.

The Idea Café

www.ideacafe.com

Get help on starting and running a business: At the Idea Café, you can find the information you need to start and run a business — such things as financial planning, sources of capital, sales and advertising, protection of intellectual property, and sources of help from Uncle Sam. You can also read interviews with personalities like Scott Adams, the creator of *Dilbert,* and Jerry Yang, the cofounder of Yahoo! The site has lots of tips for running a small business — tips you can't get from a text book at the Harvard Business School, only from someone who's actually done it.

International Business Resources on the Web

ciber.bus.msu.edu/busres.htm

Your source of information for international business: This site, at Michigan State University's Center for International Business Education and Research, is an extremely good collection of sites related to international business. Sites are categorized according to a variety of criteria, such as geographic location, government resources, statistics, company listings, indexes of business resources, trades shows and seminars, market indicators, journals, research papers, and articles. International Business Resources on the Web is extremely well researched. If you plan on expanding into international markets, come here for your research needs and market leads.

D-22 Miscellaneous

Nua Internet Surveys

www.nua.com/surveys/

Free survey results on business, demographics, social and technical trends: Now here's an example that all research organizations should follow — make your research results available for free! That's exactly what Nua Consultants and Developers have done. Why? Because they feel that the quality and quantity of their information are a reflection of their organization. Their surveys are organized into categories such as Business, Demographics, Social, and Technical. This site is clearly not to be missed.

The Mining Company

www.miningco.com

Helpful information dished out by experts in their fields: The Mining Company's approach to providing information on the Web is unique and refreshing. Like many other sites, this site provides a comprehensive listing of sites or areas of interests. But that's where the similarity ends. Each of the Mining Company's areas of interests is hosted by a Guide — a person who's an expert in that particular area. So for example, the Entrepreneur area is hosted by a Guide who has actually started a business or two and gives a first-hand account of running a business, watching for pitfalls, and taking precautions. A wonderful approach that makes Web cruising a personal experience. And if you'd like to be a Guide in your area of expertise, just follow the Apply to be a Guide link, and you'll be able to add your two cents for the world to see.

NetMarketing

www.netb2b.com

Come here to put together your online marketing plan: How do you know whether your Web design and development budget is too small, too big, or just right? Has anyone told you that maintaining a site and keeping it current is far more work than the initial setup? Where do you go to get an idea of setup and maintenance costs? What about the incremental costs — adding things like audio, video, databases, chat, and Java applets to the site? The folks at NetMarketing provide a valuable service in their attempts to answer these questions. The site also has a searchable KnowledgeBase containing tutorials, case studies, profiles, and articles on topics such as advertising, direct marketing, design, and technology.

SmartBiz

www.smartbiz.com

Tips, services, and resources for anyone running a business: The SmartBiz site is a comprehensive collection of articles, Web sites, newsgroups, mailing lists, tips, events, surveys, and statistics about starting and operating a business. The Super Store section contains a list of books, audio and video tapes, magazines, newsletters, and reports. The site isn't specifically geared to online marketing but does have some good business-related information.

Stock Exchanges around the World

**www.cnnfn.com/resources/
webconnection/exchanges/**

List of international stock exchanges:
From the African Stock Exchange to the
Zagreb Stock Exchange, this site has links
to more than 20 of the most prominent
international stock exchanges.

Zona Research

www.zonaresearch.com

$

Reports on trends and technology related
to the Internet: The Zona Research site
does not have a ton of free material; the
bulk of the material on the site is available only for a fee. However, before you
order a report, you can read a profile or
outline of the report to see whether it's
what you're looking for. Place your order
for a report directly on the Web.

Other Stuff to Check Out

www.careermosaic.com
www.salesdoctors.com
www.amazon.com
www.dilbert.com

D-24

Part V
The Part of Tens

The 5th Wave   By Rich Tennant

"I like getting complaint letters by e-mail.
It's easier to delete than to shred."

In this part . . .

Summing up many of the most important points of this book is embarrassingly easy, but crucial — especially for marketing people who often like to see important points in the form of a quick list. We do so in the form of two chapters outlining the ten advantages and ten disadvantages of online marketing. (The rest of the book has the details to help you make your online marketing presence really work.) Our last chapter points out ten great *offline* marketing resources that will help you do your best marketing work online, offline, or both.

Chapter 12

Ten Advantages of Online Marketing

In This Chapter

▶ Low barriers to entry

▶ Informational marketing works best

▶ Rapid responses rewarded

▶ Advantages to U.S. marketers

▶ Geographic barriers reduced

*O*nline marketing is still only a fraction of marketing budgets for most companies. Despite all the attention that's paid to the Internet, dismissing it as a fad or a trend is still all too easy for some people. You may well need some ammunition to help convince others that you should be spending your time, let alone your company's money, on online marketing.

Following are ten of the most important advantages of online marketing — some of which we also look at in a different light in Chapter 13, "Ten Disadvantages of Online Marketing."

Online Marketing Has Low Barriers to Entry

A great advantage of online marketing is that it has low barriers to entry. You can begin building an effective online marketing presence with tools such as a basic business Web site (Chapter 5), an Internet mailing list (Chapter 9), or presence in newsgroups and online service forums (Chapter 10) for a few hundred dollars and a moderate investment of time. Much useful online marketing work is done on the cheap. If your initial online work is successful, you can use your experience to justify building a larger, albeit more expensive, online marketing presence. For this reason, you want to always have one eye on the cost-justification for your online marketing expenditures, as we explain in Chapter 7 and Chapter 11.

Online Marketing Is Informational Marketing

Many people see marketing as an art that is less than completely honorable, and marketers as people who are willing to stretch or even invent facts to make a sale. Needless to say, this perception does not lend itself to building a relationship with customers and potential customers.

Online marketing has evolved in such a way that it avoids some of the disadvantages inherent in popular negative perceptions of offline marketing. Online marketing has evolved into *informational marketing,* that is, a style of marketing in which you build a reasonable case for your product as the best, and for you and your company as trustworthy partners with the buyer in the purchase process. In online marketing, core marketing skills, such as finding and clearly stating the user benefits of product features, are valued over other disciplines such as fast talking salesmanship or the glitz of advertising.

To find the write tone, if you'll excuse the pun, look at sponsored *advertorial* ("advertising" + "editorial") sections in *Forbes* and other business publications. The goal in advertorials is to deliver solid information that's just as true as anything in the magazine's articles, but written from the advertiser's point of view and selected to help build the case for purchasing the advertiser's product.

If you've been instilled with a tendency to express yourself in breathless superlatives over the years, as are many marketing people, you need to change your style online. Find someone who knows the online world and ask for a frank evaluation of the straightforwardness and clarity of your writing. Then edit your writing to remove anything that seems overstated or out of place.

The Online World Enables You to Respond Rapidly

The ability to respond quickly — in many cases instantly, off the top of one's head — distinguishes the best marketers from the rest in offline marketing. The ability to respond rapidly is vital online — it enables you to build a one to one relationship with your customers and potential customers and gives people the impression they're getting factual information rather than a carefully crafted sales pitch. Marketers who aren't afraid to risk occasional criticism for timely, honest responses — for instance, mentioning a competitors' products as well as one's own in answering a question in a newsgroup, as described in Chapter 10 — can do a lot to advance the interests of their companies online.

The Online World Highlights Marketing's Role

The reason marketing in general is important is that it establishes a link between products, customers, and sales. In the online world, this link gives online marketing an advantage over offline marketing in that online marketing is more immediate and obvious.

Both tactical efforts, such as redesigning Web pages for easier navigation, and strategic efforts, such as incorporating online sales, are most often in the hands of the marketing department. Marketing is highlighted in the online world to such an extent that its importance in the rest of a company's efforts is brought to the forefront as well. The increased focus that the Internet brings on the importance of marketing may make it easier for people you work with to understand the importance of marketing input in other areas such as product planning and distribution.

Be sure to keep track of your accomplishments in online marketing; they may impress a hiring manager or a potential client or customer down the road. A resume with online marketing work alongside offline marketing work shows off marketing versatility and the ability to stay on top of marketing trends.

Online Innovations Are Marketing Opportunities

The online world is built on rapid change and continues to evolve at breakneck speed. These changes are good for you as a marketer, because each change brings you new ways to communicate with your customers.

While the precursor networks to today's Internet existed over 25 years ago, services such as Usenet newsgroups, online services, the World Wide Web, and push technology have arrived steadily over time (some in the last few years). The Web itself is changing rapidly as new standards and new tools appear with dizzying rapidity. Each time new standards, new tools, or new technologies are introduced in the online world, examine them for opportunities to better communicate with your customers and potential customers.

The Online World Makes Research Easy

The online world is a tremendous resource for all kinds of research, as we describe in Chapter 2. Want to know what users are saying about your product? Scan Usenet newsgroups and online forums for comments and then send e-mail, asking for details, to a few of the people who spoke out. Want to see what your competitors are planning? Check their Web site and relevant newsgroups; you're likely to get valuable information such as their past press releases and upcoming events schedule. Sometimes secrets such as product release dates are posted by less-than-careful insiders.

Not only is online research informative, it's easy to share with others. Online information is freely available for others to verify — unlike things people might say to you on the phone or in person, though that kind of information remains valuable as well. Use online information to help convince others whenever you see a need for action.

As valuable as it is, online research is currently hampered by the fact that so many people, even in the relatively well-wired North American market, are not online, and by the lack of information on so many companies' Web sites. As the amount of information on company Web sites grows, online research will get easier and more valuable.

The Online World Is Forgiving of Mistakes

Compared to other marketing and publishing media, the online world is relatively forgiving of mistakes. If you make a typographical error in an e-mail message or a Usenet posting, few people are likely to care; it's more important to get a factually accurate and helpful response up quickly than to wait for editorial review. If you make a typographical error on a Web page, it's more embarrassing, but much easier to fix than, for instance, a printed piece — which would simply have to be thrown out if it contained any major typographical errors.

Factual errors are different, but still easier to correct online than elsewhere. If you make a factual error online, simply post the correct information and an apology for the earlier error, much as a newspaper would publish a correction. People online seem, in our experience, to appreciate the honesty displayed when an error is corrected in this manner.

Of course, no one wants to make errors online. Always use a spell checker when creating Web page content; the better Web page creation tools now include them, though it's amazing how often they seem to go unused. For other Internet services, use your best judgment. The larger the number of

people who see a given communication, and the more official it is as opposed to being your personal response or opinion, the more important it is
that you take the time to spell check and even grammar check the content.

While nearly all Web page creation tools and even some e-mail programs
have spell checkers, few have grammar checkers, which can catch subtle
errors such as using the wrong version of a word when you right (misspell-
ing intended). To use a grammar checker on your work, create your text in a
full-featured word processing program, spell check it, grammar check it, and
then copy and paste it into another tool for use online.

The Online World Is U.S.-Centric . . .

The Internet itself was begun from a network funded by the U.S. military and
expanded by further U.S. government funding supported by, among others,
then Senator, now Vice President Al Gore, who also coined the term *information superhighway*. Most of the companies that dominate the creation of
hardware, software, and services for the Internet are U.S.-based, and according to the GVU Survey described in Chapter 1, over 80 percent of frequent
users are from the U.S. So at this point in its history, the Internet is a U.S.-
dominated medium.

The point of this is not that America or Americans are somehow superior;
any American businessperson who gets smug today will have their head
handed to them by an overseas competitor tomorrow, as, for instance,
U.S. automakers learned in the 1970s. The point is that a big opportunity
exists right now for U.S.-based companies to take advantage of the current
U.S.-centric nature of the Internet and get a head start on establishing
themselves in cyberspace.

U.S.-based marketers need to be careful in using the word *American* to
describe themselves and their companies; it turns out that Canadians, and
to a lesser extent Mexicans and other South Americans, consider themselves American as well.

The fact that the online world is U.S.-centric makes life much easier for
marketers based in the United States. They can hone their skills online now,
while the Internet is still dominated by Americans, and then expand their
reach and influence as more and more citizens of other countries come
online in the future years. (We don't know if this is a *good* thing; it's just a
fact of life that you can take advantage of, if you're fortunate enough to be
based in the United States.) Some companies and professionals based in
other countries will have a great deal of catching up to do as Internet use in
their countries begins to take off.

. . . and English-centric

Because it's U.S.-centric, the online world is also English-centric. Again, this fact is a big advantage for U.S.-based online marketers. Companies and professionals that operate predominantly in other languages have a large barrier to operating successfully on the Internet. They must either operate only on the small part of the online world that's in their native tongue, or go through a constant translation process back and forth to English in order to operate in the mainstream of the online world.

Some people predict the online world will become much more varied in its support for other languages, and that's no doubt true, but the authors of this book suspect that the great bulk of online content will continue to be in English for a long time to come. It may be that tens of millions of people who have other native languages will need to learn English to participate fully on the information superhighway, the same way that they do now in the sciences and some trades.

In the longer term, automatic translation services — the ability for computers to automatically translate one language to another — may make language barriers less relevant. (The AltaVista Web site at `www.altavista.digital.com` includes automatic translation.) For now, however, automatic translation isn't good enough to completely close the gap. If you work in English, take advantage of the current predominance of English in the online world to start getting your message out now.

Online Marketing Removes Geographic Barriers

One of the most exciting but confusing things about the online world is the way in which it removes geographic barriers. In the online world, the barriers are whether people are interested in what you have to say, and helping interested people find you online. But reaching someone two time zones away costs no more than reaching someone next door. An international delicatessen in Ohio can now easily sell to customers in New York, or New Delhi.

Of course, operating in this new world requires a considerable amount of work and imagination to decide what makes sense and what doesn't. Should a local map store attempt to go statewide on the Internet? National? Global? As we mention in the previous two sections, you can get started with a U.S.-centric, English-only approach, but you also need to decide at what point you need to translate and localize content. Many vendors who've put up a Web storefront have been sadly disappointed. Others have been successful beyond their wildest dreams.

You need marketing expertise and considerable self-restraint to use the online world to grow your business without courting disaster. That's why we suggest growing one's online presence gradually. But if your situation offers a unique opportunity to expand your geographic reach — for instance, if you have a lot of expertise, a lot of money, and a unique product — consider rolling the dice and making a bigger initial effort online.

Chapter 13

Ten Disadvantages of Online Marketing

*O*nline marketing has tremendous advantages. However, online marketing also has its problems — some of which are the dark side of the good points we describe in Chapter 12. In this chapter, we tell you some of the monsters hiding in the online marketing closet — and show you how to shine a light on them and make them crawl farther back into the corner.

Online Marketing Is Different

Online marketing is definitely different from offline marketing. It's informational marketing with a vengeance — too much hype and your online readers and Web site visitors may not only turn you off, but turn on you. Online marketing's costs are hard to estimate in advance, and their benefits are still unclear, whereas in offline marketing you have years of past experience to go on. And because of the fast pace of online marketing, on any day, a competitor who's one step ahead of you — or makes a lucky bet with the company's money — may get ahead of you.

Not only is online marketing different from other marketing work you've done, each Internet technology has its own kinks and culture. If you aren't already online-savvy, you have a limited window in which to catch up; competitors who have even a year or two of online experience may be much better able to take advantage of the new medium than you are. If you don't at least start to get your hands dirty now, you'll fall farther behind. As an example of the different meaning of "experience" in the online world, the few years of online marketing experience that the authors of this book have, which would only be enough to make them knowledgeable beginners in many areas of offline marketing, are enough to make them experts in the online world.

What can you do about the problem of falling behind in online marketing? The solution is information and attitude. On the information side, this book, we humbly submit, is a good starting point for discovering what you need to know for a good start in marketing online. Experience and other resources, including some described in the Directory of online resources and Chapter 14, will do the rest. Attitudinally, the solution can best be summed up in the Latin phrase *carpe diem,* or "seize the day." The online world is a huge opportunity for marketing; don't ignore the risks and difficulties of working in this new environment, but don't let them keep you from acting either.

Internet Bandwidth Is Crowded

The Information Superhighway is like the U.S. highway system in more than just its name. Any free road tends to get overcrowded as people pile onto it; the traffic jams around our cities may well be matched by increasing frustration on the Net. The limiting factor is *bandwidth* — the speed of the connection between all the different routing and rerouting points on the Net, from the massive servers that host Web pages for companies like IBM, all the way down to the 28.8 Kbps modem built into someone's portable computer. And though many plans to increase Internet bandwidth — for the network as a whole and for specific kinds of users — exist, dozens of companies are also scheming to shove data down the newly enlarged *pipes* faster than you can say videoconferencing.

As a user, you probably understand that all these bottlenecks cause frustration. But how do they affect you as an online marketer? The answer is that you need to ignore the siren call of companies and individuals that tell you to use lots of large graphic images and multimedia files in your online presence, especially on your Web site.

The solution to crowded network wires is KISS — Keep It Simple, Silly. Do experiment with multimedia to get your feet wet and liven up your Web site, but use a light touch, and always back up your multimedia information with static text and graphics that deliver the same message. That way people who surf the Net with graphics turned off for speed's sake, or who don't wait for graphics to appear before surfing on to a new location, still get the message.

Online Efforts Can Get Expensive

A full-scale online marketing effort with a Web site, newsgroup monitoring and response, and other efforts, as spelled out in the earlier chapters of this book, can get expensive. Such an effort for a company with, say, 10 to 100 staffers may require employing several people — usually a mix of employees and contractors. Some work on the site full-time, others part-time. Web site hosting costs are either paid to an Internet Service Provider (ISP) or handled internally. In high-wage areas, the total cost of keeping half a dozen people paid, insured, and housed in offices can approach a million dollars a year. (For employees, much of the cost is hidden as benefits and facilities expenses; for contractors, you write one check for your entire expense for that person.) So be ready to spend some real money if you expand beyond a CYA (Cover Your Assets) Web and online presence like the one we describe in Chapter 5 of this book.

A million dollars is a lot of money, but marketers have certainly been known to spend that and more. Spending that much money for an online effort brings up two special challenges. The first is that the expenses can sneak up on you — given that you can create a simple online presence in your spare time for a few hundred dollars, the large expenditures needed for a larger online presence can be a shock. The second is that, when all is said and done, only a minority of your target audience is likely to be online where your online effort can reach them, as we described in Chapter 2. You have to plan and budget carefully to avoid "sticker shock" and to make sure you still have enough money left to reach people offline as well.

The truly big spending, though, comes with online commerce. Carefully plan and budget your expenditures before selling online, and read *Selling Online For Dummies* by Leslie Lundquist (IDG Books Worldwide, Inc.) to start getting an idea of what's involved.

Online Marketing Doesn't Reach Everybody

Your colleagues, press, analysts, and core customers with whom you regularly work are likely to be online. So you may think that your job of keeping all your customers informed, updated, and happy is done as soon as you put information on your Web site or answer a question in a newsgroup. Unfortunately, this just isn't so.

To avoid missing your customers, don't shut out people who are offline or have limited online capabilities. Design your online content, especially your Web pages, to be accessible to all. (If you can comfortably use your Web site with Netscape Navigator 2.0, which doesn't support recent advances like Java, frames, and so on, then you can be assured that your site is accessible to the vast majority of Web users.)

Your online audience is probably better-informed than the offline world because people online are often very interested in information. However, make sure that both your online and offline group has access to all the same information. (The GM BuyPower program, which provides people telephone access to the same information that other people get online, is a good example of providing equal access to both an online and offline customer base. See Chapter 11 for more discussion of this issue.)

Another technique is to make offline access information a part of your online presence. Examples of this include making information from your Web site available via a faxback service and adding a toll-free number to your SIG (signature) file, as described in Chapter 9. Reaching out in this way helps your online customers pass on contact information to their unconnected friends.

Getting Online Can Be Difficult

If you've ever had problems connecting to your online service or Internet Service Provider when traveling, you know that getting online can be all too difficult. While getting connected is hard enough for experienced computer users, the barriers to entry for people who don't yet use a computer are far higher — between the decision to get online and actually being online lies a purchase of at least several hundred dollars as well as several hours of setup time. (Many people also have a large learning curve ahead of them before they can use computers effectively.) So when you ask people to visit you on your Web site or otherwise get information from you online, you may be causing frustration for many people who would like to be in touch with you but can't get online right now, or who aren't online yet. So use a gentle touch when promoting your online presence, and provide alternate ways of getting information, as we describe in the preceding section.

The Online World Increases the Pressure on Marketing

In written Chinese, the character for crisis is a combination of the characters for danger and opportunity. So it is in marketing: the sudden arrival of the online world is a crisis, with many potential problems and many potential victories. Marketing is a fast-paced environment, and the online world makes it even faster. As a result, many, many opportunities for "gotchas" exist. For instance, how many people knew two or three years ago that they should drop everything and register their best choice for a domain name before someone else beat them to it?

Coupled with the increased pace of change is the reality that marketing departments almost always seem understaffed, and the people who are on staff never seem to be given enough money to do the job. (One of the authors worked in an environment where the marketing budget for a Fortune 100 company was cut to nearly zero one quarter — and the next quarter's budget used the near-zero budget as its starting point.)

In dealing with the online world, you may find yourself feeling like you're always behind. Often, this feeling is brought about by the fact that dealing with something new or cool (like the Internet) can draw you away from your actual marketing goals. One way to overcome this potential stumbling block is to make a priority list and stick to it unless you have justification to change. If you stick to your priorities, you do a better job, and you have a little energy left for the occasional tight deadline, like adding the latest product ("What do you mean you haven't added the new liver-flavored ice cream bars to the Web site yet? They hit shelves tomorrow!") to your marketing Web site.

Justifying the Cost of Online Efforts Is Hard

Measuring the impact of marketing expenses is difficult, but at least some widely accepted rules exist for what's reasonable in offline media. Also, people in your company get a kick out of seeing and hearing ads on TV and radio. If the decision-makers in your company aren't entirely comfortable with the online world, they may not get as much of a thrill from a Web site, let alone a newsgroup posting. ***Hint:*** Don't suggest that they scan `alt.barney.dinosaur.die.die.die`, which is described in Chapter 10, or they might really think the Internet is not something on which they want to spend their time — or the company's money.

The cost-justification effort is made more difficult by some of the costly processes that you may want to implement in order to make your online presence shine. These processes include:

- ✔ **Automating as many parts of your online presence as possible.** For example, using an e-mail autoresponder program to respond to e-mail messages sent to your Web site (Chapter 8). Automating your online processes costs time and money up front, and answering the messages individually doesn't seem to cost any money at all because the expense is hidden in your salary. (Not answering the messages costs even less — that is, in terms of hard dollar costs.) However, the opportunities you miss and the bad impressions that you leave by not responding quickly to requests for information can be very expensive in terms of lost future sales.

- ✔ **Outsourcing work to consultants and companies that specialize in online work.** Although hiring outside consultants results in hard dollar costs in a form that many executives loathe — that is, medium-sized and large checks written to consultants — it can save you money in the long run. An outside consultant may be able to set up your marketing Web site in a couple of days, while doing it in-house may take weeks. (We explain outsourcing in Chapter 6.)

These concerns are why we address the issue of cost-justifying your online presence (at greatest length in Chapter 11). We strongly recommend that you adapt our advice and your own experience into an ongoing effort to actively demonstrate the benefits of your online presence. Possible ways to demonstrate benefits include counting the number of times people click on items in your Web site, counting downloads of files that you offer, polling your online visitors about the impact of your Web site on their buying behavior, and counting responses to special offers you make on your Web site. Even when no one's asking, keep gathering information about the benefits of your online presence so that you're ready when they do ask.

Making Misteaks Online Is Easy

Any time that you do something new, you're bound to make mistakes. Typos are bad and embarrassing, but easy to fix. The real challenge comes when you're put on the spot to answer tough questions — fast.

In the immediacy of the online world, you're often asked to explain complicated issues online almost to the minute the issues arise — why didn't your company ship a product on time? What are your plans for speeding up deliveries? When are you finally going to start doing customer service right? If you admit wrongdoing, you may embarrass yourself or others in your company; if not, you can look ignorant, defensive, or clueless.

The approach we take online is to apologize a lot when we do anything that irritates a customer or partner, and always ask for clarification — is there some way you can perform a needed task with the current product? What happened to you when you spoke with our customer service department? The answers to these kinds of questions help you address real problems better, and also lets the air out of wiseacres who may not even be customers or don't have any real problems with you, but just like to throw bombs online.

When all is said and done, you have to ask others in your company to be tolerant of any mistakes that you make online, and you have to be tolerant of the mistakes that others in your company may make. The online world is a relatively new medium that's highly public and demands rapid responses, always a formula for potential embarrassment. You can reduce errors of judgment, as well as typing and other mistakes, by typing an answer, then reading it out loud to yourself. You may be surprised how your own words sound when you read them back to yourself. But whatever you do, mistakes happen — prepare to be flexible and discover as you go along.

Guilt by Association

Because of all the junk in the online world, including pornography, slander, libel, and hateful talk, many people have a bad impression of the online world. The way that you conduct yourself and how you present your company online can do one of two things. You can reinforce people's negative stereotypes, leading them to very quickly form a low opinion of your company, your products, and maybe even your parentage, or you can confound them, making a positive impression, and create a high opinion of your company and your products.

Like other media before it — Newton Minow, the Chairman of the Federal Communications Corporation called television a "vast wasteland" back in the 1960s — the Internet is bound to face some criticism as it grows and develops. If you conduct yourself with class and professionalism online, you and your company can be seen as exceptions, even if the public at large believes that lies, half-truths, and junk are the online rule.

The Uncertain Future of the Online World

Usually, a fairly high degree of predictability exists between what happens one year and what happens the next. But the entire future of the online world seems continually up in the air. As a result, knowing how big a bet to put down on your online presence is hard.

Our answer to the rapid rate of change online is to move cautiously but quickly — cautiously in that you shouldn't make large investments at first, but quickly in that you can and should establish a modest, easy to use online presence as soon as possible. Then you can combine the advice you get in this book and elsewhere with your own increasing experience to create an online presence that works best for you and your own unique set of customers.

Chapter 14

Ten Offline Marketing Resources

*N*o matter how much the online world grows, most of the world's information will still be in books and magazines for the foreseeable future. This book's Directory has scores of great online marketing resources; this chapter is the source for some good offline resources. Several marketing classics listed in this chapter can help you to get a firm grasp of the essentials of marketing in any medium, online or offline.

Paying close attention to offline marketing vehicles such as television ads can help you sharpen and transfer your skills to the online world. As you gain experience in online marketing, you look at traditional media — books, magazines, radio, television, and others — in a whole new way.

All the books recommended in this chapter are available online through amazon.com, the online bookseller, at `www.amazon.com`, or Barnes and Noble, the book superstore chain with a large online presence as well, at `www.barnesandnoble.com`. Both of these Web sites are also great places to shop for books that may fit your specific job interests more closely.

Crossing the Chasm

Crossing the Chasm by Geoffrey Moore (HarperBusiness) isn't about online marketing at all, but rather about the general marketing of high-technology products to mainstream customers. The online marketing world rests on a high-tech base, and has the technologically oriented elite at its core. Therefore, a book on high-technology marketing having some valuable lessons for use online makes sense. Moore's book definitely does. Its successor, *Inside the Tornado* by Geoffrey Moore (HarperBusiness), is valuable as well, but of the two, *Crossing the Chasm* is the classic.

The key lesson of *Crossing the Chasm* is Moore's insights into why most high-technology products fail to reach a broad market and instead stay stuck in niches — and how to get one's products unstuck. Reading *Crossing the Chasm* can help you to understand what you're doing online, why, and what to do next. If you don't look at any other offline marketing resource, look at this one.

Trade Associations

Every profession or industry that we can think of has a trade or professional association, from dentists and decorators to car dealers and computer companies. Many of these associations have marketing sections or groups that exchange marketing information and hold meetings. These associations are great resources for finding out what has and hasn't worked for others online in your industry.

If you're not familiar with all the associations that cover your field — national, regional, and local — talk with a colleague or check one of many directories of associations, available at most library reference desks. And if you want an online pointer to these offline associations, try the Yahoo! association listing online at www.yahoo.com/Business_and_Economy/ Organizations/Trade_Associations/.

The trade association for marketing professionals across all industries is the American Marketing Association (AMA), over 50,000 members strong. The AMA has local chapters in many cities and is another good way to compare experiences with others, while building your online and offline marketing skills. You can find your local American Marketing Association chapter at www.ama.org.

Note the .org, for a nonprofit organization, not .com for a commercial entity, at the end of the URL. (The domain ama.com was registered to a company called Imprint Media Communications in Louisville, Kentucky, in 1995, but is not in use as a Web site at this writing.) The American Marketing Association was sharp enough to beat the American Medical Association, which of course has the same acronym, to the right URL for themselves! Chapter 4 describes how to choose and register the right domain name for your company.

Marketing: An Introduction and Marketing For Dummies

Marketing: An Introduction by Philip Kotler and Gary Armstrong (Prentice-Hall) is a marketing textbook that starts by looking at human needs as the basis of marketing — a good thing to think about in analyzing your online marketing efforts — then covers all the basics of marketing, from market segmentation and public relations to designing new products. Reading all this with an eye to its application online is a mind-opening experience.

If the textbook approach isn't your cup of tea, an excellent marketing book written in the Dummies style may be more up your alley — if you don't mind our mixing British and American metaphors. *Marketing For Dummies* by Alexander Hiam (IDG Books Worldwide, Inc.) is an excellent introduction to marketing and a valuable companion to this book.

Trade Publications

Another good source of trade-specific marketing information is your industry trade publications, whether they're weekly tabloids, monthly magazines, or the occasional newsletter. Articles frequently offer marketing tips or profiles of what other companies are doing. Your trade or professional association, or your colleagues, can point you in the right direction.

Also look at Internet-specific trade publications such as the weekly *Internet World* and the monthly *NetGuide*. Go to a high-technology-oriented bookstore, or the magazine section in a computer superstore, and you may see as many as a dozen such publications or more. These resources can help make you become familiar with what's happening online.

Marketing trade publications are also a good resource for online marketing. The American Marketing Association, mentioned in the "Trade Associations" section earlier in this chapter, puts out several publications, including *Marketing News, the Journal of Marketing, Services Marketing Today, Ad News,* and *Advertising Age.* As their names suggest, these publications are largely advertising-oriented, but also cover trends useful to general marketers as well.

Statistical Abstract of the United States and American Demographics

American Demographics is a magazine that addresses consumer trends and is therefore valuable to anyone in marketing. This magazine is also a useful aid to your thinking as you look at the differences between the demographics of the online world, as described in Chapter 1, and the demographics of the offline world. You can find American Demographics online at www.marketingtools.com/publications/ad/index.htm.

For definitive information on the U.S. population, the *Statistical Abstract of the United States* is available from the U.S. Government in book or CD-ROM form. The *Statistical Abstract* is a great way to back up your plans and proposals with information that's about as authoritative as you can get in a fast-changing field like marketing. You can get the book from the American Demographics bookstore: Follow the link on the top of the American Demographics home page at www.marketingtools.com/publications/ad/index.htm.

News Radio

News radio is fairly analogous to the online world in general, and the World Wide Web in particular. Basically, news radio stations are delivering information to attract listeners who then hear the commercials that pay the station bills. You can think of your Web site the same way: You're attracting the person by providing information that interests them and also delivering your sales and marketing messages encouraging them to buy your product. Listen to news radio with an ear to understanding how they mix many different kinds of information along with commercials in a way designed to keep you listening.

The writing style for your Web site may be improved if you borrow from the writing style for news radio — lots of short pieces of information, each capable of standing alone, with nothing extraneous in them. CNET news.com, which you can find online at news.com, is an example of a news radio-type approach translated to the Web.

Try reading your Web pages and other online writing aloud — if it sounds slow and ponderous, it probably won't compel people to keep reading, and they're likely to surf off somewhere else.

The Pocket Marketer and Anything by Ries and Trout

Billed as "your portable professional real-world marketing companion," *The Pocket Marketer* is a vest-sized paperback by Brian Scott Sockin and Janet Gorttalio (Warner Books) that's a great quick-and-dirty guide to marketing terminology and processes. Originally published in 1992, this book is full of practical information, tools, and charts that you can use directly for your online and offline marketing efforts. This book is also nice to have as a reference when marketers around you are engaging in marketingspeak.

If marketing had gods, Al Ries and Jack Trout would be right up there with Geoffrey Moore, mentioned earlier in this chapter. All books written by this marketing duo are easy, fun reads full of marketing strategy tips with lots of real-life examples. Good titles include their classic *Positioning: The Battle for Your Mind* (Warner Books), as well as *Marketing Warfare* (McGraw-Hill), *Bottom-Up Marketing* (Plume) and *The 22 Immutable Laws of Marketing* (HarperBusiness). All are available in paperback and nicely challenge common marketing assumptions. They're worth reading — and re-reading.

Any Big Magazine Rack

Imagine a big magazine rack with sewing thread used to connect information from one magazine to related information in others. By the time you were done connecting all the related pieces, you'd have, well, a web of information links. This idea was part of the thinking behind the creation of the World Wide Web, and you can see it in action today in any bookstore.

Most of the Web is very magazine-like — pages of information mixing text and graphics, the text written in a compact style for easy skimming or scanning, and ads interspersed throughout. (One may argue that the Web has an advantage over magazines in the form of multimedia, but we've never seen a scratch-and-sniff insert on a Web page, so that's at least one "multi" medium where magazines have an advantage.)

You can pick out magazines you like, then compare them to your Web site. Look for layout and graphic design ideas in the magazine that you can apply to the Web. Find an article you like in a magazine, then compare the writing in it to the writing on your Web site; you may be able to find ways to improve the quality of writing on your Web site by using ideas you get from magazine articles.

Linking is the single biggest difference between the Web and magazines, given that no such thing as a hypertext link exists in print — you have to physically turn the pages to get somewhere else! Look at your Web site for ways to use linking that give your site an edge over magazines.

The High-Tech Marketing Companion

Companies with high-tech products usually face a two-step marketing process: First, educate the customer as to what a product category does, then sell them their specific product. *The High-Tech Marketing Companion* (Addison-Wesley), edited by Dee Kiamy, includes tips and advice specifically for high-tech marketers faced with these problems on everything from market research and positioning to product naming and distribution. Contributors include long-time technology marketers such as Geoffrey Moore, author of *Crossing the Chasm* (mentioned earlier in this chapter) and even a relative unknown named Frank Catalano. Though this trade paperback was originally published in 1993 and some information is slightly dated, it's still a worthwhile read.

Television Advertising

What do you do when you have 30 seconds of someone's attention — *if* you can entice them not to click a button and surf away from you? TV has had this problem for decades, and the ways in which they meet (or fail to meet) this challenge are very educational for online marketers. Think of someone giving your online messages their attention 15–30 seconds at a time — and realize that if they aren't enthralled at the end of each brief chunk of time, they go somewhere else. Study TV ads and then see if you can apply the things that do and don't work for you, as a TV viewer, to your own online presence. (But expect people to be a bit surprised when they see you channel-surfing with your remote control to find commercials, rather than to avoid them!)

Part VI

Appendix

"Come on Walt—time to freshen the company Web page."

In this part . . .

We were able to put the only additional information you need in a single Appendix that covers using the CD-ROM that comes with this book. The CD-ROM has great Windows and Macintosh software that will speed and make easier the task of creating your online presence. Enjoy!

Appendix

About the CD-ROM

- -

*H*ere's some of what you can find on the *Marketing Online For Dummies* CD-ROM:

- ✔ MindSpring Internet service sign-up software
- ✔ LISTSERV, the popular e-mail mailing list creation software
- ✔ WinZip and ZipIt file compression utilities

System Requirements

Your computer must meet the minimum system requirements listed below to run the software on the CD-ROM. If your computer doesn't meet these requirements, you may have trouble running some of the software.

- ✔ **A PC with a 486 or faster processor, or a Mac OS computer with a 68040 or faster processor.**
- ✔ **Microsoft Windows 3.1 or later, or Mac OS system software 7.5 or later.**
- ✔ **At least 8MB of RAM installed on your computer.** For best performance, we recommend that Windows 95-equipped PCs and Mac OS computers with PowerPC processors have at least 16MB of RAM installed.
- ✔ **At least 60MB of hard disk space available to install all the PC programs or 25MB of hard disk space available to install all the Mac OS programs from this CD-ROM.** (You need less space if you don't install all the programs.)
- ✔ **A CD-ROM drive — double-speed (2X) or faster.**
- ✔ **A monitor capable of displaying 256 colors or grayscale.**
- ✔ **A modem with a speed of at least 14,400 bps.**

For more information on the basics, see *PCs For Dummies,* 5th Edition, by Dan Gookin; *Windows 95 For Dummies,* 2nd Edition, by Andy Rathbone; *Windows 3.11 For Dummies,* 3rd Edition, by Andy Rathbone; or *Macs For Dummies,* 5th Edition, by David Pogue, all published by IDG Books Worldwide, Inc.

What's On the CD-ROM

The CD-ROM that comes with this book contains a variety of interesting software for accessing various Internet services and for creating and publishing content on the Internet. The CD-ROM includes *freeware,* which you can use with no further payment; *shareware,* which is free to use during an evaluation period but requires payment if you use it beyond the evaluation period; and tryout versions of commercial software. The CD also includes a list of useful Web links and other Internet service links for more online marketing information and resources.

This appendix lists the contents of the CD-ROM by software category. Much of the software works only after you run an installation program.

The Internet is full of freeware, shareware, and trial versions of commercial programs. Use the search techniques we describe in Chapter 2 to help you find additional software to suit your needs.

The publisher and the authors have taken all reasonable precautions to ensure that these files are not damaged nor infected by a computer virus. Even so, we recommend that you take the following precautions before installing any software: Make sure you have a current backup of your hard drive and scan any program file for viruses before running it.

Using the CD with Microsoft Windows

To install the items from the CD to your hard drive, follow these steps.

1. **Insert the CD into your computer's CD-ROM drive.**

2. **Windows 3.1 or 3.11 users: From Program Manager, choose File⇨Run.**

   Windows 95 users: Click the Start⇨Run.

3. In the dialog box that appears, type D:\SETUP.EXE.

Most of you probably have your CD-ROM drive listed as drive D under My Computer in Windows 95 or the File Manager in Windows 3.1. Type in the proper drive letter if your CD-ROM drive uses a different letter.

4. Click OK.

A license agreement window appears.

5. Since we're sure you want to use the CD, read through the license agreement, nod your head, and then click the Accept button. After you click Accept, you'll never be bothered by the License Agreement window again.

From here, the CD interface appears. The CD interface is a little program that shows you what is on the CD and coordinates installing the programs and running the demos. The interface basically lets you click a button or two to make things happen.

6. The first screen you see is the Welcome screen. Click anywhere on this screen to enter the interface.

Now you are getting to the action. This next screen lists categories for the software on the CD.

7. To view the items within a category, just click the category's name.

A list of programs in the category appears.

8. For more information about a program, click the program's name.

Be sure to read the information that appears. Sometimes a program requires you to do a few tricks on your computer first, and this screen tells you where to go for that information, if necessary.

9. To install the program, click the appropriate Install button. If you don't want to install the program, click the Go Back button to return to the previous screen.

You can always return to the previous screen by clicking the Go Back button. This feature enables you to browse the different categories and products and decide what you want to install.

As soon as you click an Install button, the interface program drops to the background and the CD begins installation of the program you chose.

10. To install other items, repeat Steps 7, 8 and 9.

11. When you're finished installing programs, click the Quit button to close the interface.

You can eject the CD now. Carefully place it back in the plastic jacket of the book for safekeeping.

Using the CD with the Mac OS

To install the items from the CD to your hard drive, follow these steps.

1. **Insert the CD into your computer's CD-ROM drive.**

   In a moment, an icon representing the CD you just inserted appears on your Mac desktop. Chances are, the icon looks like a CD-ROM.

2. **Double-click the CD icon to show the CD's contents.**

3. **Double-click the Read Me First icon.**

   This text file contains information about the CD's programs and any last-minute instructions you need to know about installing the programs on the CD that we don't cover in this appendix.

4. **To install most programs, just drag the program's folder from the CD window and drop it on your hard drive icon.**

5. **Some programs come with installer programs — with these programs, you simply open the program's folder on the CD, and double-click the icon with the word "Install" or "Installer."**

   After you have installed the programs that you want, you can eject the CD. Carefully place it back in the plastic jacket of the book for safekeeping.

The Software for Windows

Accessing the 'Net

MindSpring Internet Access is a free commercial product that gets you signed up to the MindSpring Internet Service Provider. If you don't already have Internet access, MindSpring is an excellent ISP that offers unlimited Internet access for a low monthly fee.

System: Windows 95

Browsing the Web

Internet Explorer 4.0 is a free commercial product that lets you surf the Web and access push channels, e-mail, newsgroups, FTP sites, and more from one well-integrated interface.

System: Windows 95

Bookmark Converter is freeware that converts and merges bookmark files between Internet Explorer and Netscape Navigator.

System: Windows 3.1 and up

WebTurbo is a free program that works with Internet Explorer or Netscape Navigator to enable site previewing (allowing you to better understand how a Web site is put together) and enhanced searching.

System: Windows 95 and NT

Inforia Quest 1.0 is a trial version of an Internet search program that's actually fun to use.

System: Windows 95 and NT

Web links with URLs for the sites listed in the *Marketing Online For Dummies Internet Directory.*

E-mailing

LISTSERV for Windows 95 is the most famous e-mail mailing list administration program. This version is shareware that allows you to run several mailing lists simultaneously.

System: Windows 95

And more

Free Agent 1.11 is a free and excellent newsreader program that enables you to read Usenet newsgroups.

System: Windows 3.1, Windows 95

Start Right Marketing is a trial version of software that explains basic sales and marketing principles.

System: Windows 3.1 and up

Milestones, Etc. is a trial version of project planning software that you can use for planning your online marketing presence.

System: Windows 3.1 and up

WinZip is a shareware version of the popular file decompression utility. WinZip allows you to unzip files you download from the Internet as well as compress files for uploading or attaching to e-mail.

System: Windows 3.1 and up

The Software for Macintosh

License Agreement

Read Me First

Links.HTM with URLs for the sites listed in the *Marketing Online For Dummies Internet Directory.*

ZipIt! is a compression utility that allows Macintosh users to create and expand files compressed using the popular ZIP compression format.

Rumor Mill 1.11 is shareware that acts as a news server for small newsgroups.

Internet Explorer 4.0 is a free commercial product that lets you surf the Web and access push channels, e-mail, newsgroups, FTP sites, and more from one well-integrated interface.

If You Have Software Problems

We've done our best to find and deliver programs that work well on most computers that have the minimum system requirements. However, some programs may not work properly on your computer for one reason or another.

The two likeliest problems are that you don't have enough RAM to run the program that you want to use alongside other programs already running on your computer, or that the other programs you have running are affecting the installation or running of a program. If you get error messages like Not enough memory or Setup cannot continue, or if the installation program, the program that you've successfully installed, or your computer just *stops,* try one or more of these methods and then try running the software again:

✔ **Turn off anti-virus software.** Turn off any anti-virus software you have running on your computer and re-install or re-run the new software. Some installation programs behave in a way similar to some viruses and may trigger your anti-virus program to prevent the installation from completing. (Be sure to turn the anti-virus software on again after you have your program installed!)

✔ **Close other programs.** Close all running programs before installing or running the software. Installation programs typically update files and programs; if you keep other programs running, installation may not work properly. In addition, the more programs you're running, the less memory is available for the smooth installation or running of additional programs.

✔ **Add RAM.** Add more RAM to your computer, either yourself or by having a local computer store do it. RAM is inexpensive these days and you can, at the time of this writing, add 8MB of RAM for under $100, including installation. Adding more memory can really help your computer run faster and run more programs simultaneously without slowing down or crashing.

If you still have trouble installing or running the software from the CD-ROM, please call the IDG Books Worldwide Customer Service phone number: 800-762-2974 (outside the U.S.: 317-596-5261).

Index

• E •

(continued)

• F •

(continued)

• *O* •

(continued)

• Z •

IDG Books Worldwide, Inc., End-User License Agreement

READ THIS. You should carefully read these terms and conditions before opening the software packet(s) included with this book ("Book"). This is a license agreement ("Agreement") between you and IDG Books Worldwide, Inc. ("IDGB"). By opening the accompanying software packet(s), you acknowledge that you have read and accept the following terms and conditions. If you do not agree and do not want to be bound by such terms and conditions, promptly return the Book and the unopened software packet(s) to the place you obtained them for a full refund.

1. **License Grant.** IDGB grants to you (either an individual or entity) a nonexclusive license to use one copy of the enclosed software program(s) (collectively, the "Software") solely for your own personal or business purposes on a single computer (whether a standard computer or a workstation component of a multiuser network). The Software is in use on a computer when it is loaded into temporary memory (RAM) or installed into permanent memory (hard disk, CD-ROM, or other storage device). IDGB reserves all rights not expressly granted herein.

2. **Ownership.** IDGB is the owner of all right, title, and interest, including copyright, in and to the compilation of the Software recorded on the disk(s) or CD-ROM ("Software Media"). Copyright to the individual programs recorded on the Software Media is owned by the author or other authorized copyright owner of each program. Ownership of the Software and all proprietary rights relating thereto remain with IDGB and its licensers.

3. **Restrictions on Use and Transfer.**

   (a) You may only (i) make one copy of the Software for backup or archival purposes, or (ii) transfer the Software to a single hard disk, provided that you keep the original for backup or archival purposes. You may not (i) rent or lease the Software, (ii) copy or reproduce the Software through a LAN or other network system or through any computer subscriber system or bulletin-board system, or (iii) modify, adapt, or create derivative works based on the Software.

   (b) You may not reverse engineer, decompile, or disassemble the Software. You may transfer the Software and user documentation on a permanent basis, provided that the transferee agrees to accept the terms and conditions of this Agreement and you retain no copies. If the Software is an update or has been updated, any transfer must include the most recent update and all prior versions.

4. **Restrictions on Use of Individual Programs.** You must follow the individual requirements and restrictions detailed for each individual program in the "What's On the CD-ROM" section of this Book. These limitations are also contained in the individual license agreements recorded on the Software Media. These limitations may include a requirement that after using the program for a specified period of time, the user must pay a registration fee or discontinue use. By opening the Software packet(s), you will be agreeing to abide by the licenses and restrictions for these individual programs that are detailed in the "What's On the CD-ROM" section and on the Software Media. None of the material on this Software Media or listed in this Book may ever be redistributed, in original or modified form, for commercial purposes.

5. Limited Warranty.

(a) IDGB warrants that the Software and Software Media are free from defects in materials and workmanship under normal use for a period of sixty (60) days from the date of purchase of this Book. If IDGB receives notification within the warranty period of defects in materials or workmanship, IDGB will replace the defective Software Media.

(b) **IDGB AND THE AUTHOR OF THE BOOK DISCLAIM ALL OTHER WARRANTIES, EXPRESS OR IMPLIED, INCLUDING WITHOUT LIMITATION IMPLIED WARRANTIES OF MERCHANTABILITY AND FITNESS FOR A PARTICULAR PURPOSE, WITH RESPECT TO THE SOFTWARE, THE PROGRAMS, THE SOURCE CODE CONTAINED THEREIN, AND/OR THE TECHNIQUES DESCRIBED IN THIS BOOK. IDGB DOES NOT WARRANT THAT THE FUNCTIONS CONTAINED IN THE SOFTWARE WILL MEET YOUR REQUIREMENTS OR THAT THE OPERATION OF THE SOFTWARE WILL BE ERROR FREE.**

(c) This limited warranty gives you specific legal rights, and you may have other rights that vary from jurisdiction to jurisdiction.

6. Remedies.

(a) IDGB's entire liability and your exclusive remedy for defects in materials and workmanship shall be limited to replacement of the Software Media, which may be returned to IDGB with a copy of your receipt at the following address: Software Media Fulfillment Department, Attn.: *Marketing Online For Dummies,* IDG Books Worldwide, Inc., 7260 Shadeland Station, Ste. 100, Indianapolis, IN 46256, or call 800-762-2974. Please allow three to four weeks for delivery. This Limited Warranty is void if failure of the Software Media has resulted from accident, abuse, or misapplication. Any replacement Software Media will be warranted for the remainder of the original warranty period or thirty (30) days, whichever is longer.

(b) In no event shall IDGB or the author be liable for any damages whatsoever (including without limitation damages for loss of business profits, business interruption, loss of business information, or any other pecuniary loss) arising from the use of or inability to use the Book or the Software, even if IDGB has been advised of the possibility of such damages.

(c) Because some jurisdictions do not allow the exclusion or limitation of liability for consequential or incidental damages, the above limitation or exclusion may not apply to you.

7. U.S. Government Restricted Rights. Use, duplication, or disclosure of the Software by the U.S. Government is subject to restrictions stated in paragraph (c)(1)(ii) of the Rights in Technical Data and Computer Software clause of DFARS 252.227-7013, and in subparagraphs (a) through (d) of the Commercial Computer–Restricted Rights clause at FAR 52.227-19, and in similar clauses in the NASA FAR supplement, when applicable.

8. General. This Agreement constitutes the entire understanding of the parties and revokes and supersedes all prior agreements, oral or written, between them and may not be modified or amended except in a writing signed by both parties hereto that specifically refers to this Agreement. This Agreement shall take precedence over any other documents that may be in conflict herewith. If any one or more provisions contained in this Agreement are held by any court or tribunal to be invalid, illegal, or otherwise unenforceable, each and every other provision shall remain in full force and effect.

Installation Instructions

· ·

*F*or information on installing the software from the CD-ROM included with this book, see the Appendix.

IDG BOOKS WORLDWIDE BOOK REGISTRATION

We want to hear from you!

Register This Book and Win!

Visit **http://my2cents.dummies.com** to register this book and tell us how you liked it!

✔ Get entered in our monthly prize giveaway.

✔ Give us feedback about this book — tell us what you like best, what you like least, or maybe what you'd like to ask the author and us to change!

✔ Let us know any other *...For Dummies*® topics that interest you.

Your feedback helps us determine what books to publish, tells us what coverage to add as we revise our books, and lets us know whether we're meeting your needs as a *...For Dummies* reader. You're our most valuable resource, and what you have to say is important to us!

Not on the Web yet? It's easy to get started with *Dummies 101*®: *The Internet For Windows*® *95* or *The Internet For Dummies*,® 4th Edition, at local retailers everywhere.

Or let us know what you think by sending us a letter at the following address:

...For Dummies Book Registration
Dummies Press
7260 Shadeland Station, Suite 100
Indianapolis, IN 46256-3945
Fax 317-596-5498

BUSINESS AND
**GENERAL
REFERENCE
BOOK SERIES
FROM IDG**

COMPUTER
**BOOK SERIES
FROM IDG**